P9-AON-470

TOMARE!

[STOP!]

You're going the wrong way!

Manga is a completely different type of reading experience.

To start at the *beginning*, go to the *end*!

That's right! Authentic manga is read the traditional Japanese way—from right to left. Exactly the *opposite* of how American books are read. It's easy to follow: Just go to the other end of the book, and read each page—and each panel—from the right side to the left side, starting at the top right. Now you're experiencing manga as it was meant to be!

A Kodansha Comics Trade Paperback Original.

Arisa volume 10 copyright © 2012 Natsumi Ando
English translation copyright © 2013 Natsumi Ando

Published in the United States by Kodansha Comics, an imprint of Kodansha USA Publishing, LLC, New York.

Publication rights for this English edition arranged through Kodansha Ltd., Tokyo.

First published in Japan in 2012 by Kodansha Ltd., Tokyo.

ISBN 978-1-61262-251-4

Printed in the United States of America.

www.kodanshacomics.com

9 8 7 6 5 4 3 2 1

Translator: Ben Applegate
Lettering: April Brown

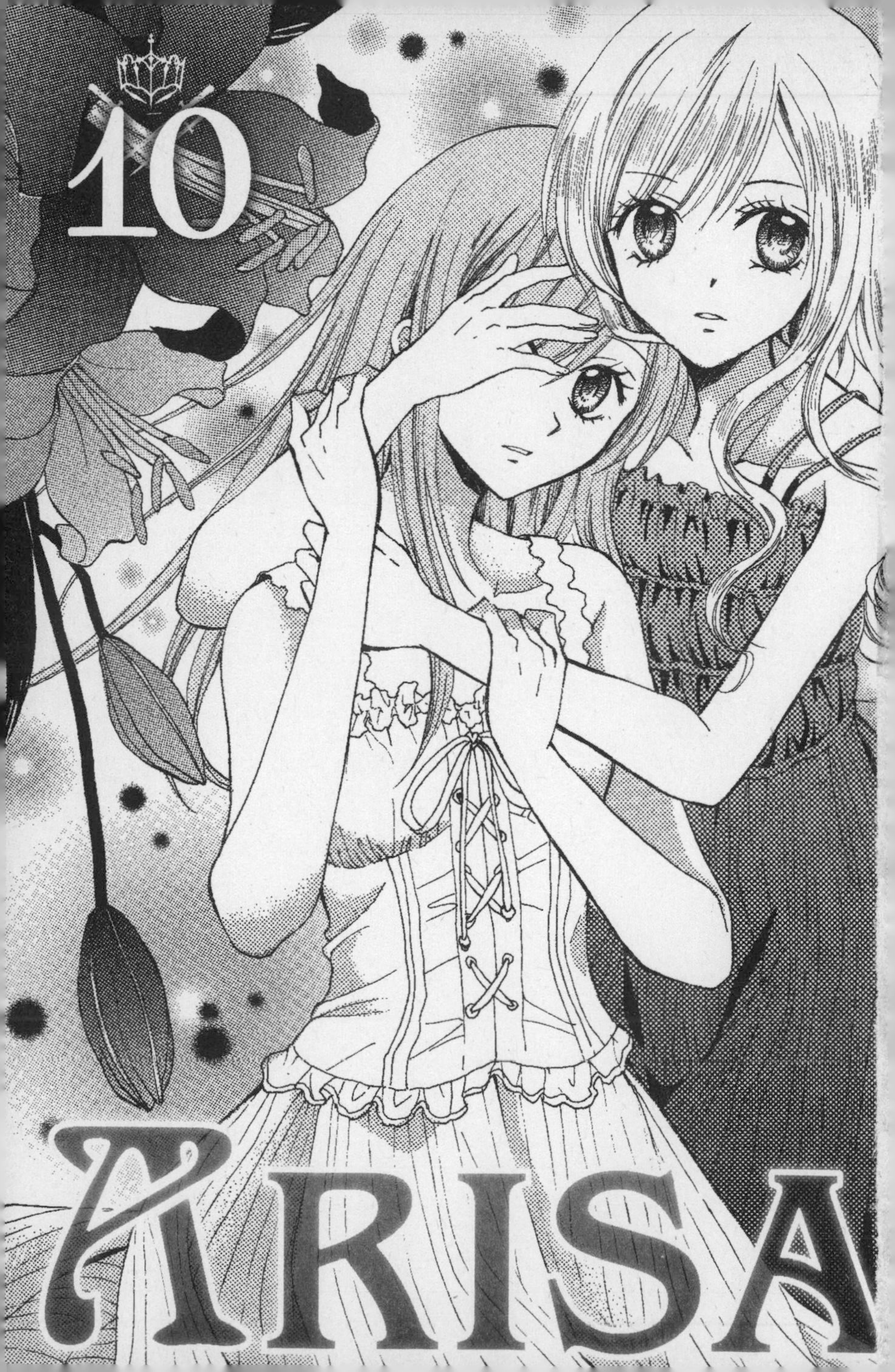
10
ARISA

Contents

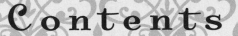

ARISA

Chapter 35: The Clockwork Clown 5

Chapter 36: A Bouquet for K ...43

Chapter 37: The Two Kings ...83

Chapter 38: The King's Smile ...121

The story so far

Tsubasa and Arisa are twin sisters separated by their parents' divorce. They finally reunited after three years of being apart, but their happy time together came to a sudden end when Arisa jumped out her bedroom window right in front of Tsubasa, leaving behind a mysterious card...

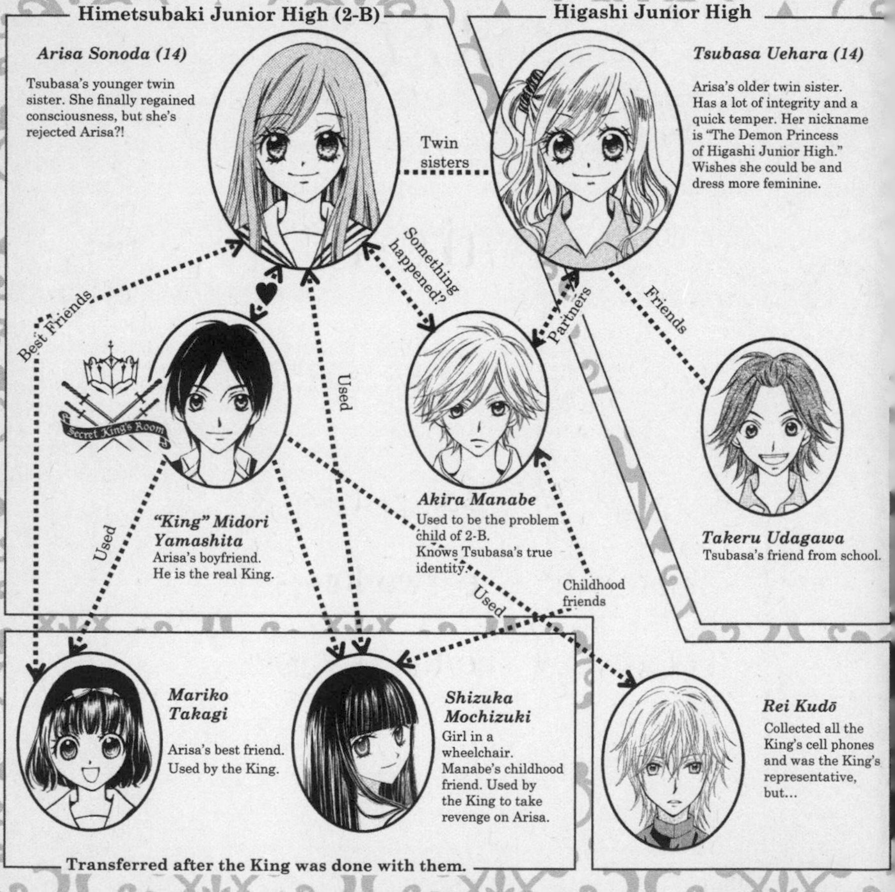

Himetsubaki Junior High (2-B)
Higashi Junior High
Arisa Sonoda (14)
Tsubasa's younger twin sister. She finally regained consciousness, but she's rejected Arisa?!
Twin sisters
Tsubasa Uehara (14)
Arisa's older twin sister. Has a lot of integrity and a quick temper. Her nickname is "The Demon Princess of Higashi Junior High." Wishes she could be and dress more feminine.
Something happened?
Partners
Friends
Best Friends
Used
Secret King's Room
"King" Midori Yamashita
Arisa's boyfriend. He is the real King.
Akira Manabe
Used to be the problem child of 2-B. Knows Tsubasa's true identity.
Takeru Udagawa
Tsubasa's friend from school.
Used
Childhood friends
Used
Mariko Takagi
Arisa's best friend. Used by the King.
Shizuka Mochizuki
Girl in a wheelchair. Manabe's childhood friend. Used by the King to take revenge on Arisa.
Rei Kudō
Collected all the King's cell phones and was the King's representative, but...
Transferred after the King was done with them.

In order to discover the secrets Arisa was hiding, Tsubasa pretended to be her and attended Himetsubaki Junior High. There she found a mysterious Internet presence known as "The King" supporting Class 2-B. Later, Arisa finally awoke from her long sleep. She seemed unstable, and said she couldn't remember anything, but after receiving something from Midori, her attitude changed completely, becoming cold. Meanwhile, at Midori's suggestion, Tsubasa broke into Kudō's room to try to discover Arisa's secret. However, it turned out to be a trap laid by King Midori! At last, Midori revealed his true identity to Tsubasa. Now she's locked in with a bomb, and time is running out...!

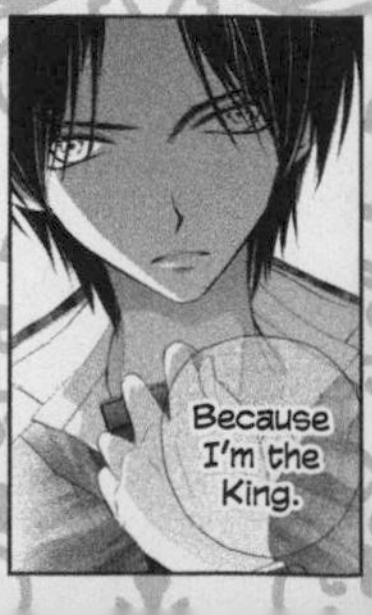

Because I'm the King.

Special Thanks

T. Nakamura, H. Kishimoto
M. Nakata & Kawamoto-sama
of the
Nakayoshi editorial dept.
&
"Red Rooster"
Takashi Shimoyata-sama
&
Ginnansha-sama

Please send mail to:
Natsumi Andō
c/o Kodansha Comics
451 Park Ave. South, 7th floor
New York, NY 10016

My latest troubles

While I'm preparing food my dog attacks me with great enthusiasm...

It's always right on the back of my knees, so it's like my dog is trying to knock me over for fun...

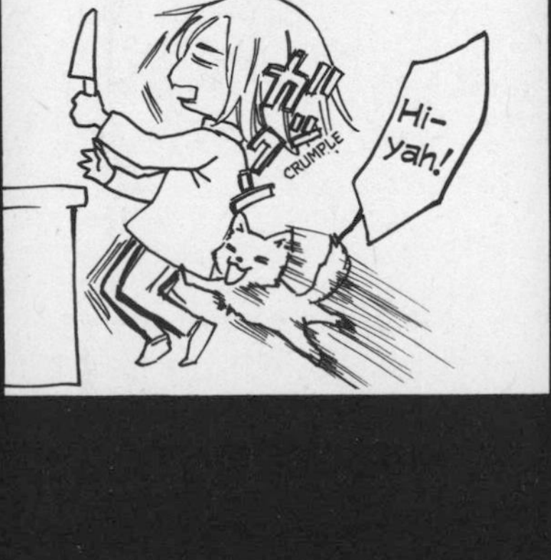
CRUMPLE
Hi-yah!

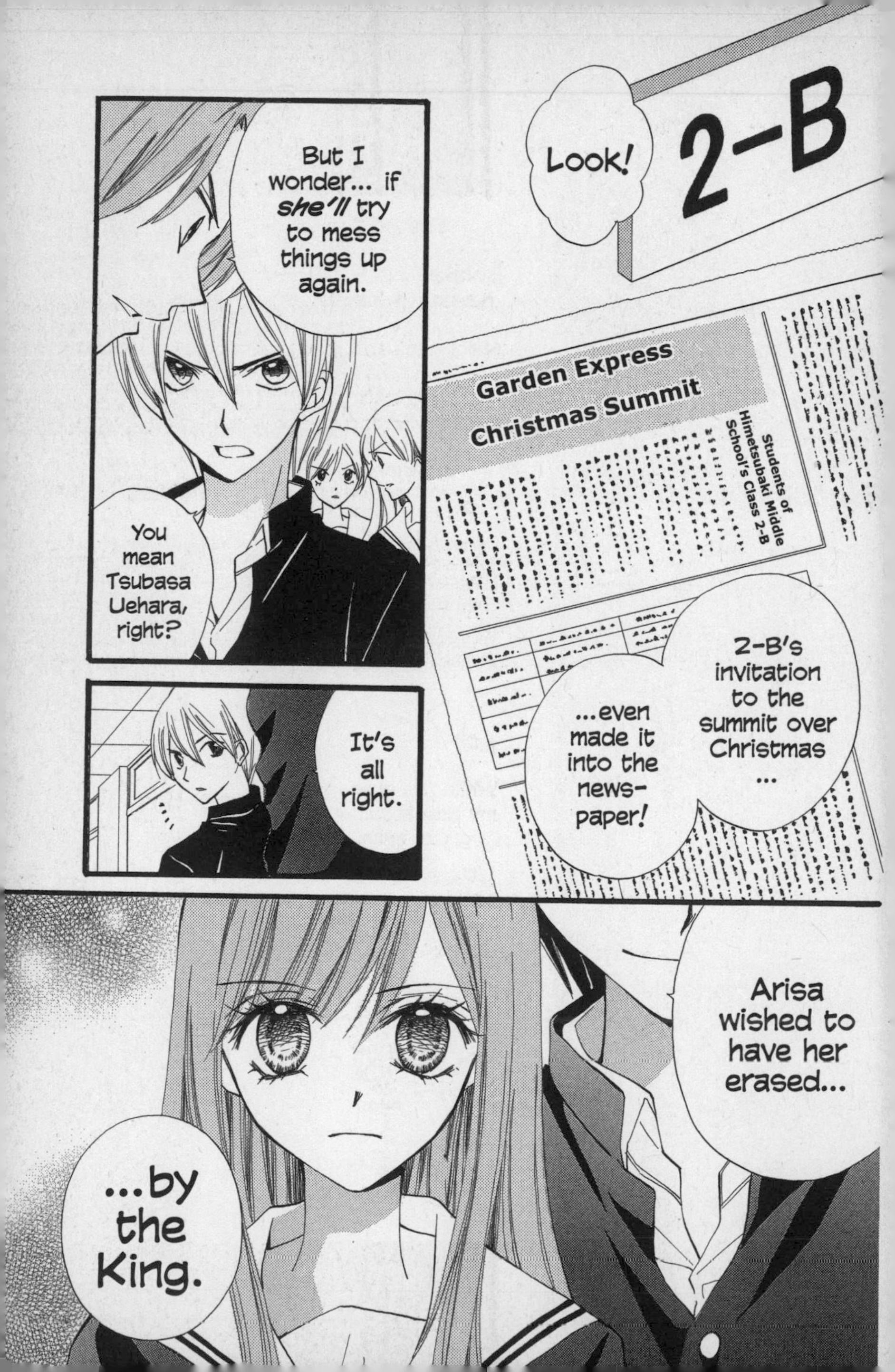

Look!
2-B
Garden Express
Christmas Summit
Students of Himetsubaki Middle School's Class 2-B
2-B's invitation to the summit over Christmas ...
...even made it into the news-paper!
But I wonder... if *she'll* try to mess things up again.
You mean Tsubasa Uehara, right?
It's all right.
Arisa wished to have her erased...
...by the King.

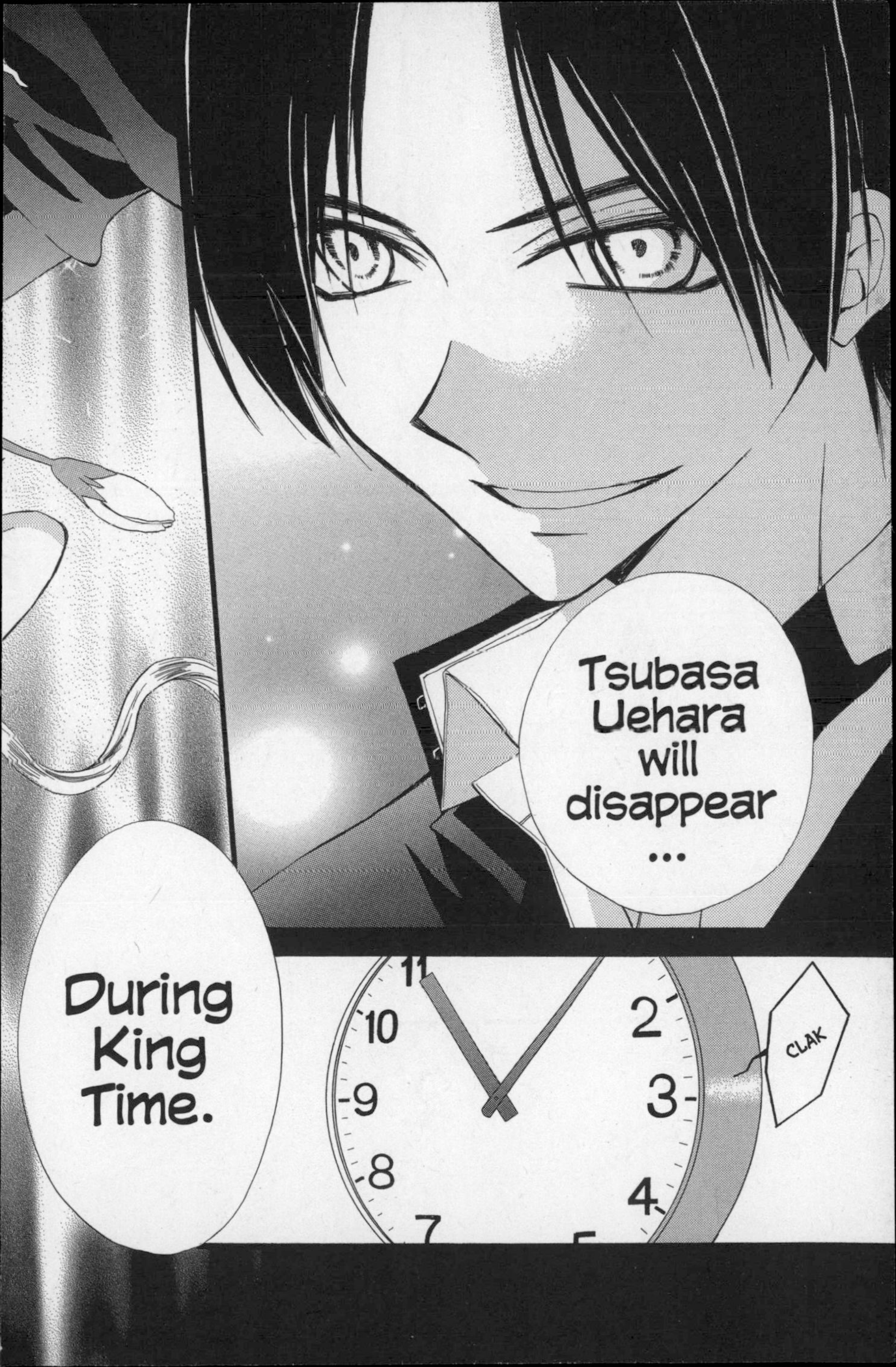
Tsubasa Uehara will disappear ...
During King Time.
CLAK

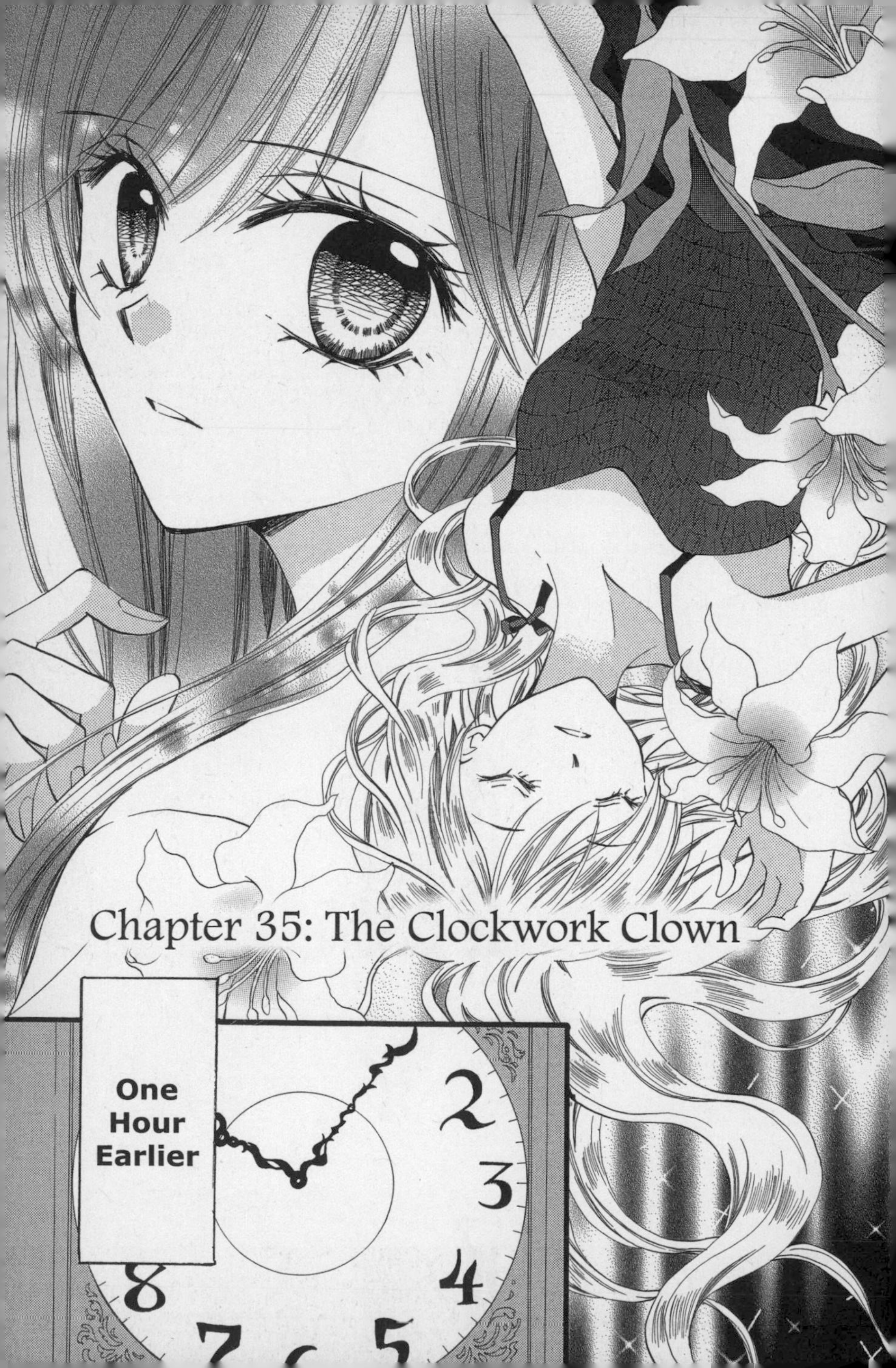
Chapter 35: The Clockwork Clown
One Hour Earlier

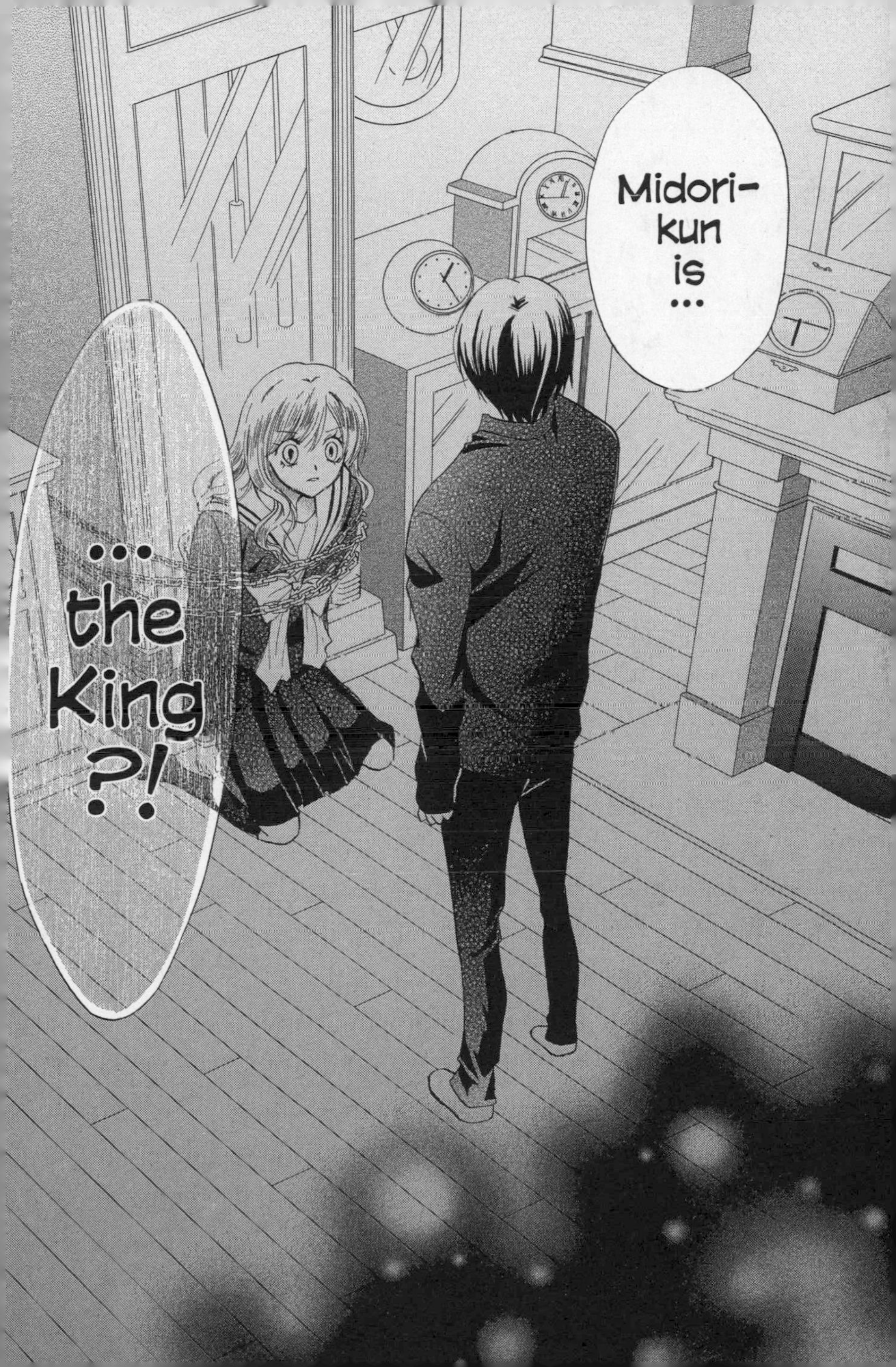

Midori-kun is ...
... the King ?!

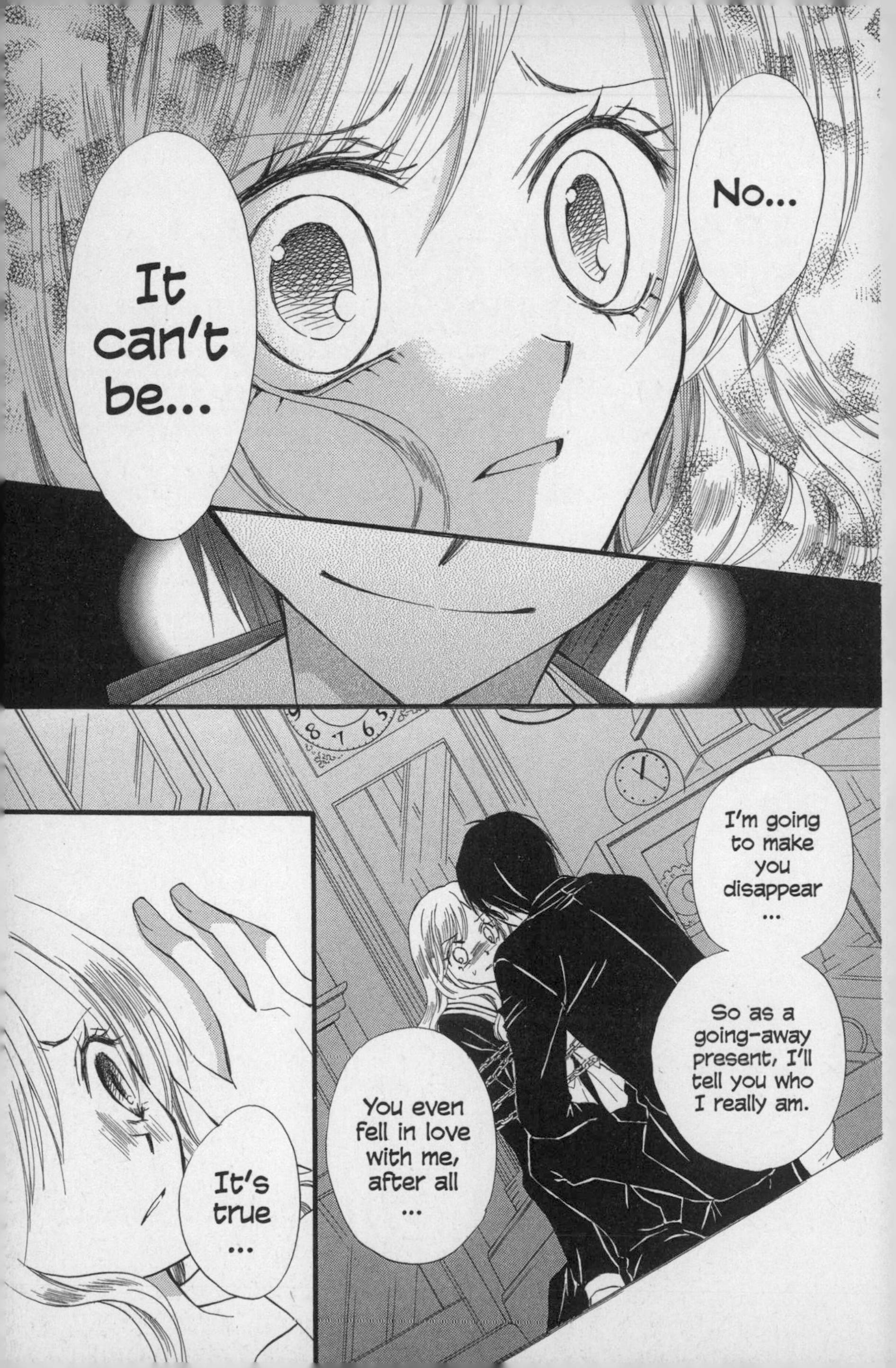
No...
It can't be...
I'm going to make you disappear ...
So as a going-away present, I'll tell you who I really am.
You even fell in love with me, after all ...
It's true ...

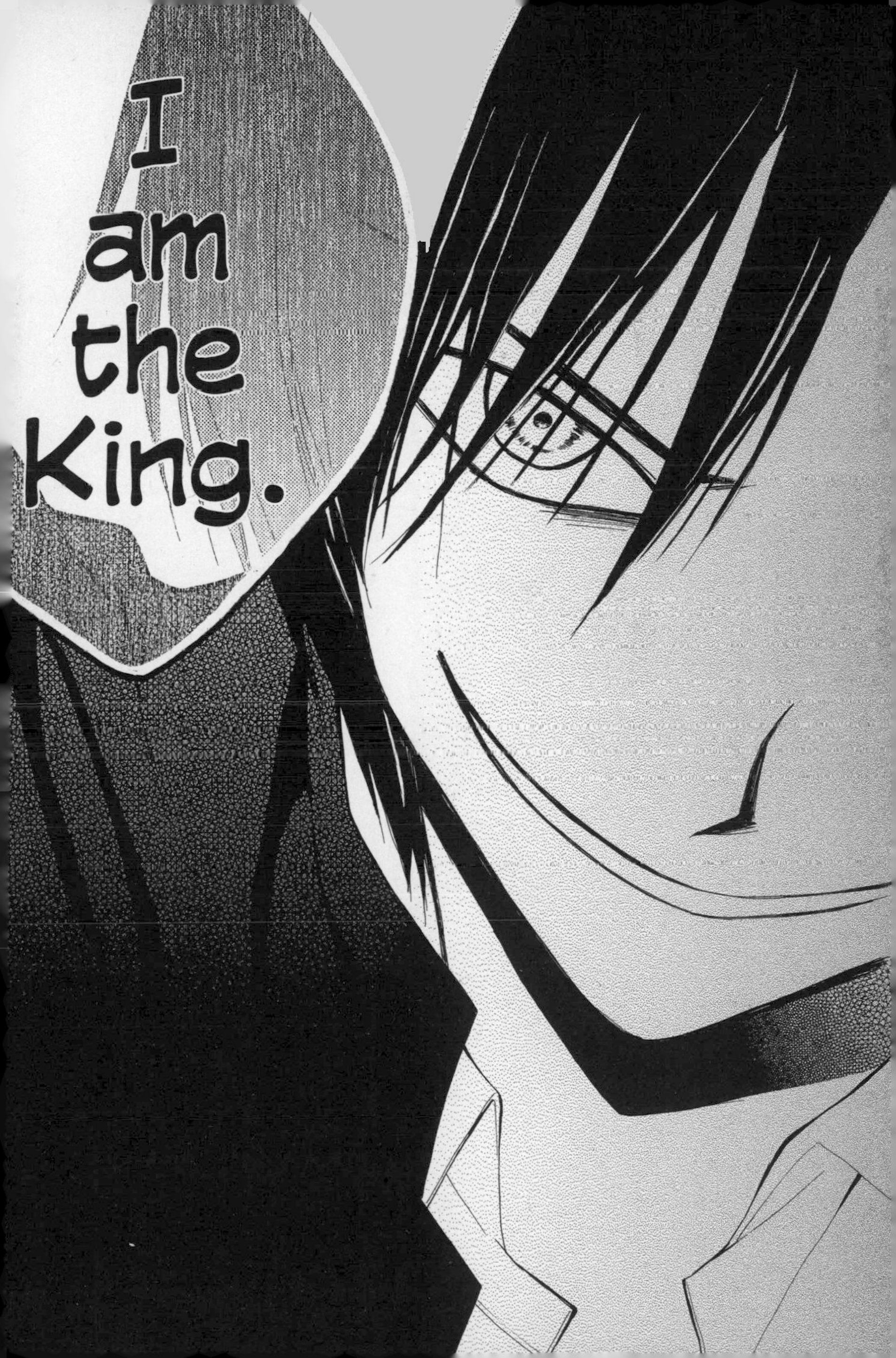
I am the King.

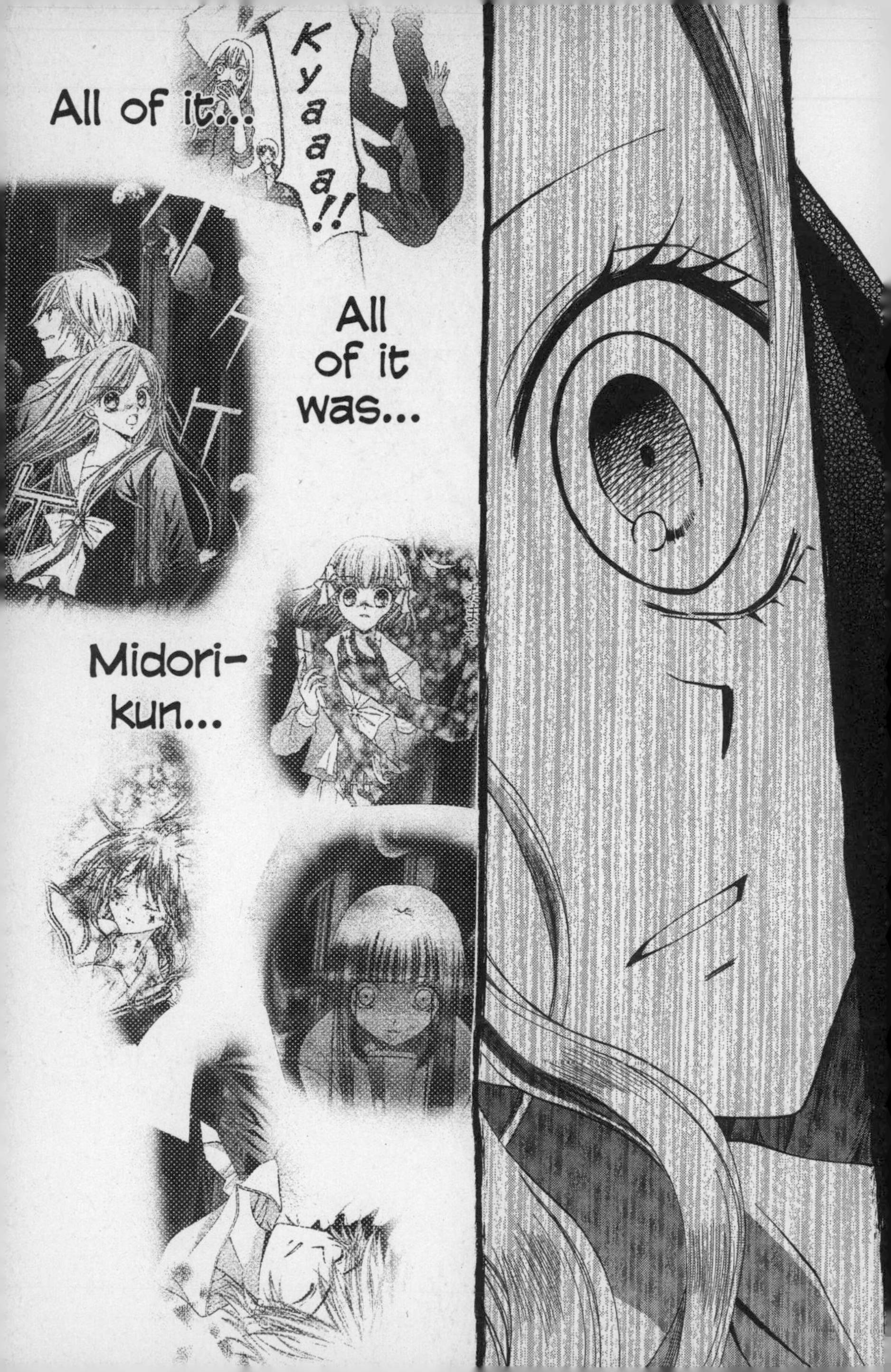
Kyaaa!!
All of it...
All of it was...
Midori-kun...

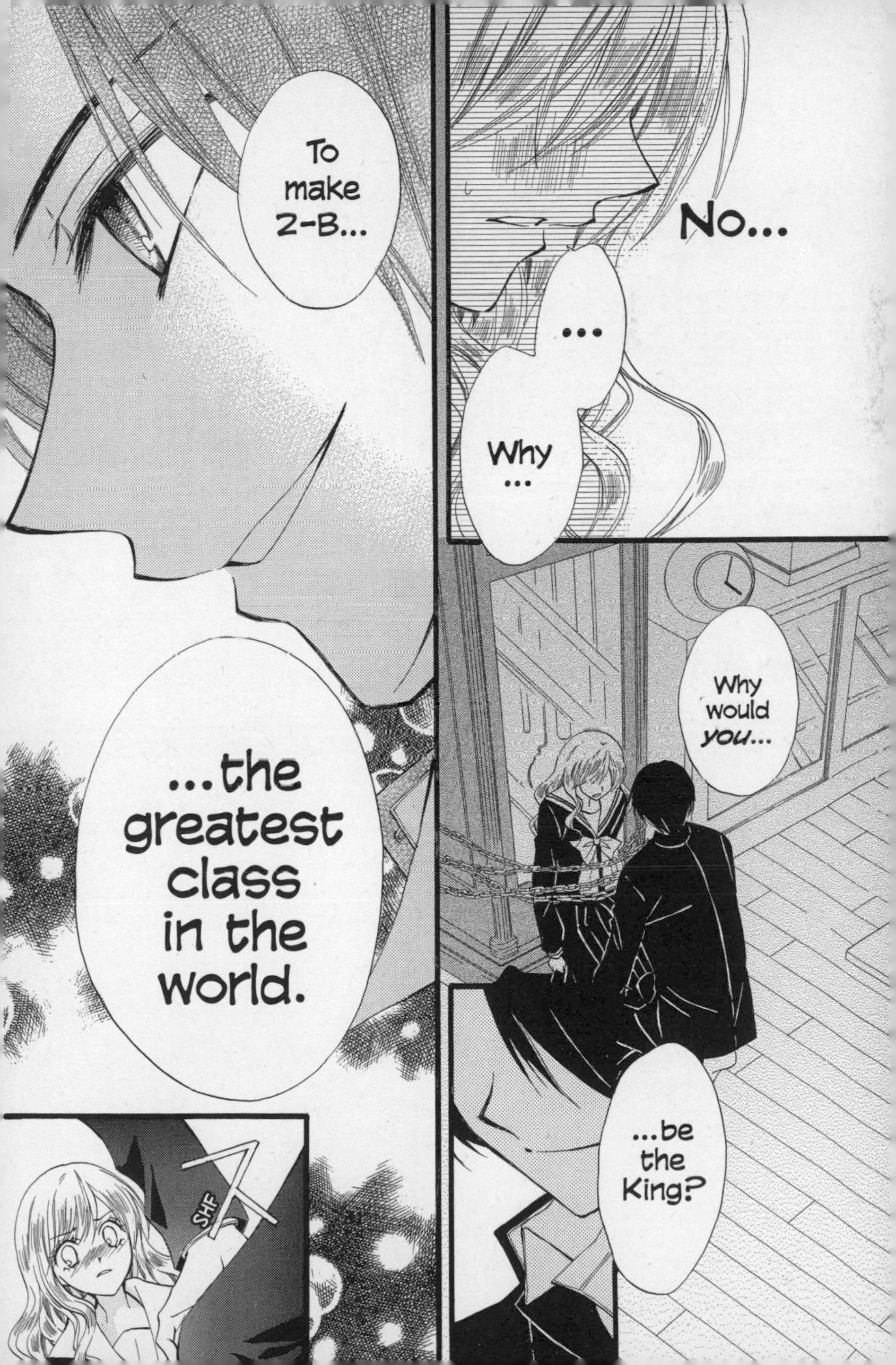
No...
...
Why...
Why would *you*...
...be the King?
To make 2-B...
...the greatest class in the world.
SHF

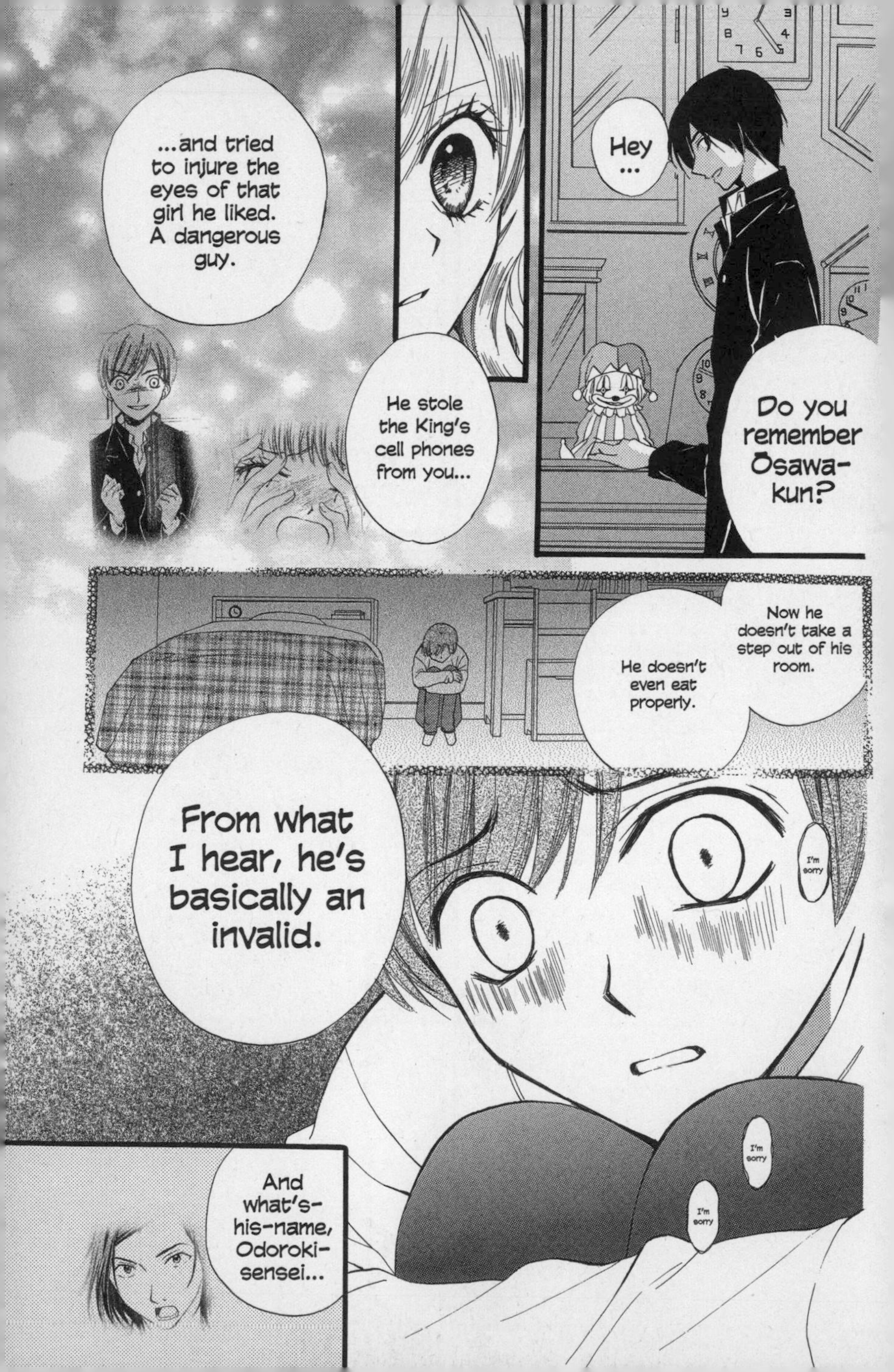
Hey ...
Do you remember Ōsawa-kun?
He stole the King's cell phones from you...
...and tried to injure the eyes of that girl he liked. A dangerous guy.
Now he doesn't take a step out of his room.
He doesn't even eat properly.
From what I hear, he's basically an invalid.
I'm sorry
I'm sorry
I'm sorry
And what's-his-name, Odoroki-sensei...

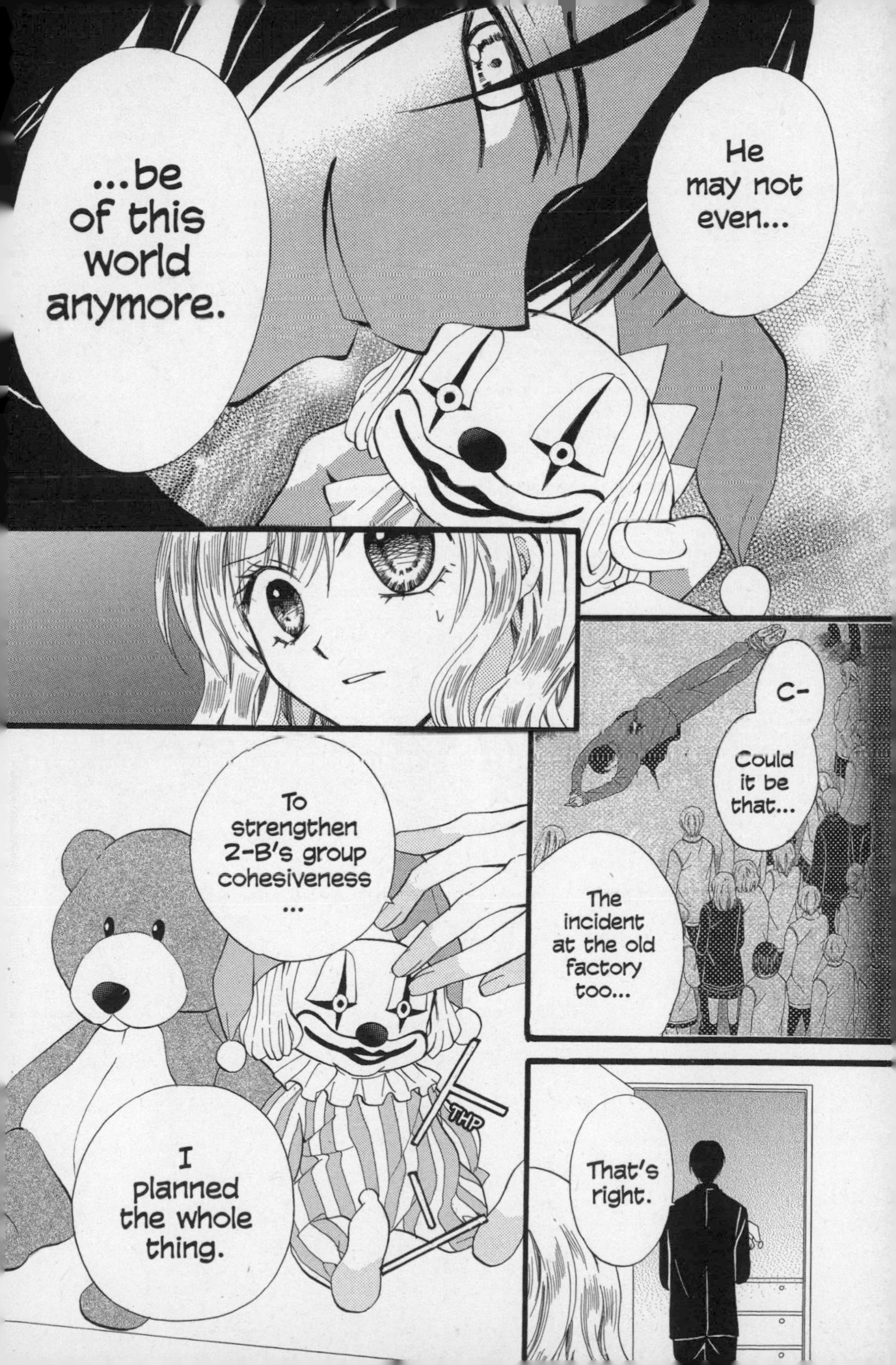

He may not even...
...be of this world anymore.
C-
Could it be that...
The incident at the old factory too...
That's right.
To strengthen 2-B's group cohesiveness ...
THP
I planned the whole thing.

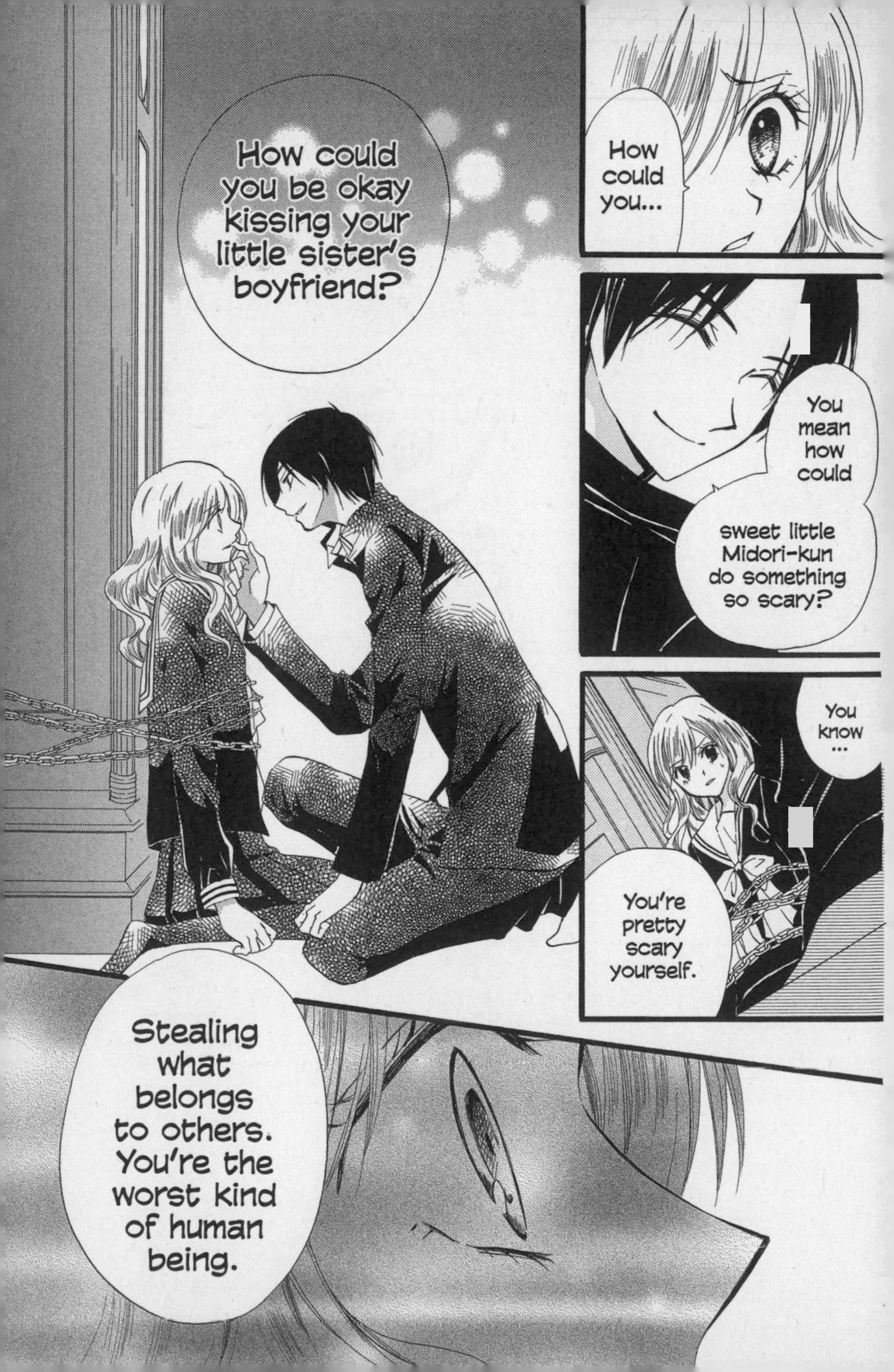
How could you...
You mean how could
sweet little Midori-kun do something so scary?
You know...
You're pretty scary yourself.
How could you be okay kissing your little sister's boyfriend?
Stealing what belongs to others. You're the worst kind of human being.

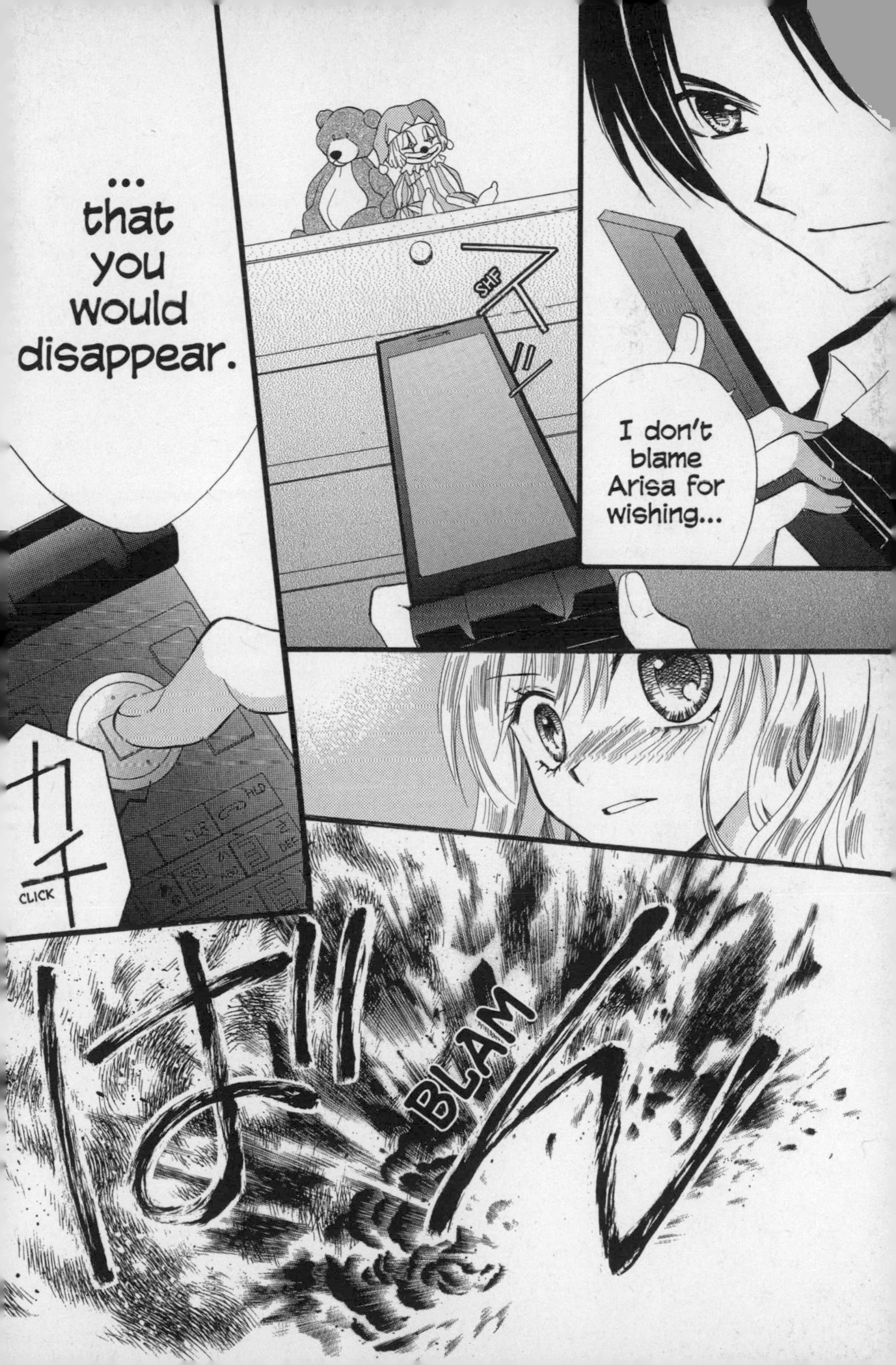
I don't blame Arisa for wishing...
SHF
... that you would disappear.
CLICK
BLAM

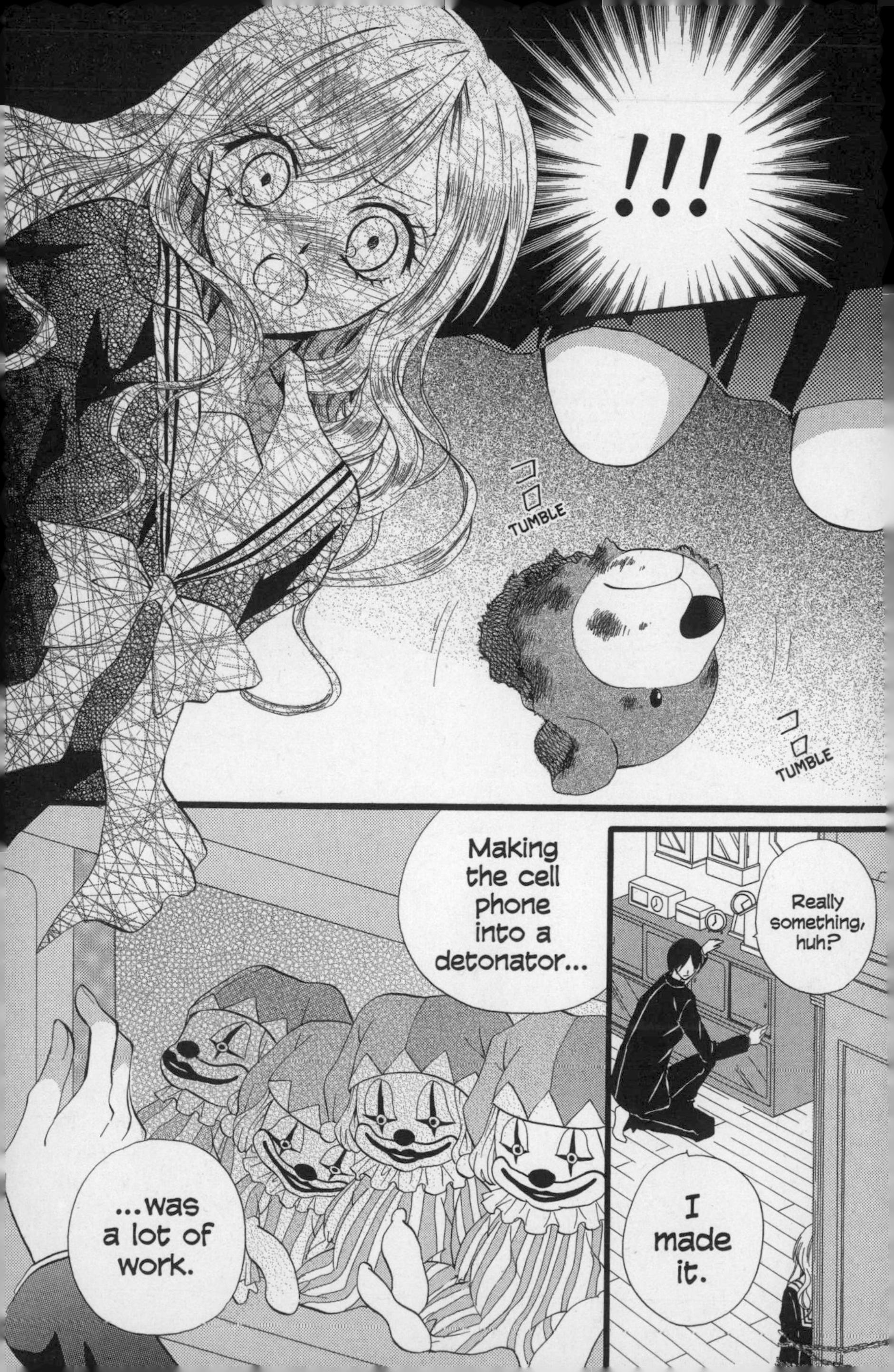
!!!
コロ
TUMBLE
コロ
TUMBLE
Really something, huh?
I made it.
Making the cell phone into a detonator...
...was a lot of work.

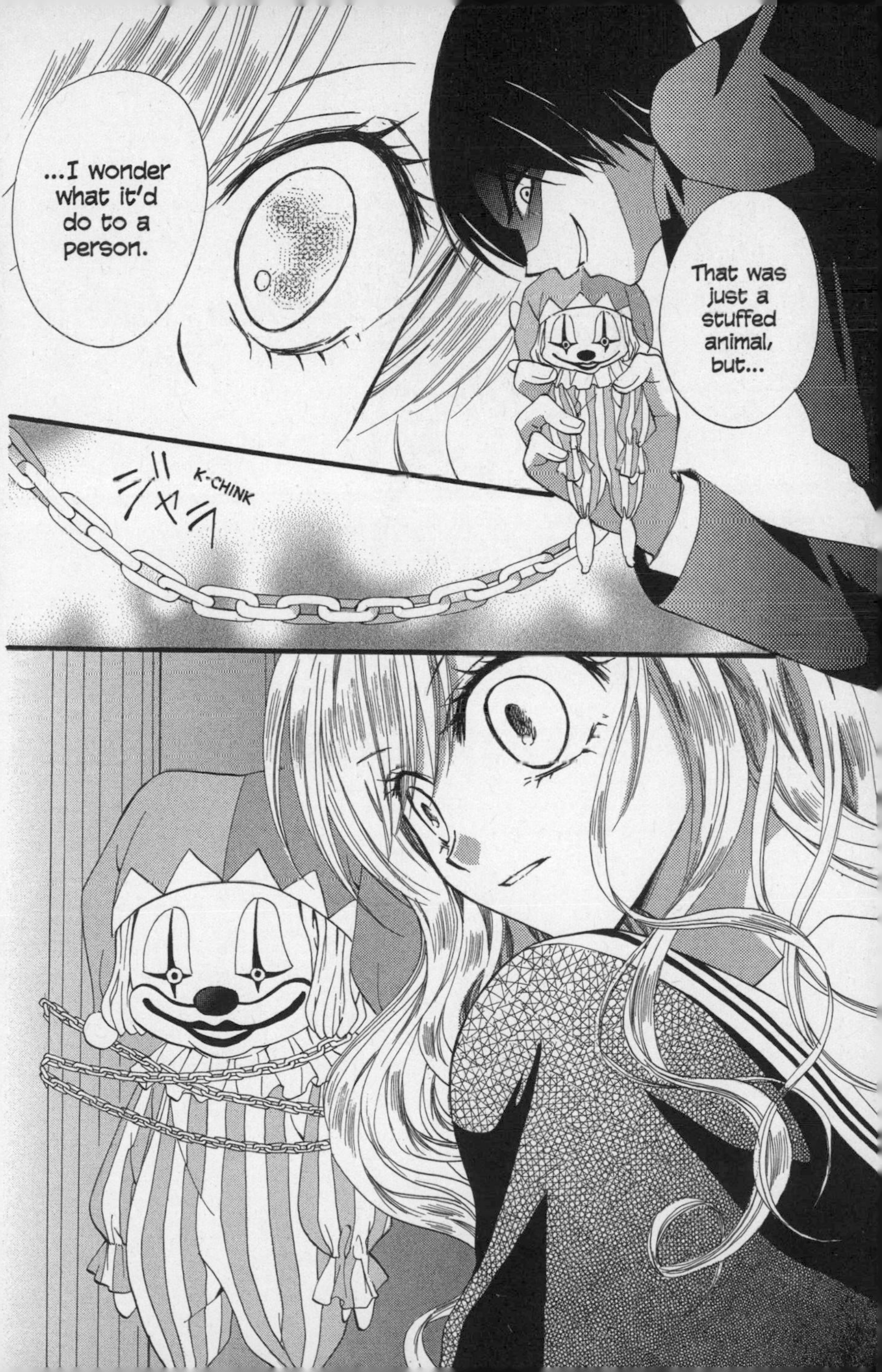
That was just a stuffed animal, but...
...I wonder what it'd do to a person.
ジャラ
K-CHINK

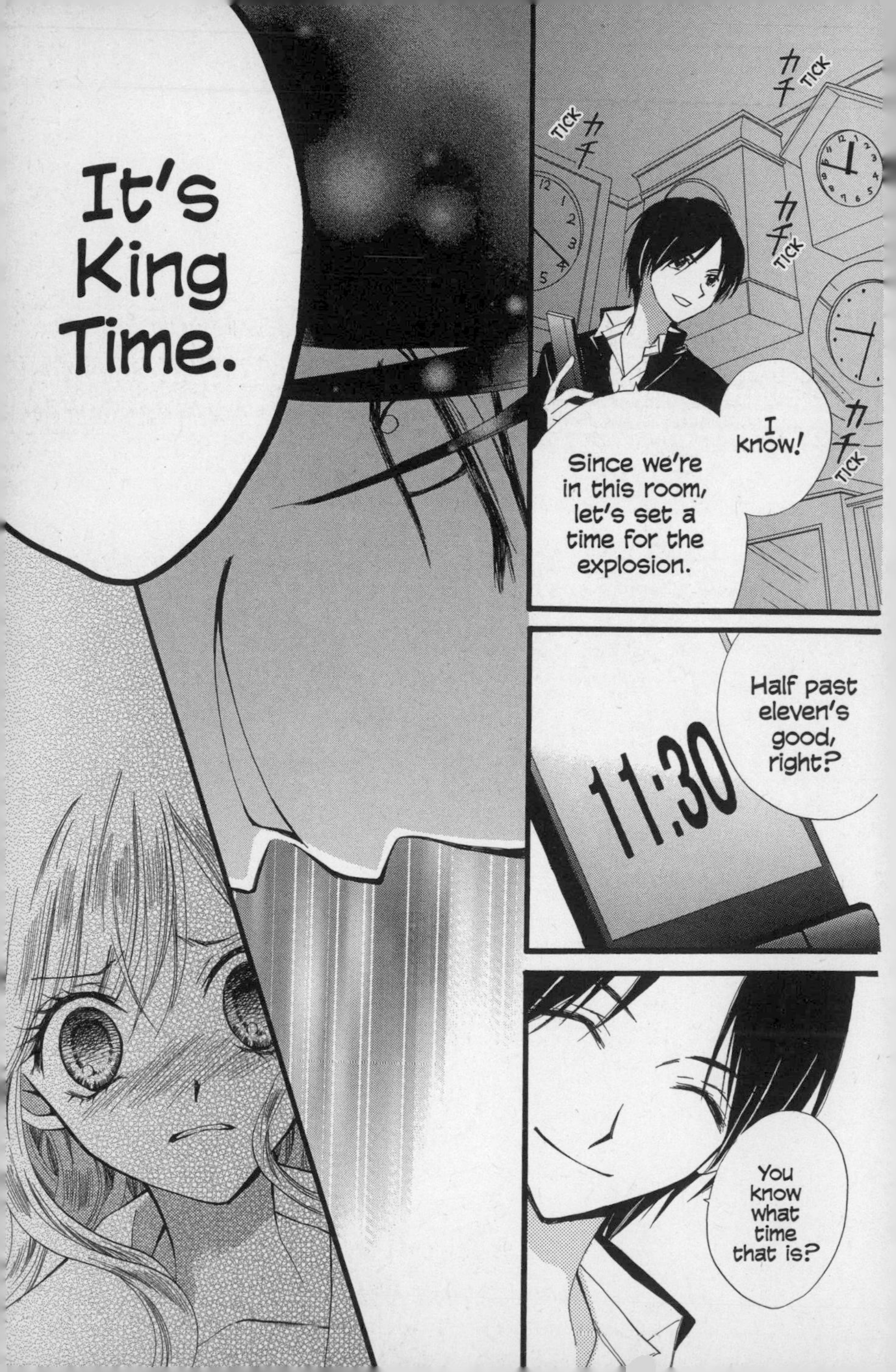
TICK
TICK
TICK
TICK
I know!
Since we're in this room, let's set a time for the explosion.
11:30
Half past eleven's good, right?
You know what time that is?
It's King Time.

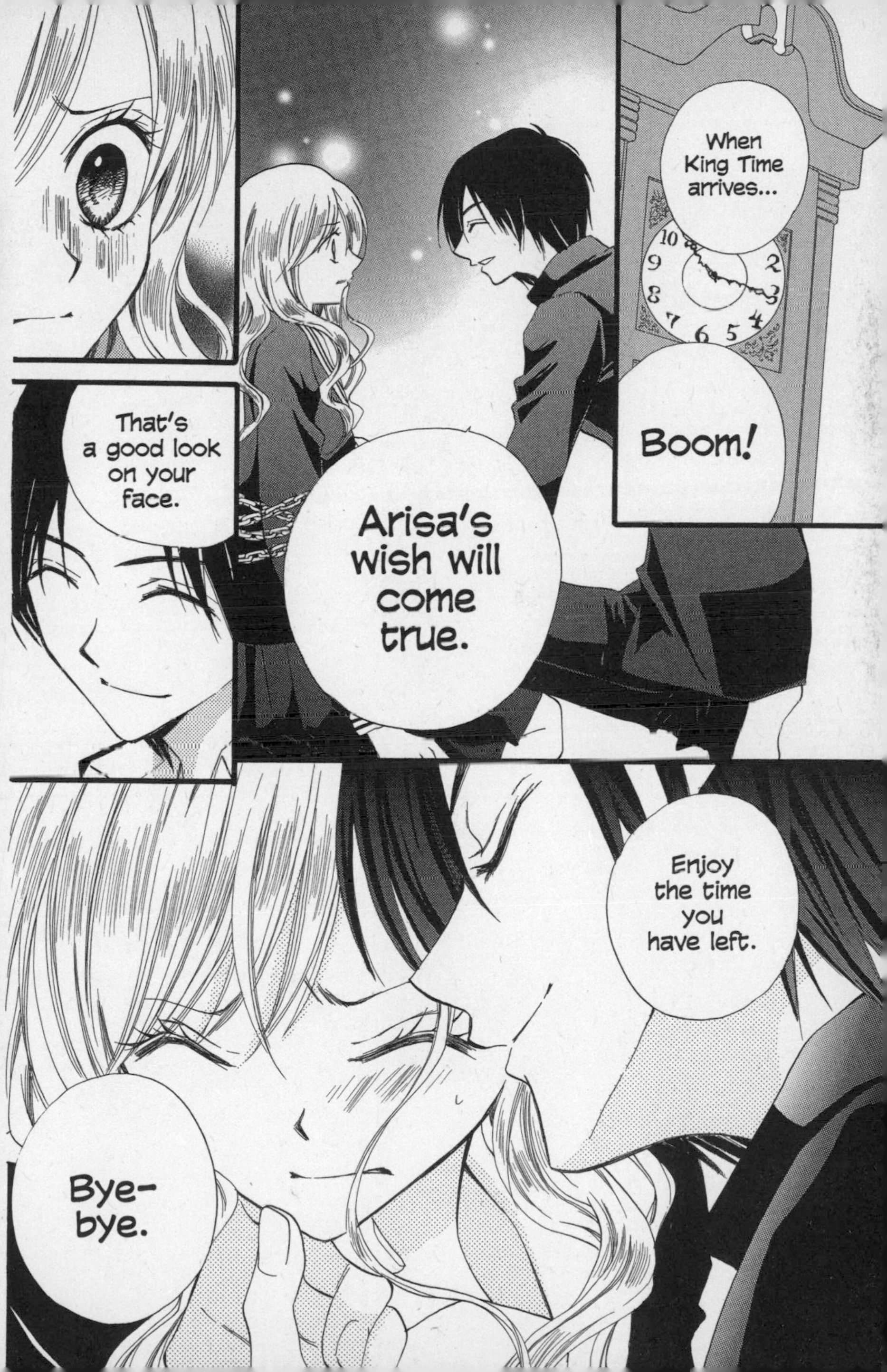
When King Time arrives...
Boom!
Arisa's wish will come true.
That's a good look on your face.
Enjoy the time you have left.
Bye-bye.

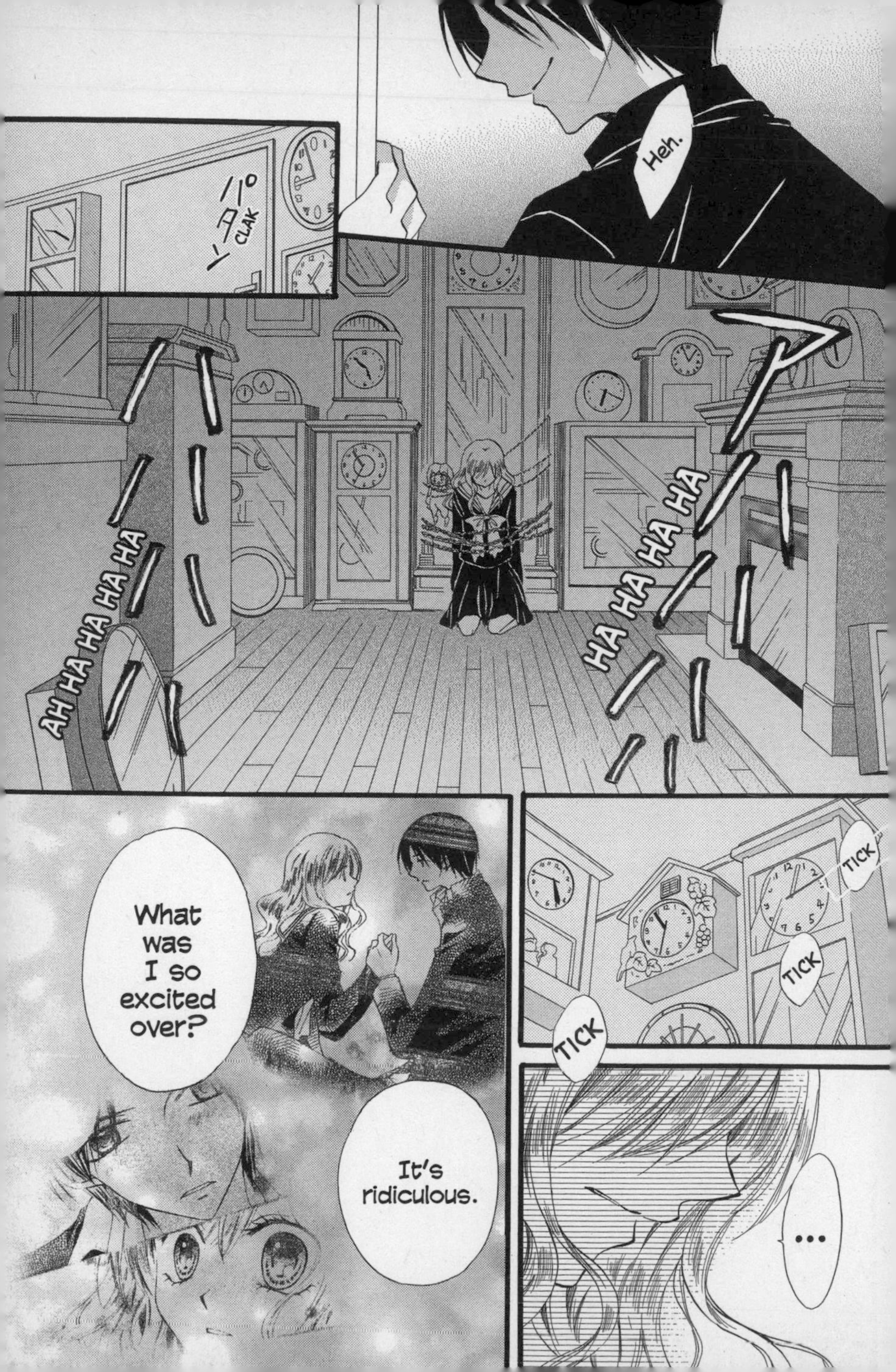
Heh.
CLAK
HA HA HA HA
AH HA HA HA HA
TICK
TICK
TICK
...
What was I so excited over?
It's ridiculous.

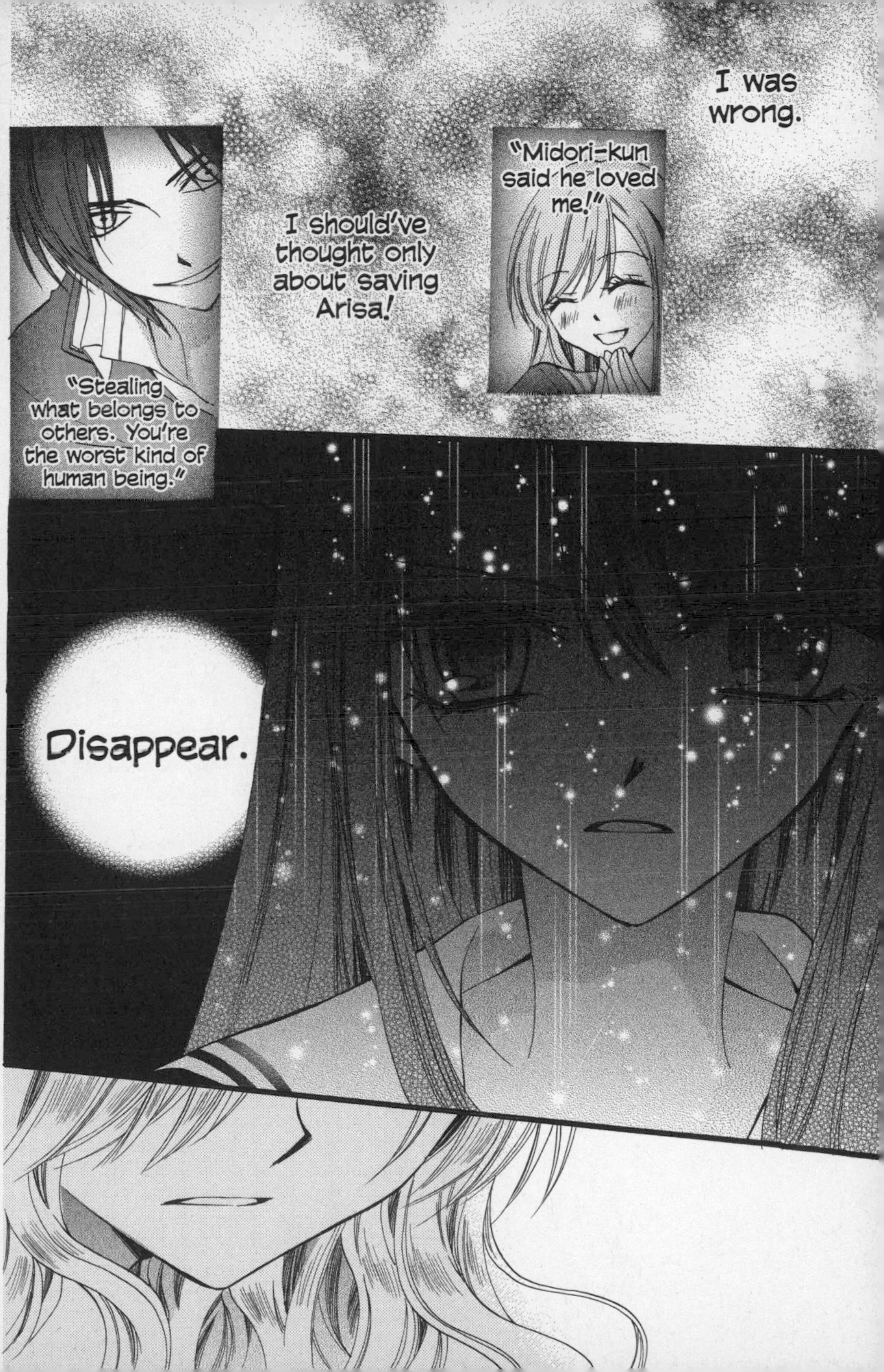

I was wrong.
"Midori-kun said he loved me!"
I should've thought only about saving Arisa!
"Stealing what belongs to others. You're the worst kind of human being."
Disappear.

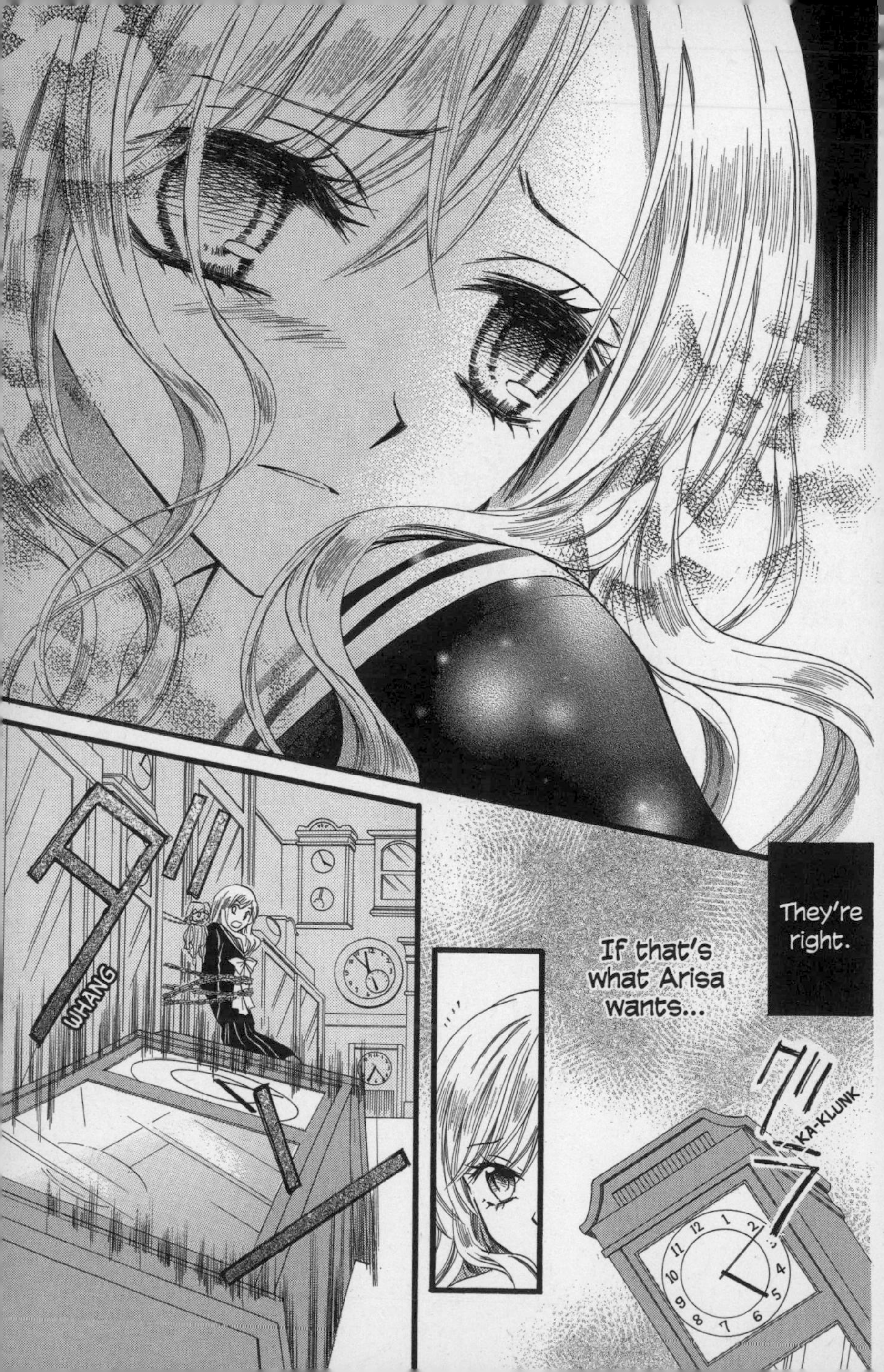

They're right.
If that's what Arisa wants...
KA-KLUNK
WHANG

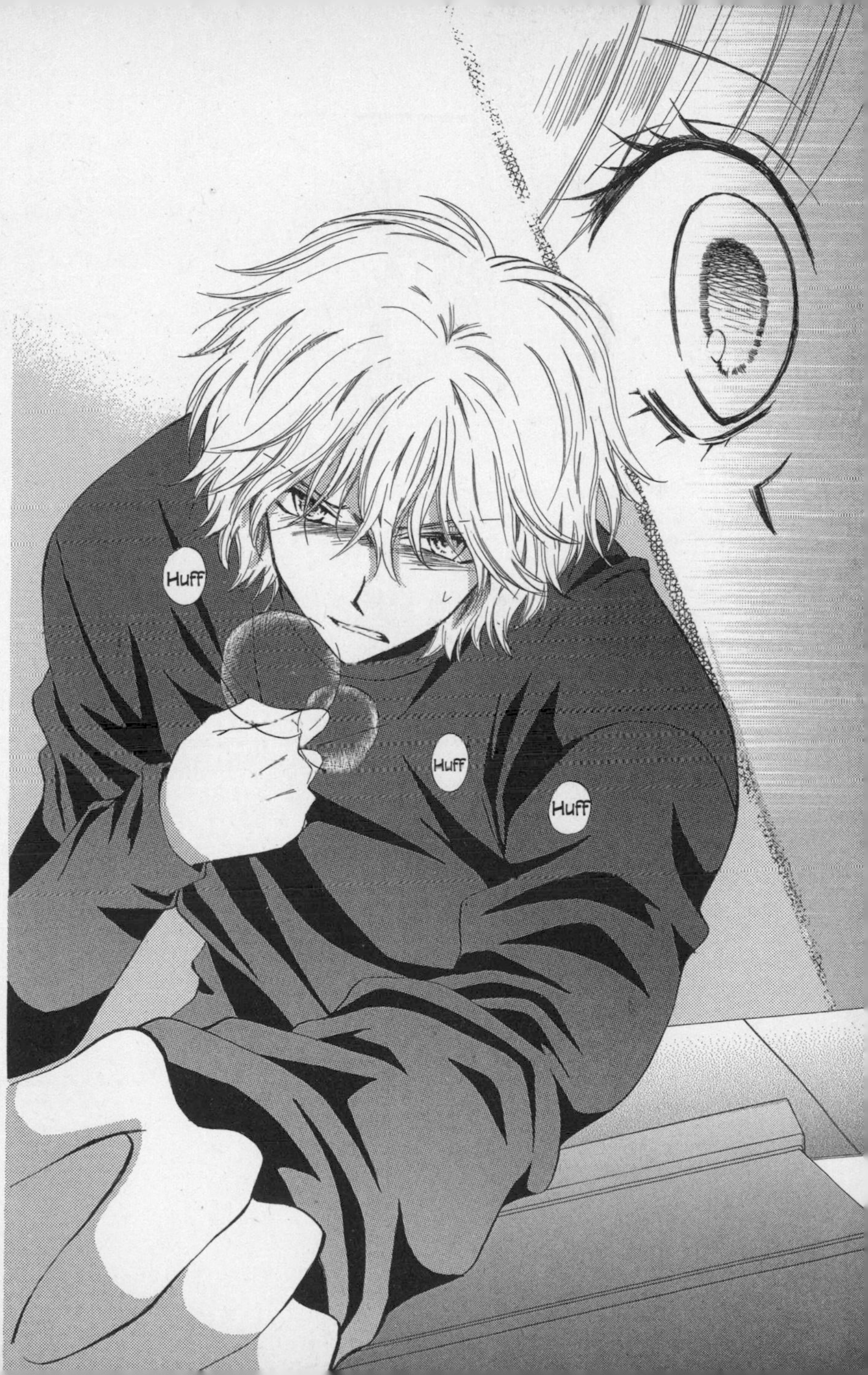
Huff
Huff
Huff

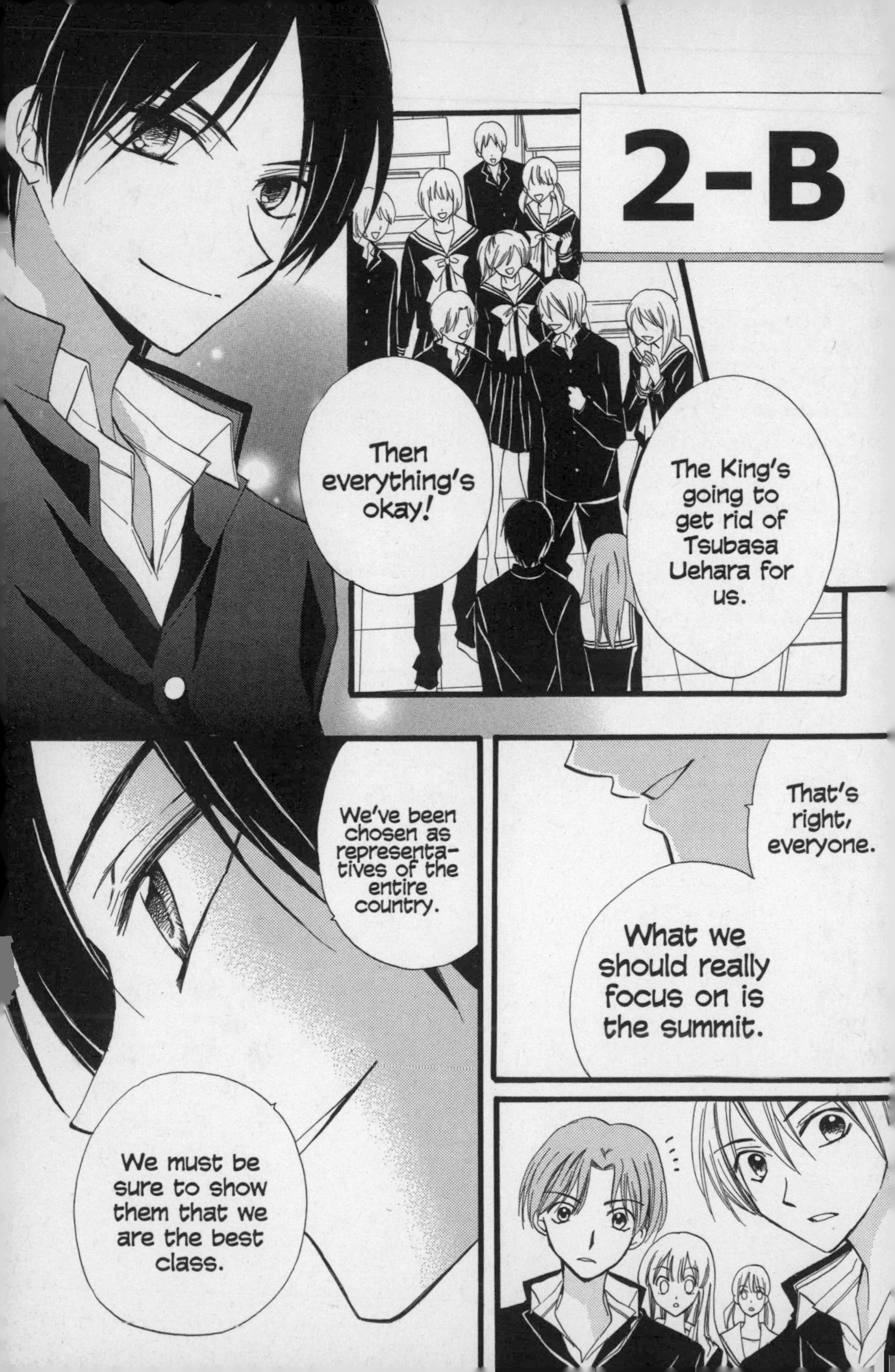
2-B
The King's going to get rid of Tsubasa Uehara for us.
Then everything's okay!
That's right, everyone.
What we should really focus on is the summit.
We've been chosen as representa-tives of the entire country.
We must be sure to show them that we are the best class.

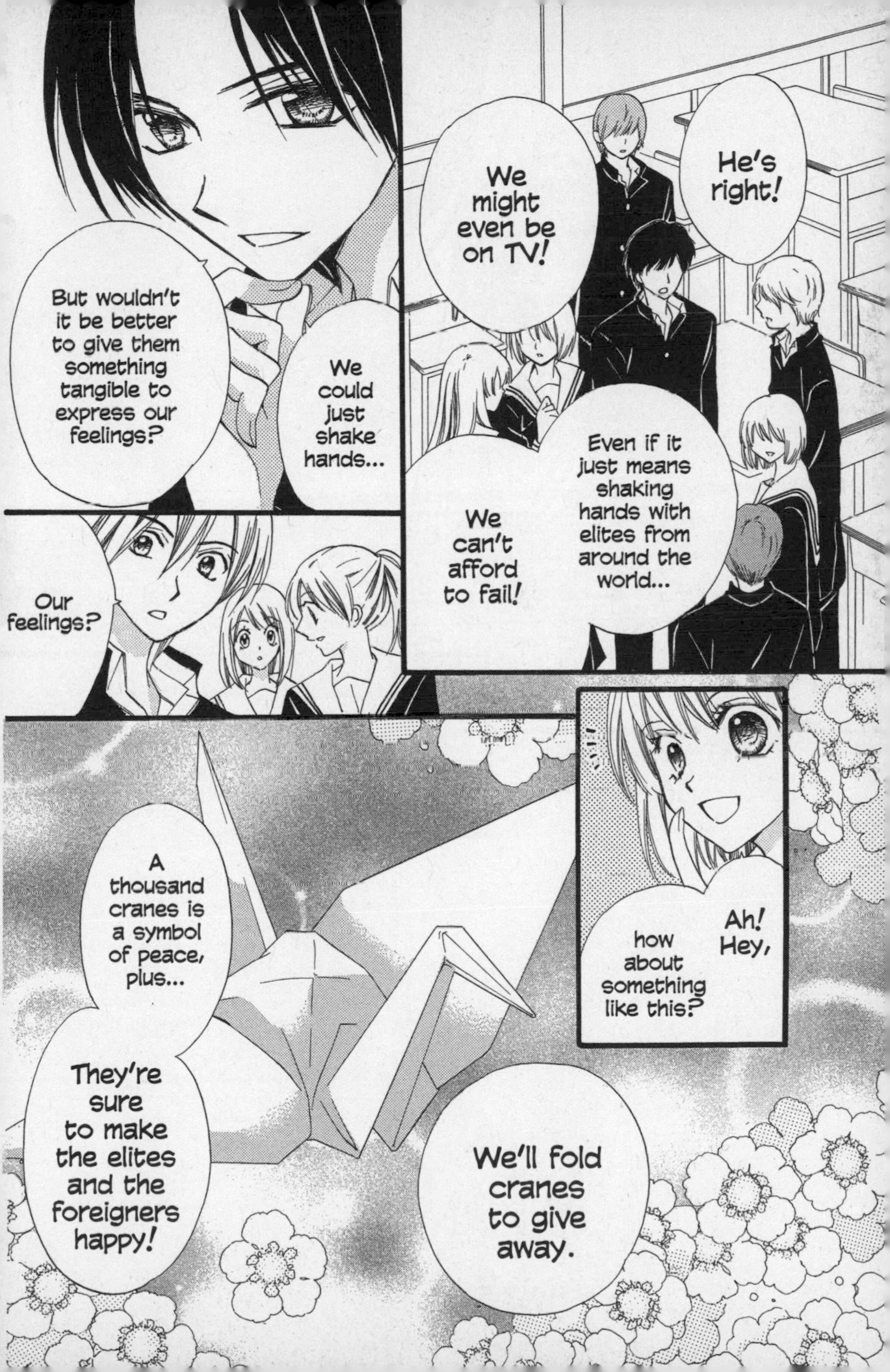
He's right!
We might even be on TV!
Even if it just means shaking hands with elites from around the world...
We can't afford to fail!
We could just shake hands...
But wouldn't it be better to give them something tangible to express our feelings?
Our feelings?
Ah! Hey, how about something like this?
We'll fold cranes to give away.
A thousand cranes is a symbol of peace, plus...
They're sure to make the elites and the foreigners happy!

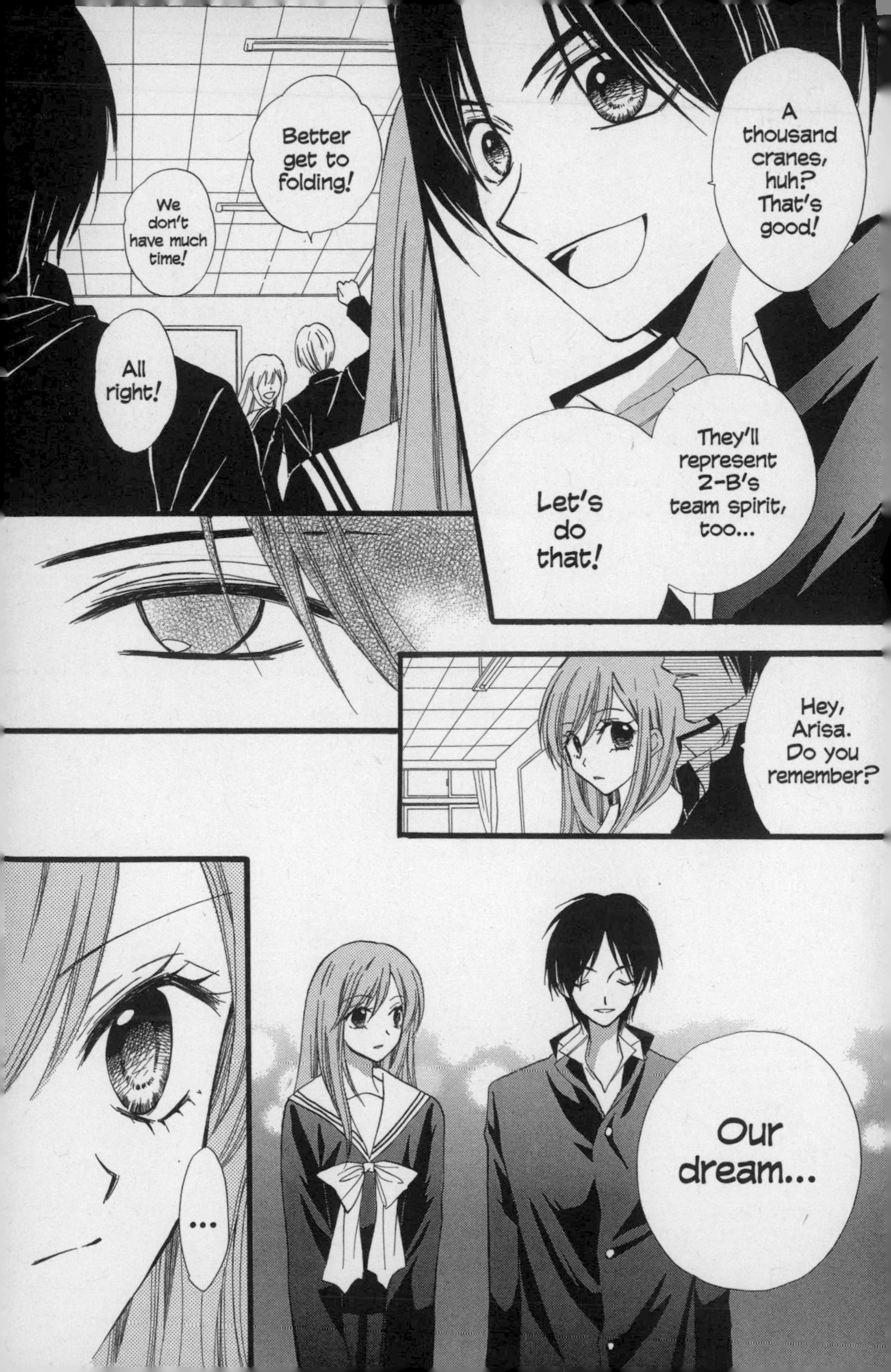

A thousand cranes, huh? That's good!
They'll represent 2-B's team spirit, too...
Let's do that!
Better get to folding!
We don't have much time!
All right!
Hey, Arisa. Do you remember?
Our dream...
...

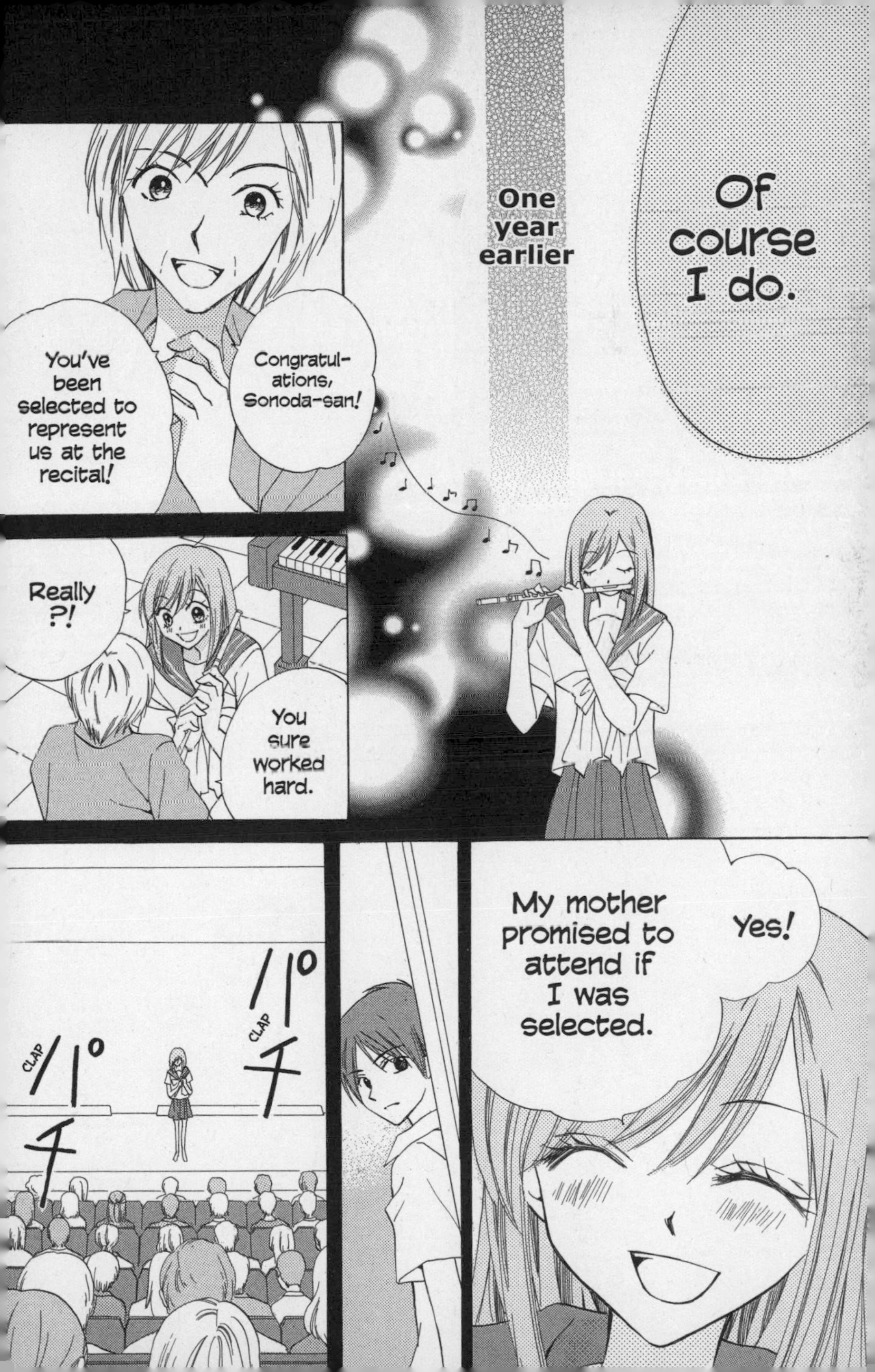
Of course I do.
One year earlier
Congratulations, Sonoda-san!
You've been selected to represent us at the recital!
Really ?!
You sure worked hard.
Yes!
My mother promised to attend if I was selected.
CLAP
CLAP

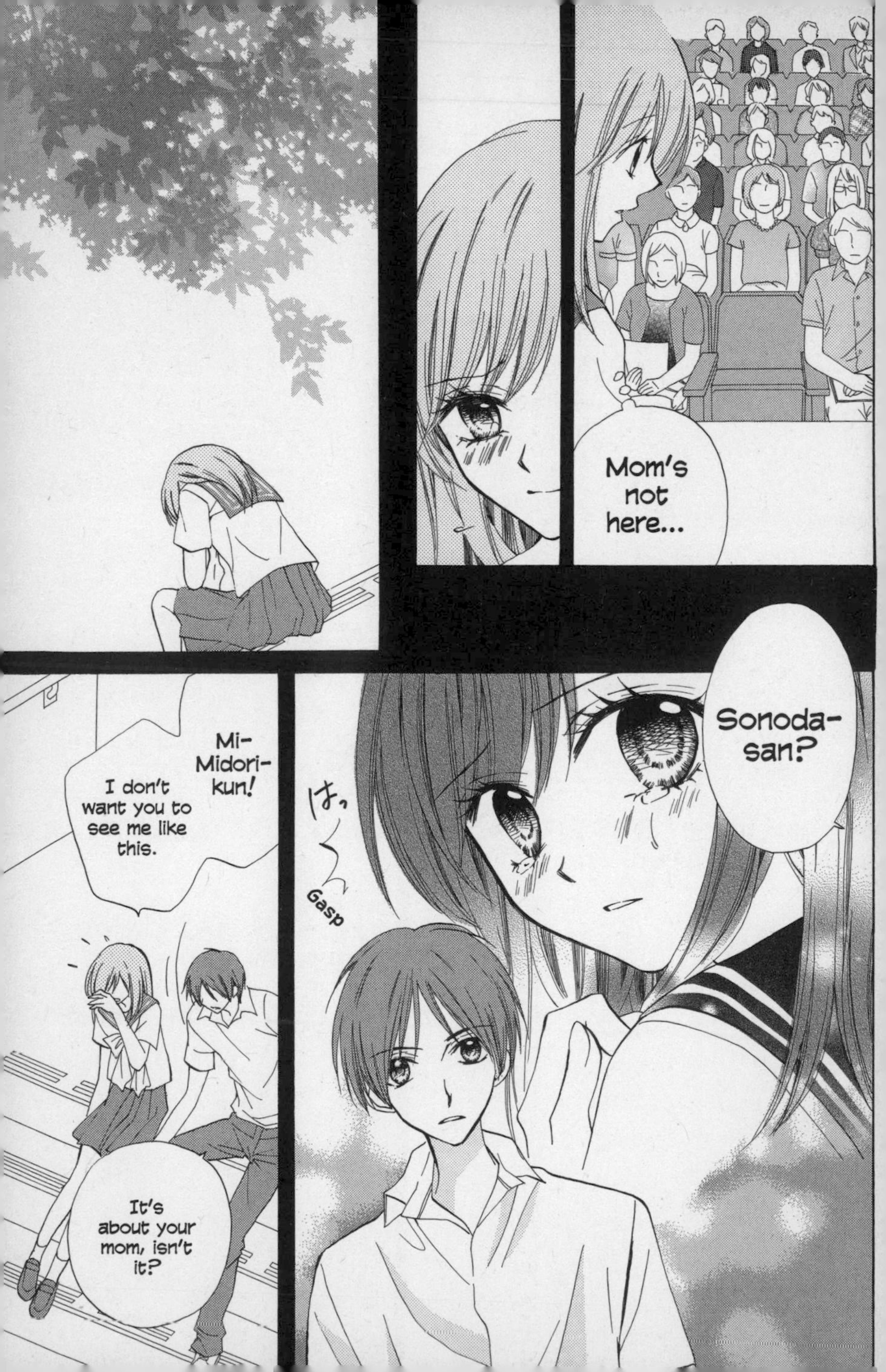
Mom's not here...
Sonoda-san?
はっ
Gasp
Mi-Midori-kun!
I don't want you to see me like this.
It's about your mom, isn't it?

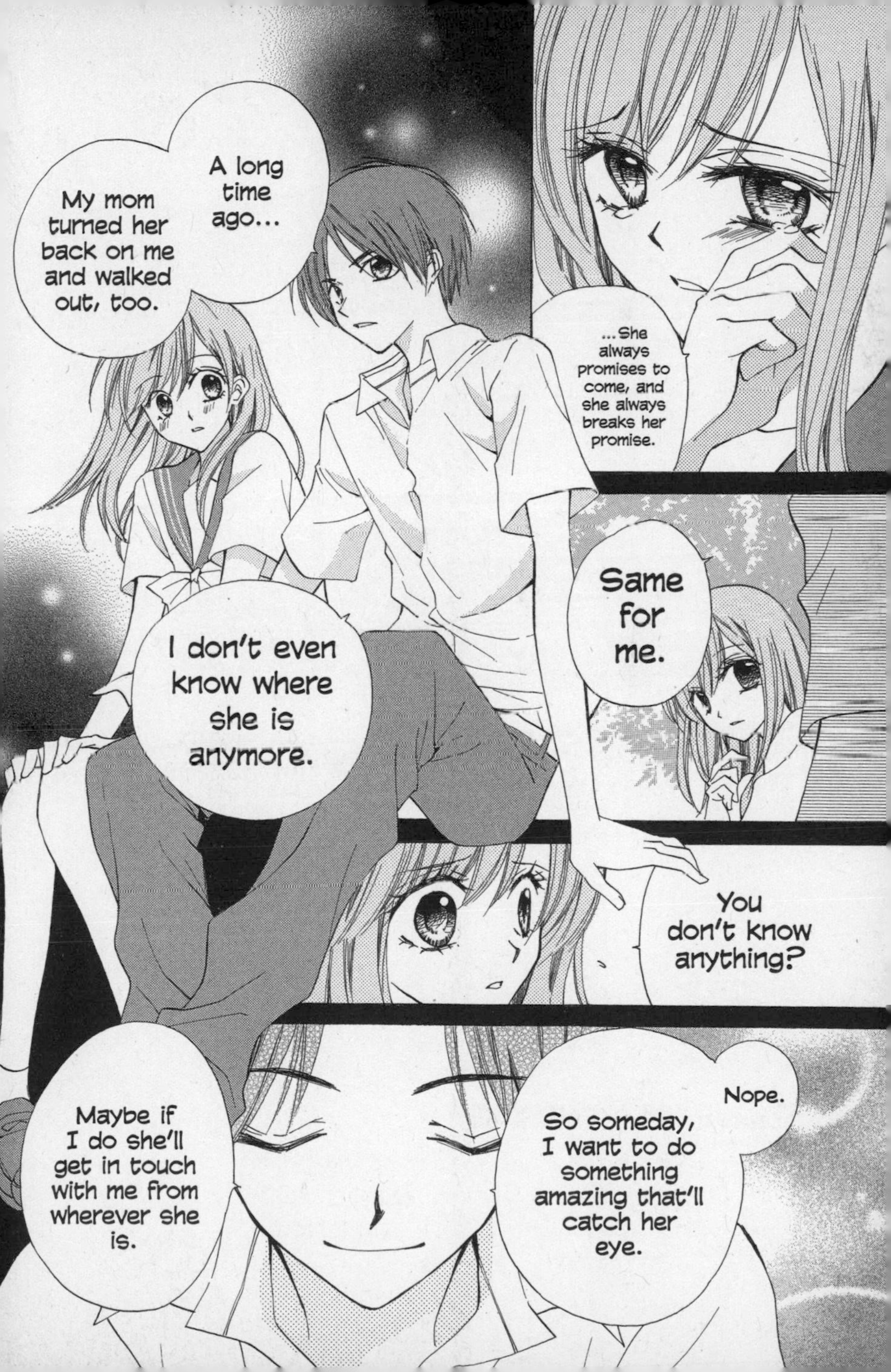
...She always promises to come, and she always breaks her promise.
A long time ago...
My mom turned her back on me and walked out, too.
I don't even know where she is anymore.
Same for me.
You don't know anything?
Nope.
So someday, I want to do something amazing that'll catch her eye.
Maybe if I do she'll get in touch with me from wherever she is.

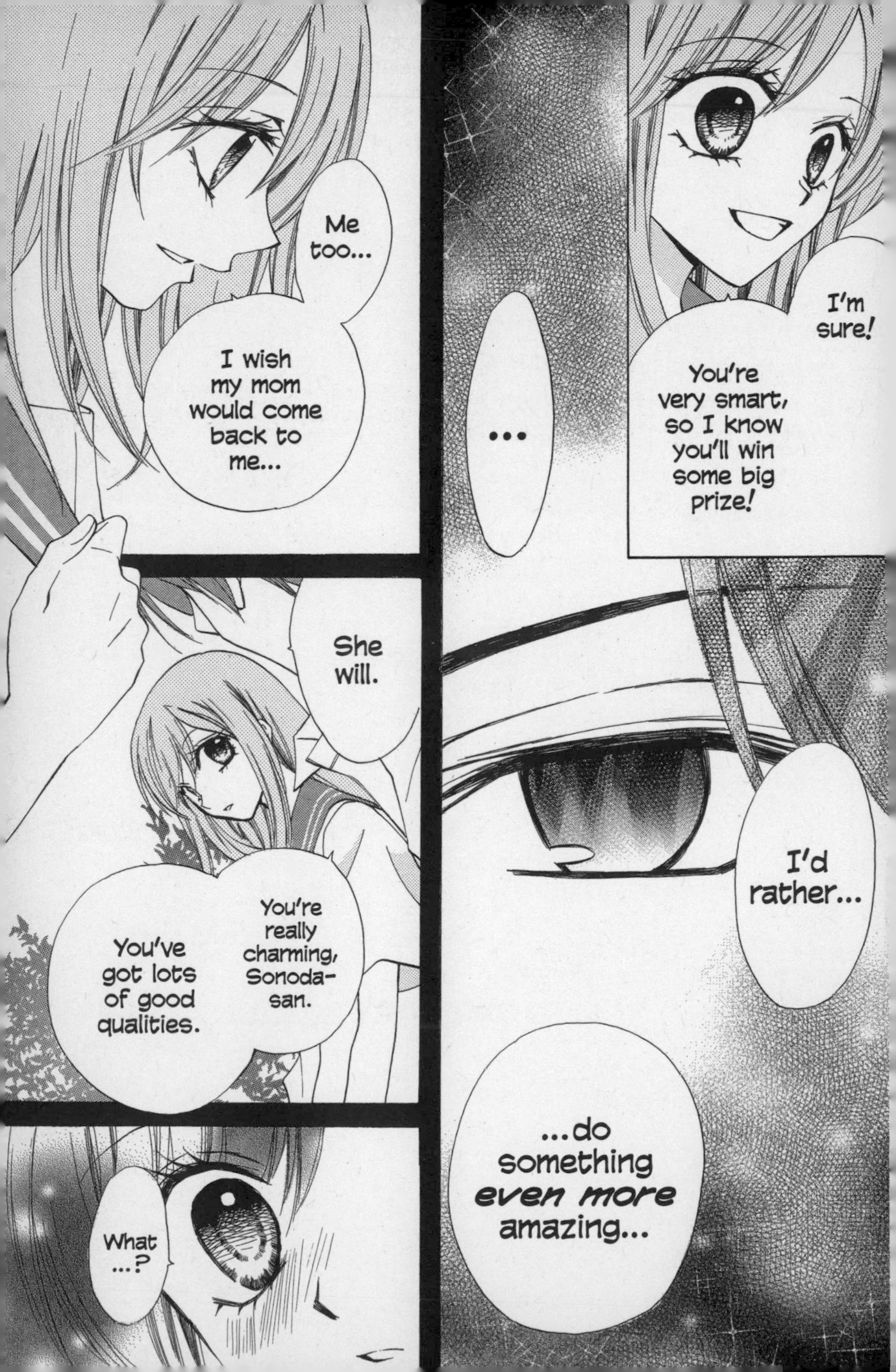
I'm sure!
You're very smart, so I know you'll win some big prize!
...
I'd rather...
...do something *even more* amazing...
Me too...
I wish my mom would come back to me...
She will.
You're really charming, Sonoda-san.
You've got lots of good qualities.
What ...?

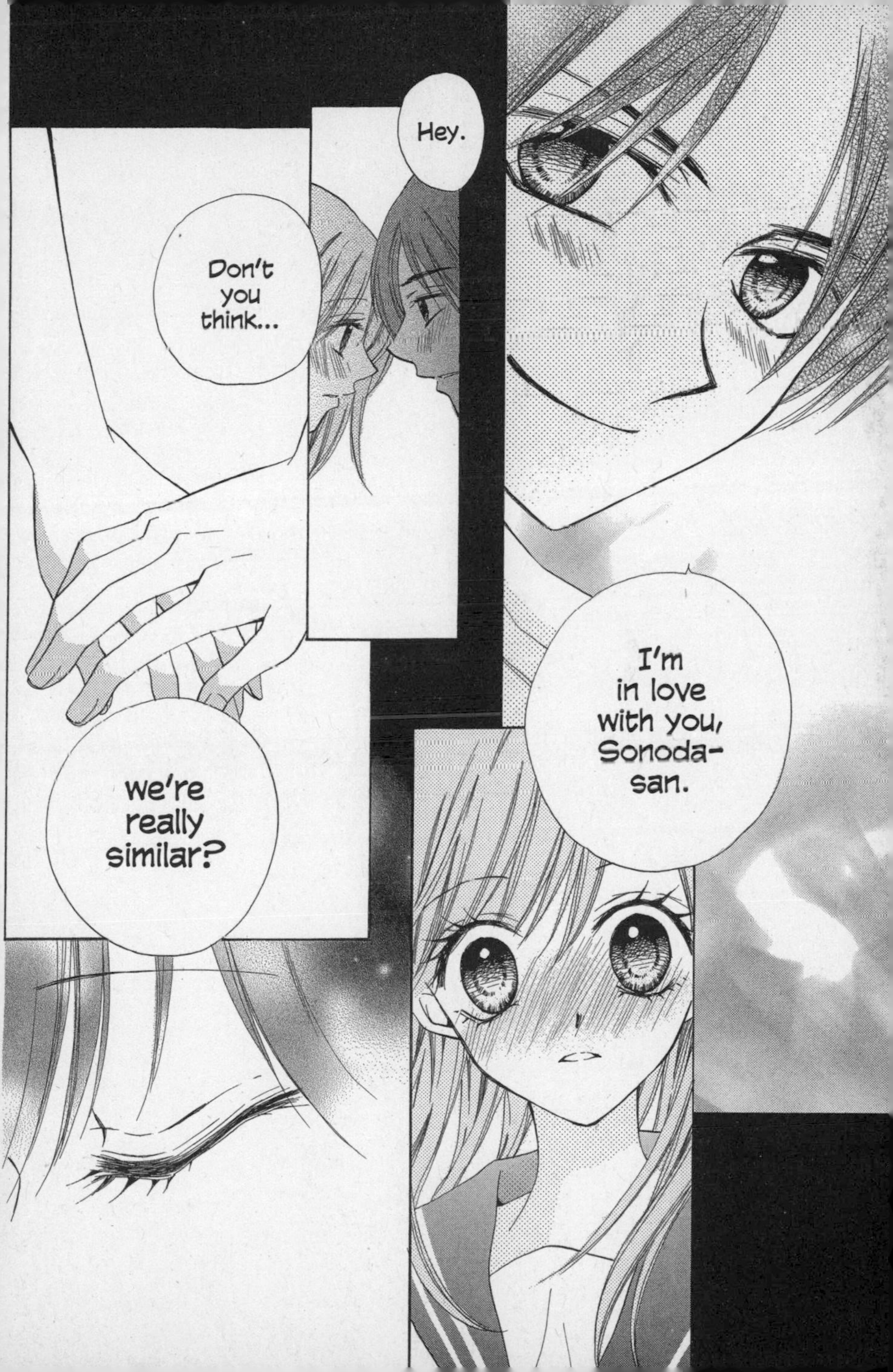
Hey.
Don't you think...
we're really similar?
I'm in love with you, Sonoda-san.

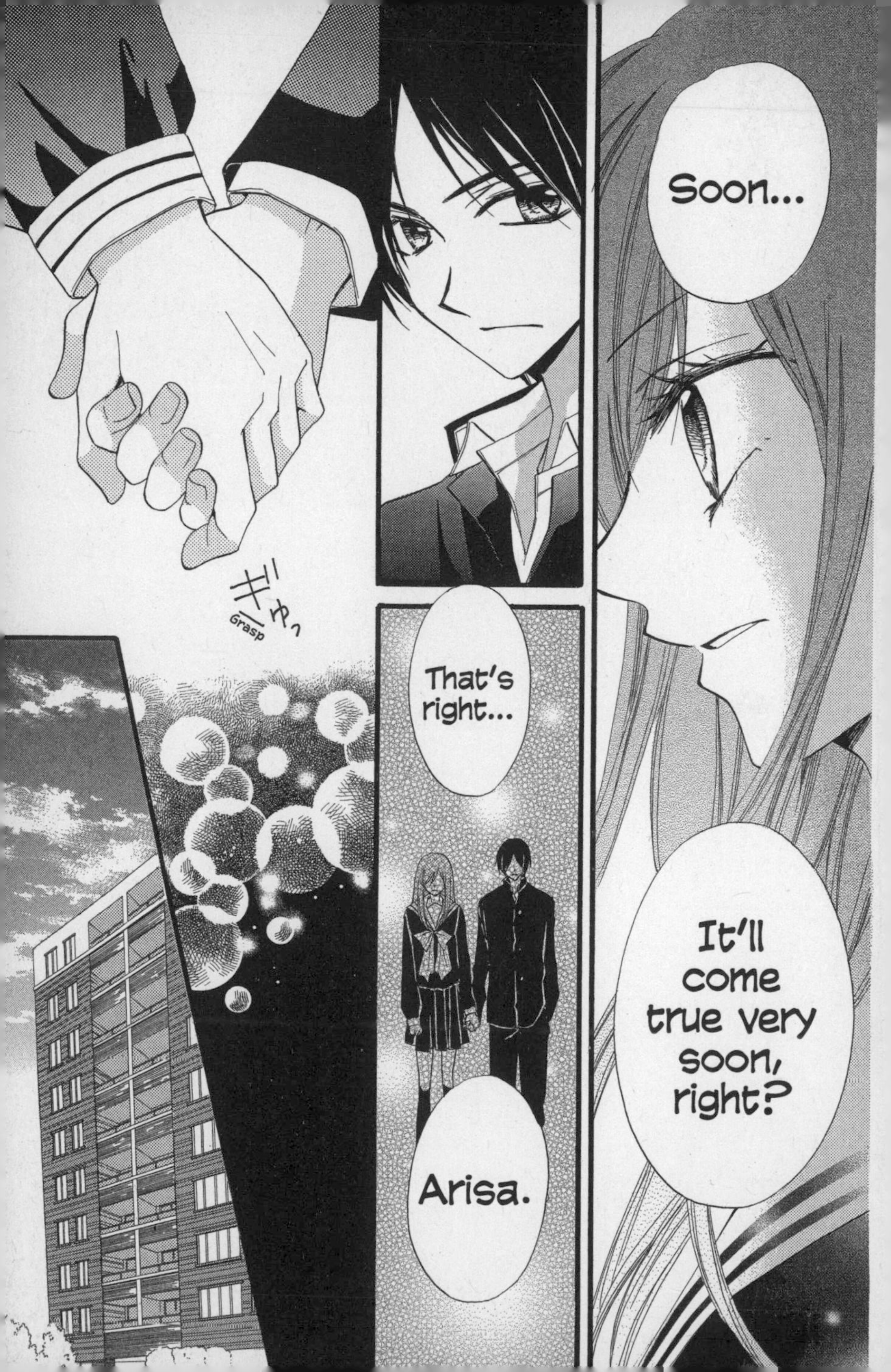
Soon...
It'll come true very soon, right?
ギュッ
Grasp
That's right...
Arisa.

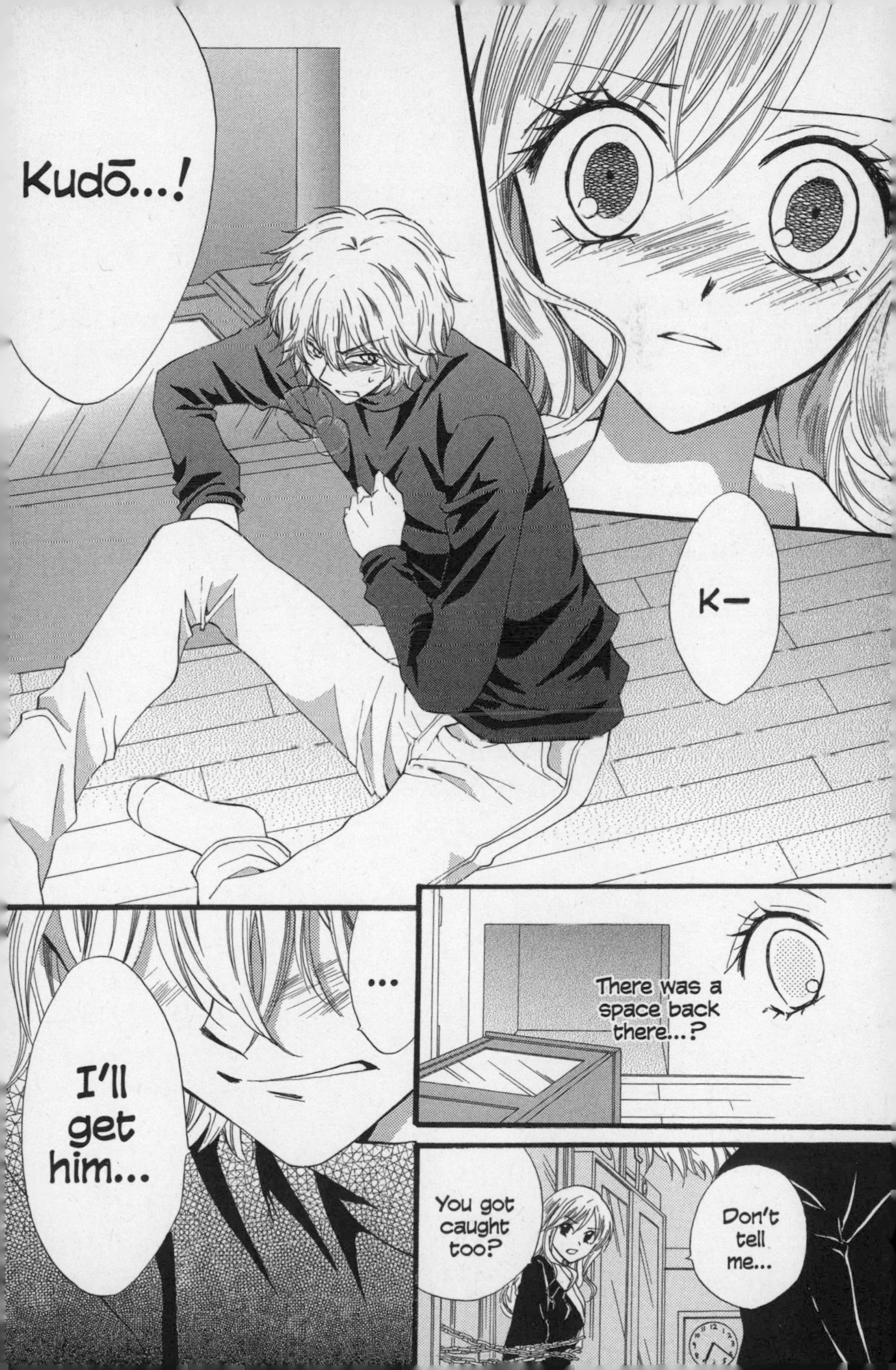
K—
Kudō...!
There was a space back there...?
Don't tell me...
You got caught too?
...
I'll get him...

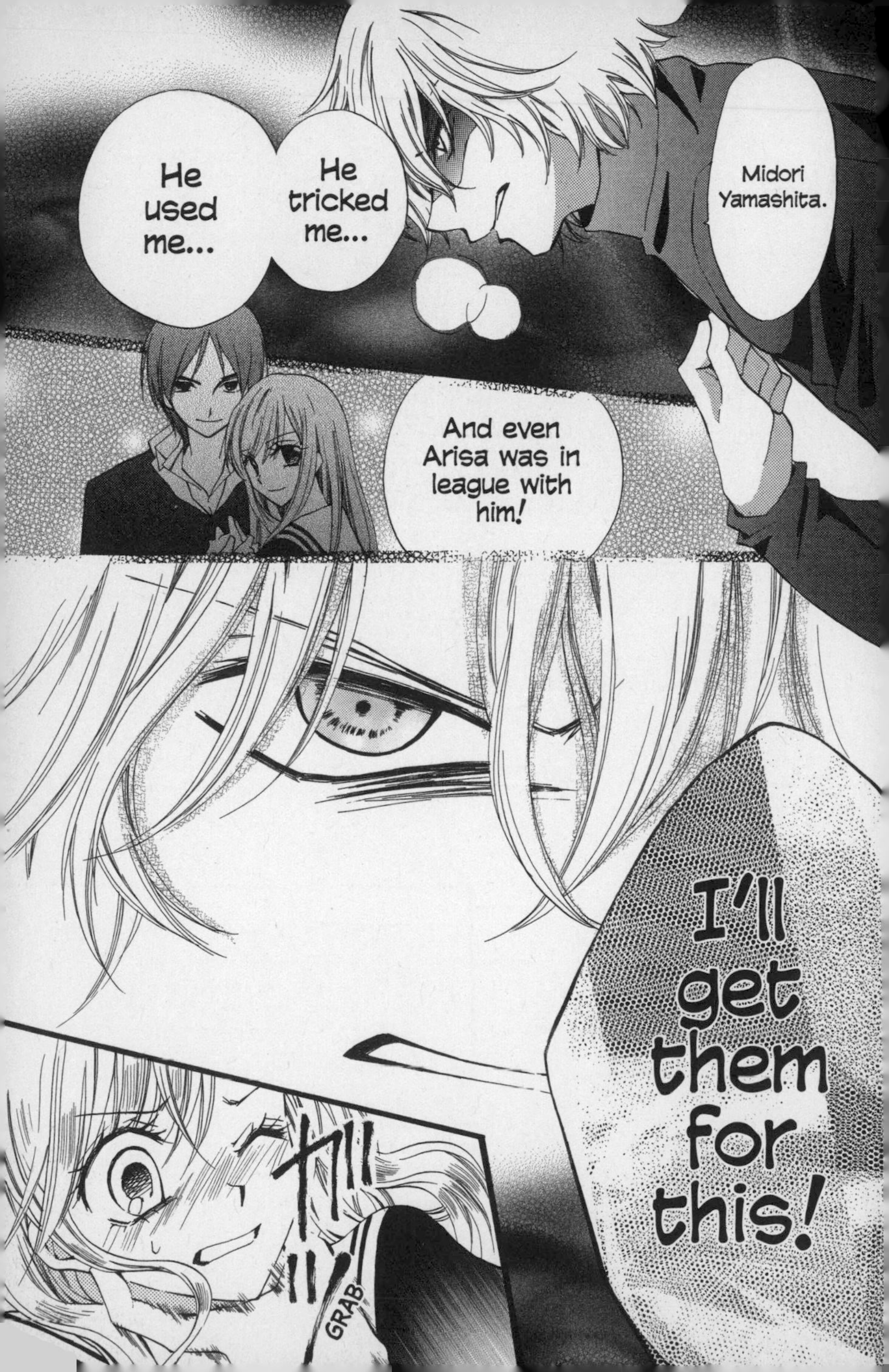
Midori Yamashita.
He tricked me...
He used me...
And even Arisa was in league with him!
I'll get them for this!
GRAB

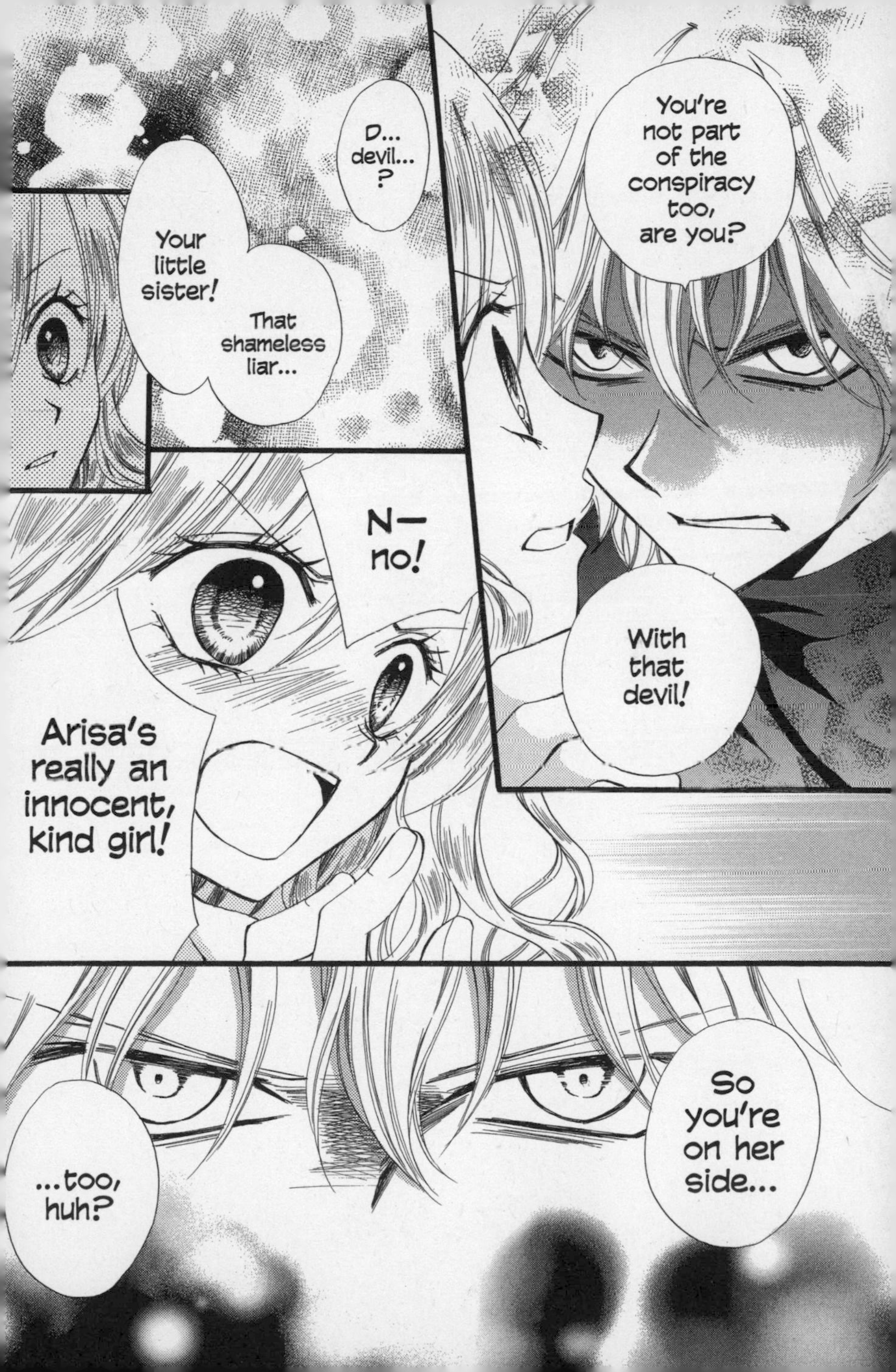
You're not part of the conspiracy too, are you?
With that devil!
D... devil...?
Your little sister!
That shameless liar...
N— no!
Arisa's really an innocent, kind girl!
So you're on her side...
...too, huh?

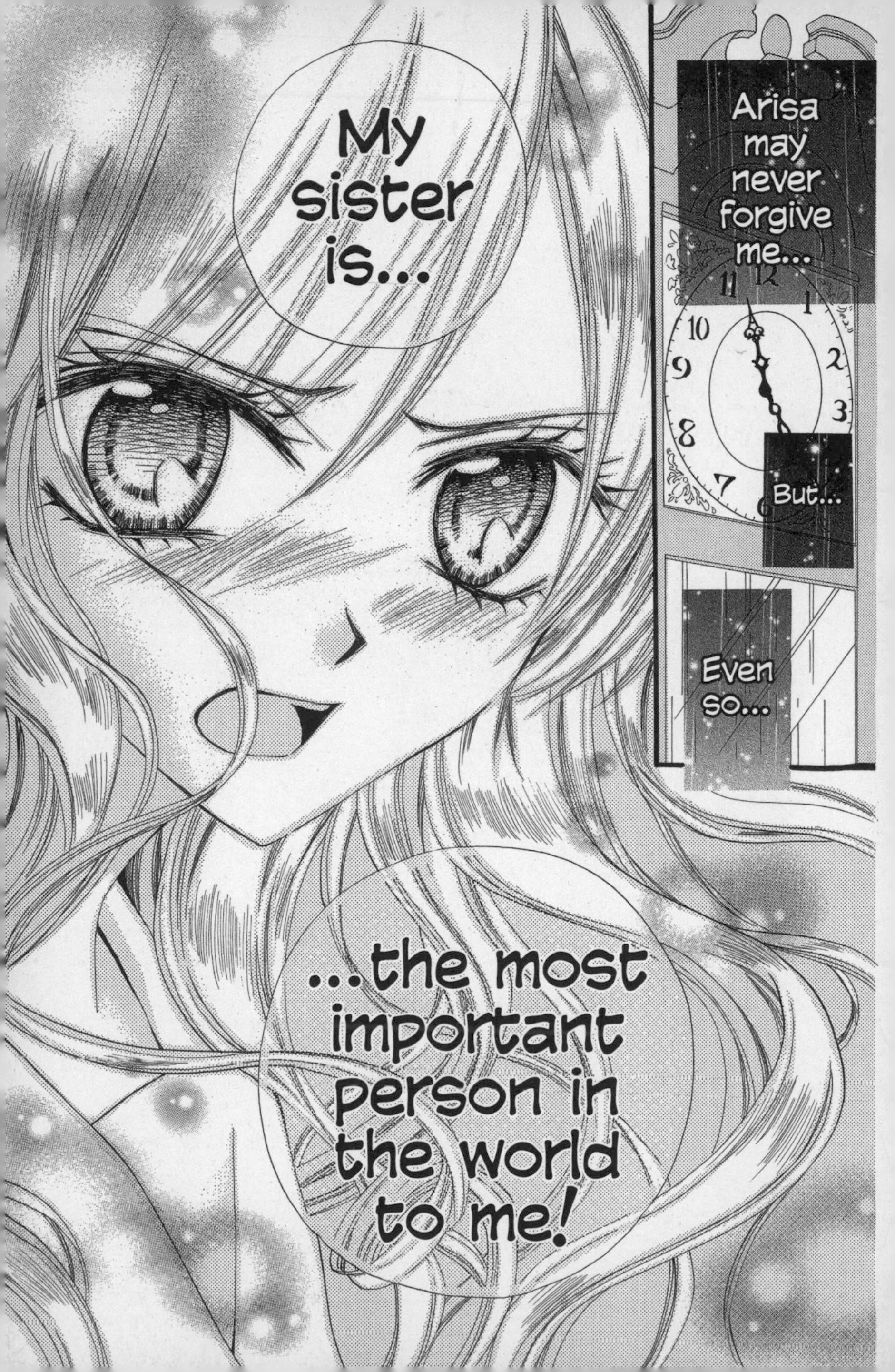

Arisa may never forgive me...
But...
Even so...
My sister is...
...the most important person in the world to me!

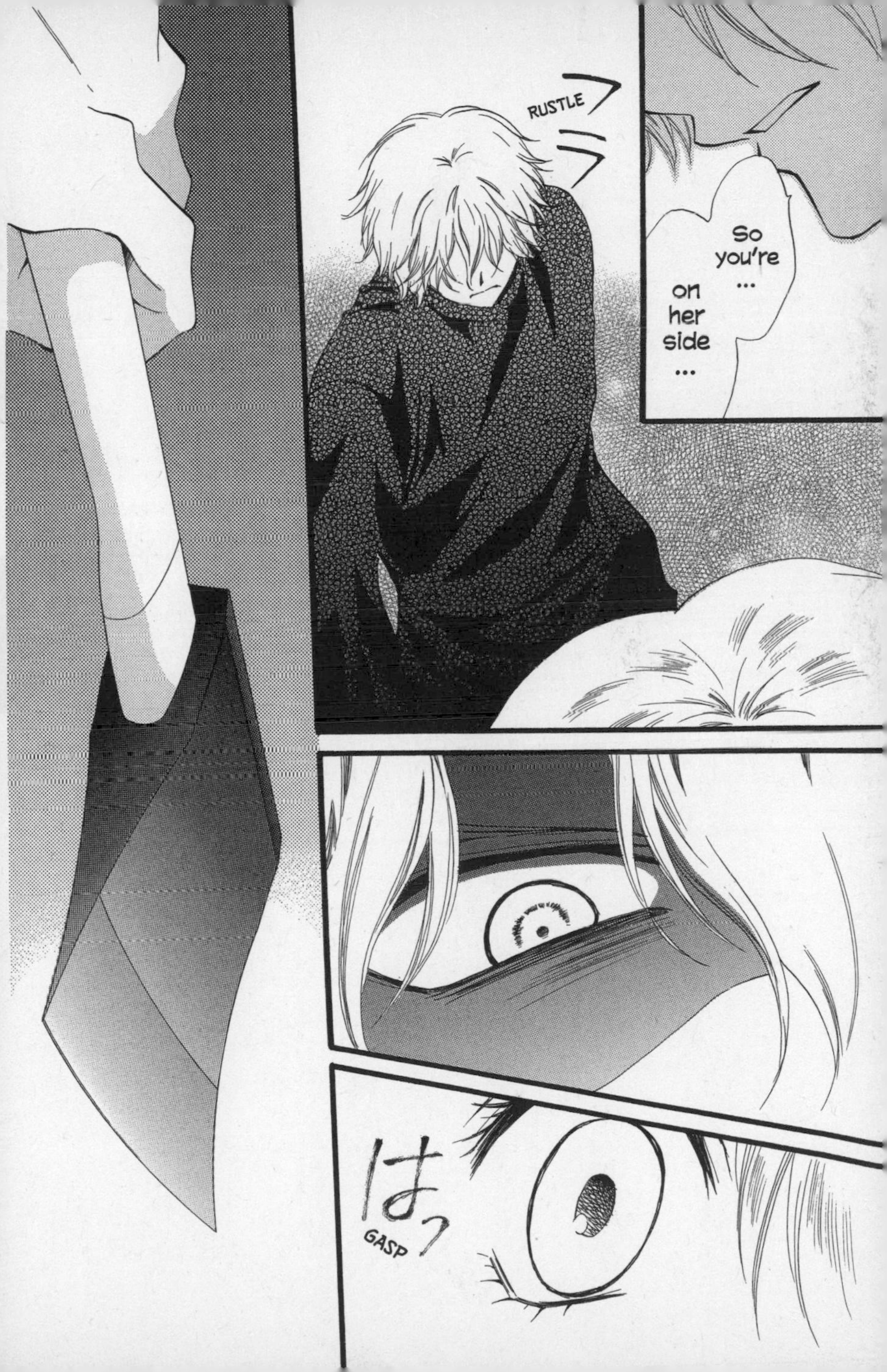
So you're ... on her side ...
RUSTLE
はっ
GASP

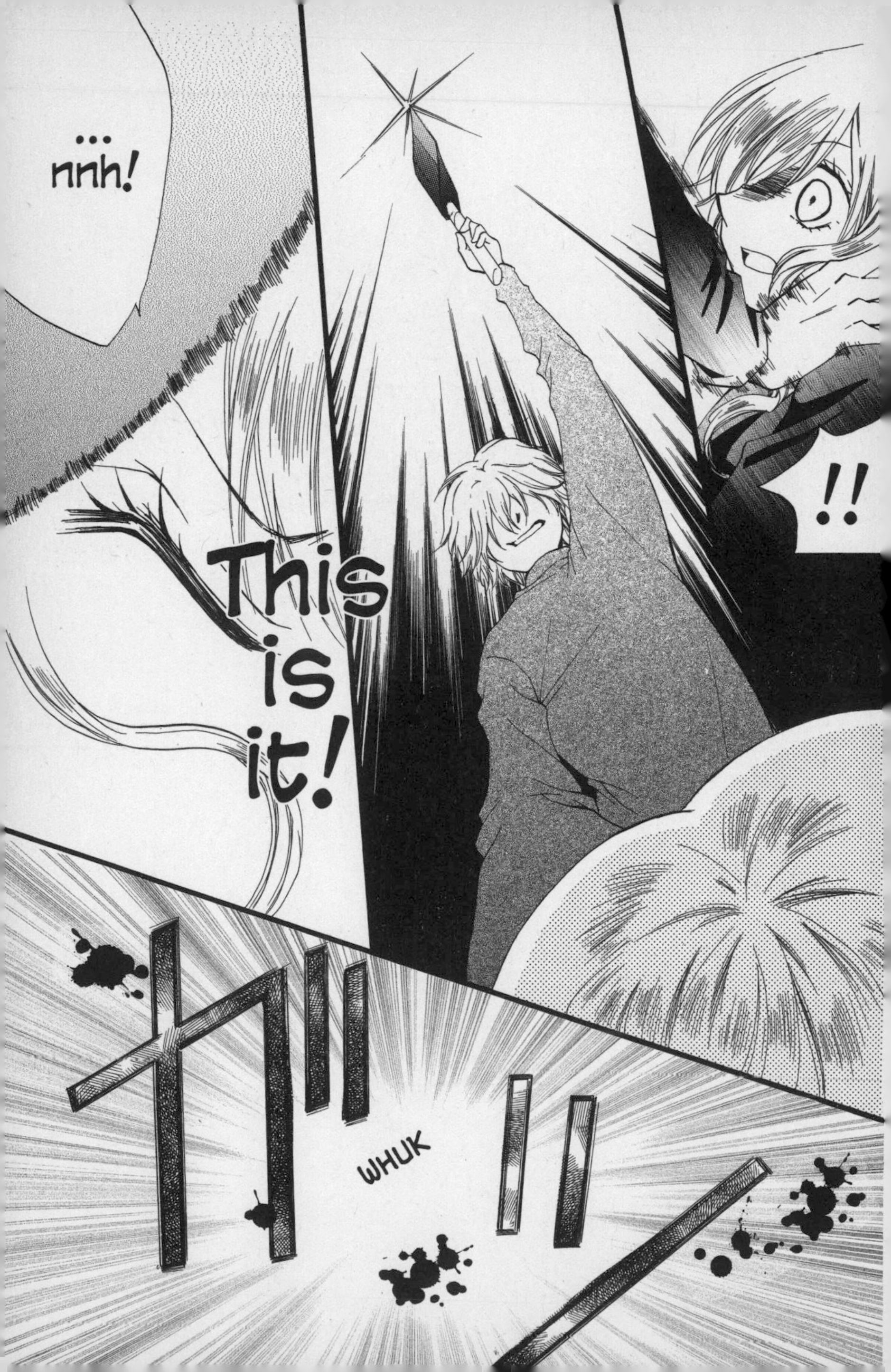
!!
This is it!
...nnh!
WHUK

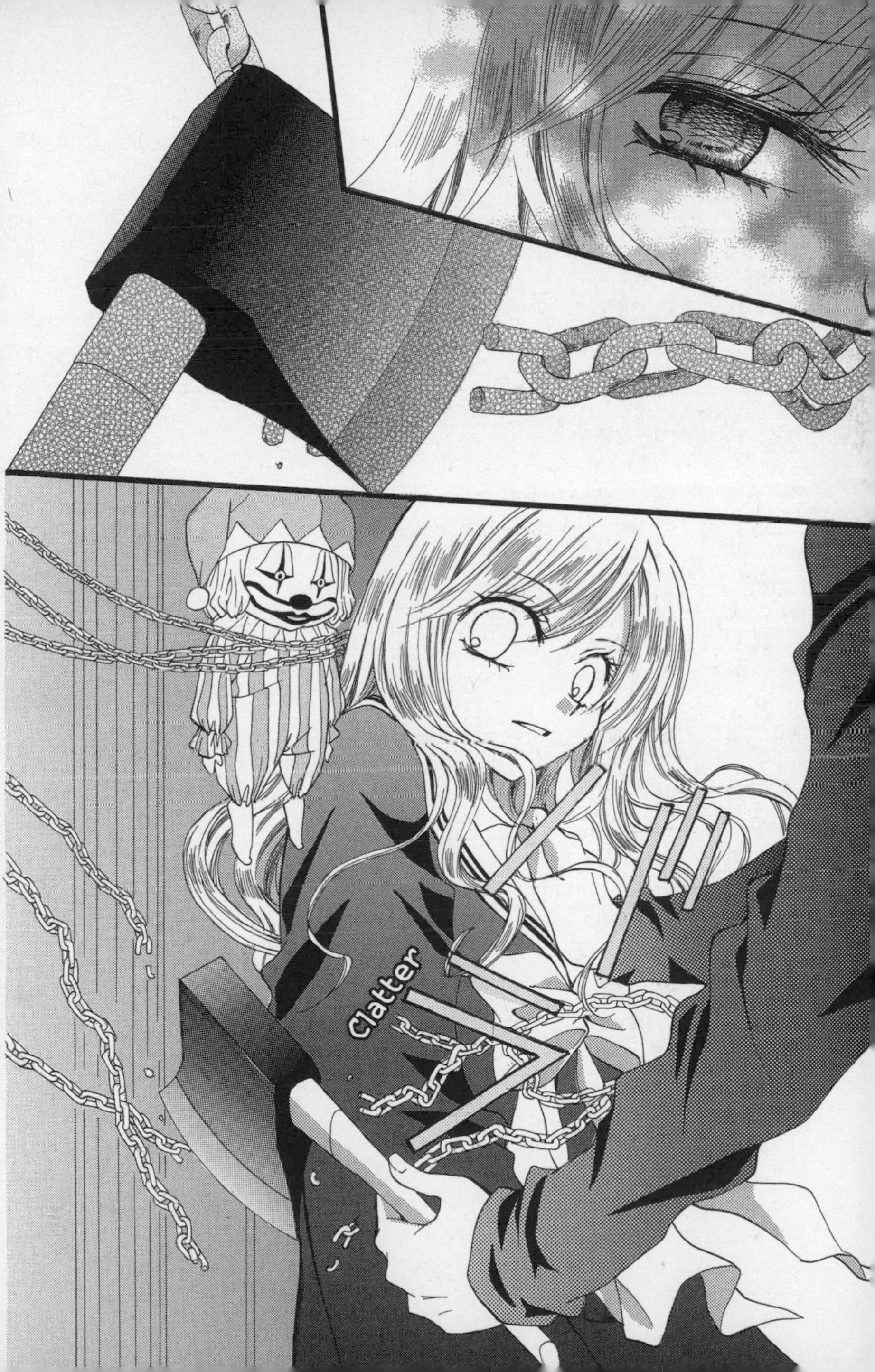
Clatter

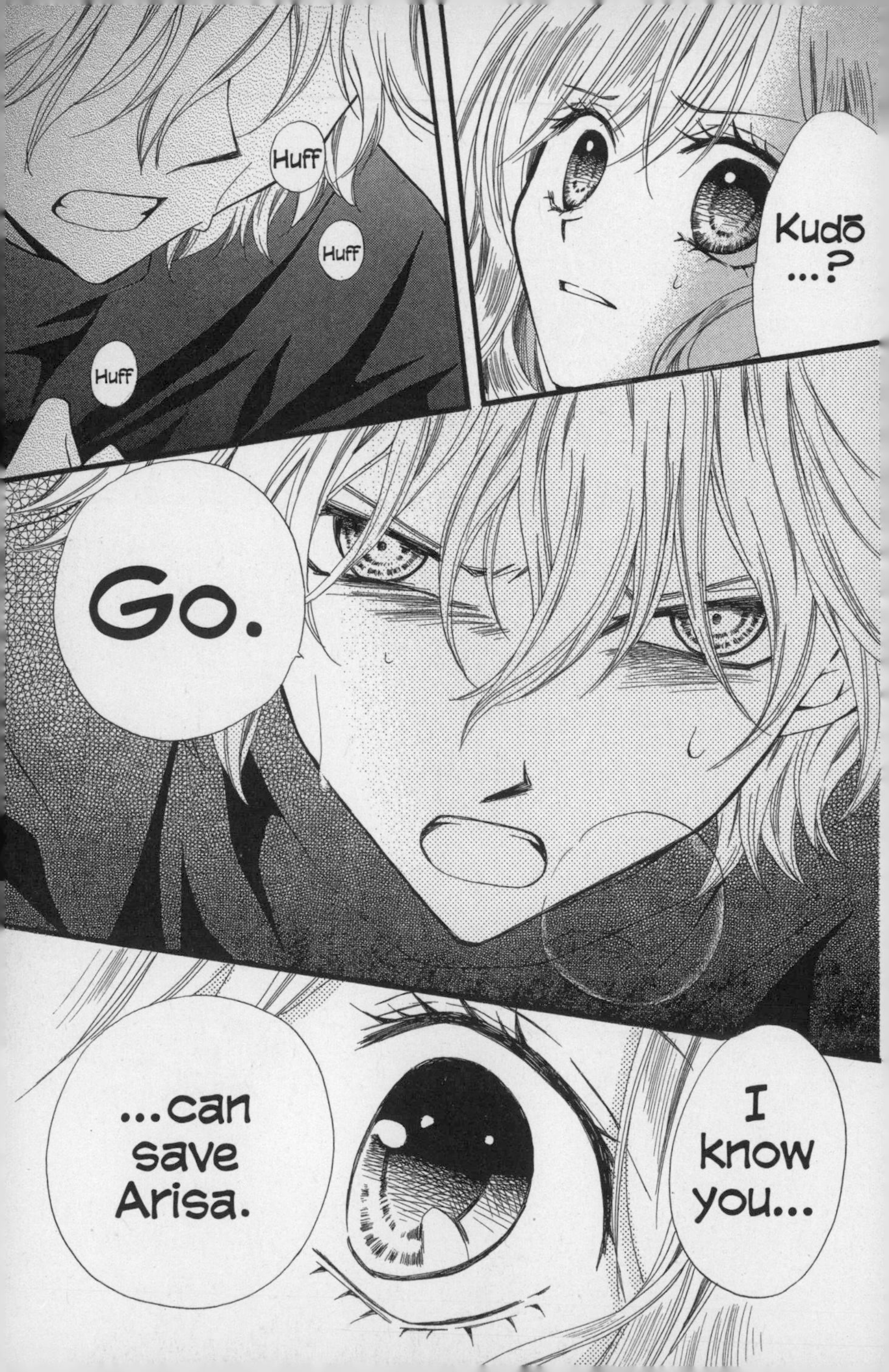
Kudō ...?
Huff
Huff
Huff
Go.
I know you...
...can save Arisa.

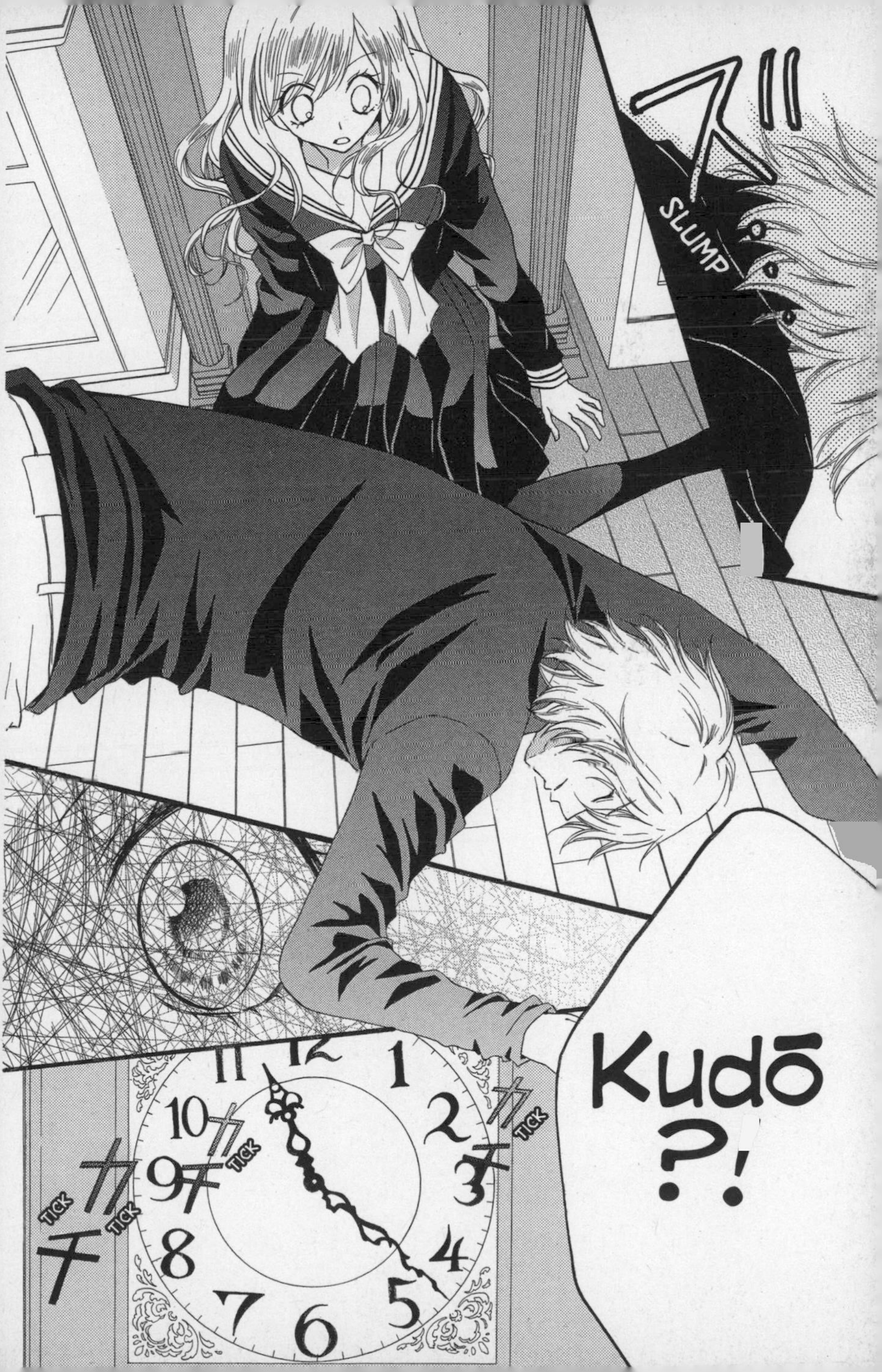
SLUMP
Kudō ?!
TICK
TICK
TICK
TICK

Chapter 36: A Bouquet for K

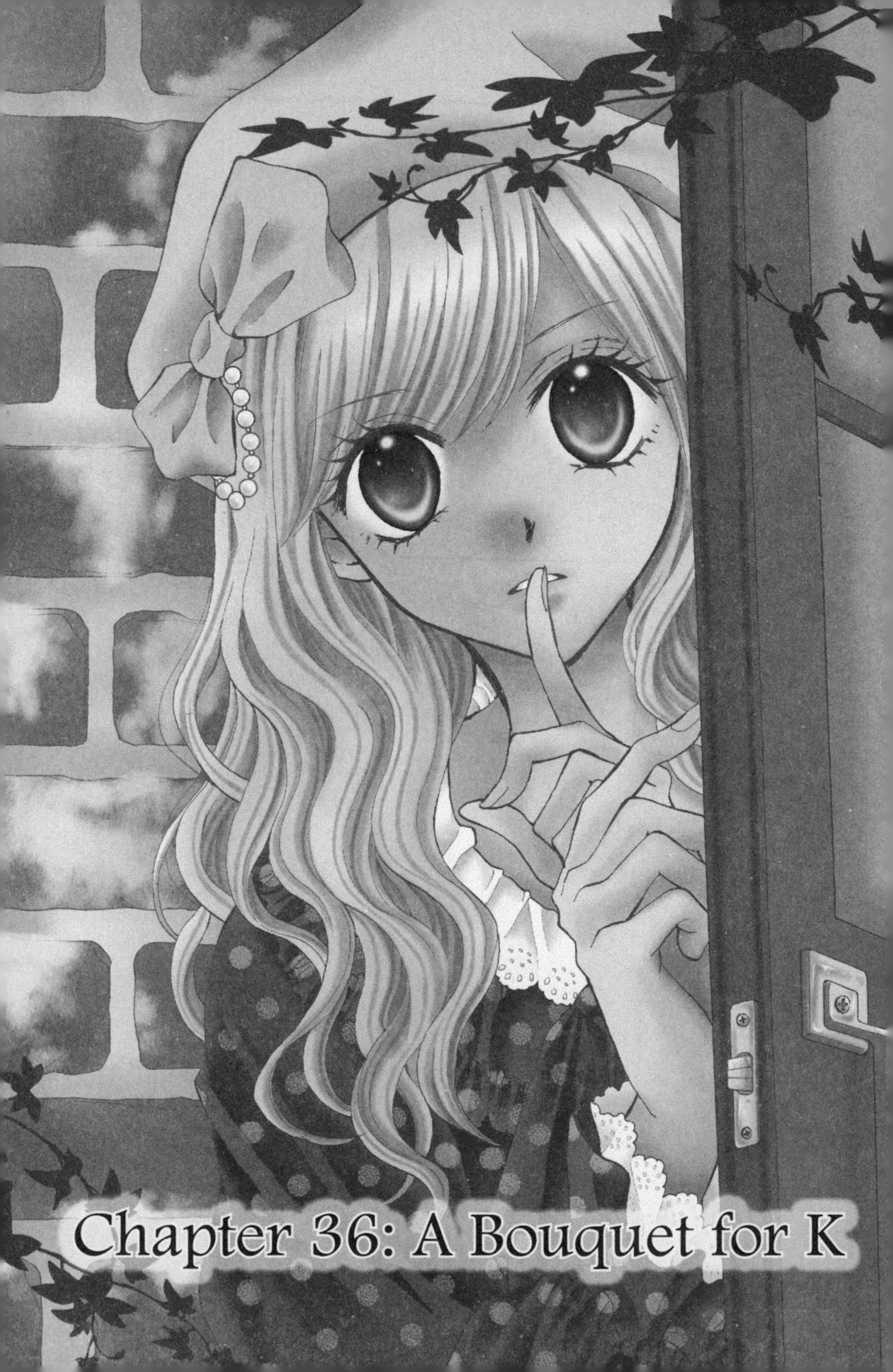

ARISA

アリサ

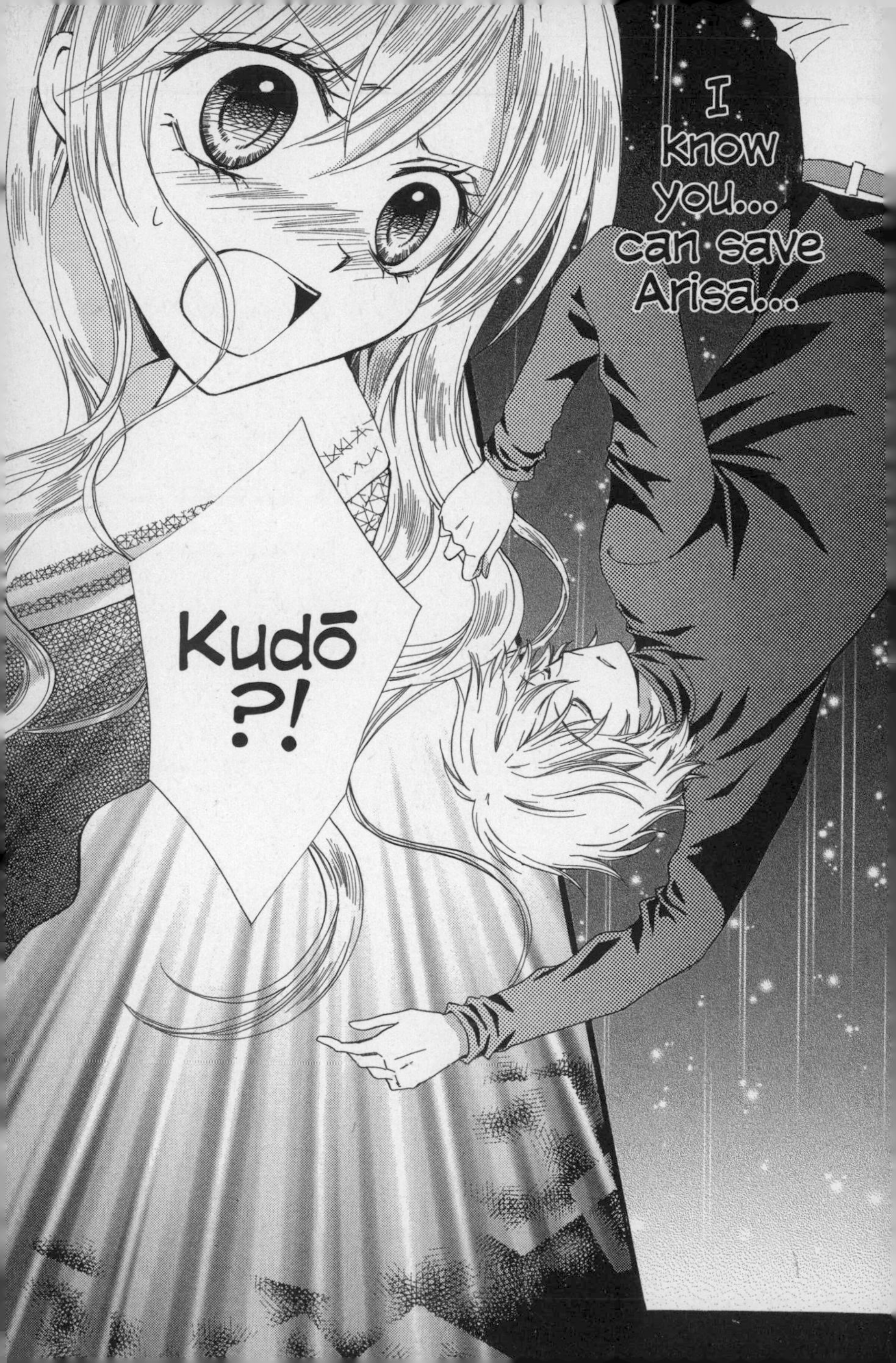
I know you... can save Arisa...
Kudō ?!

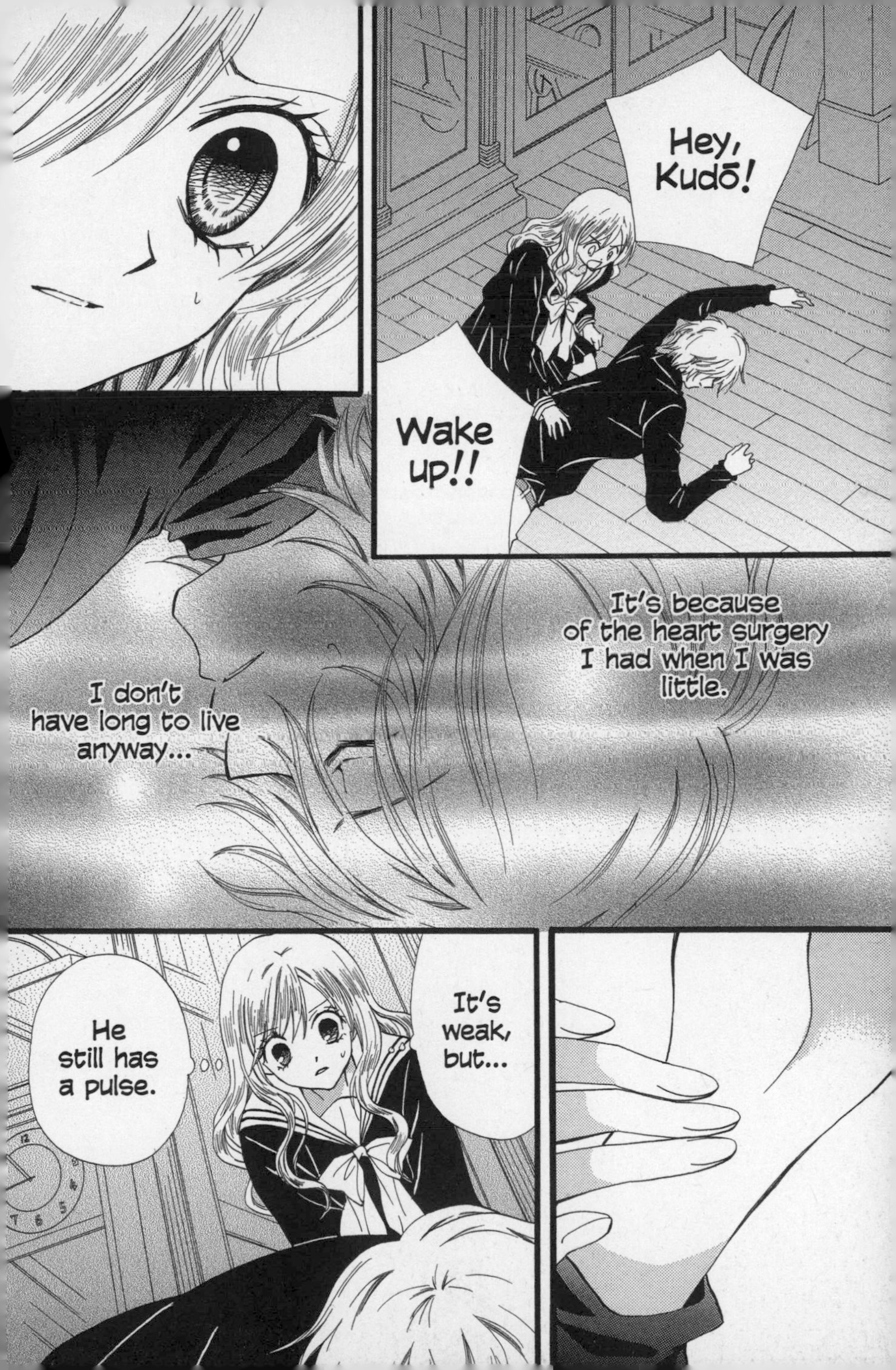
Hey, Kudō!
Wake up!!
It's because of the heart surgery I had when I was little.
I don't have long to live anyway...
It's weak, but...
He still has a pulse.

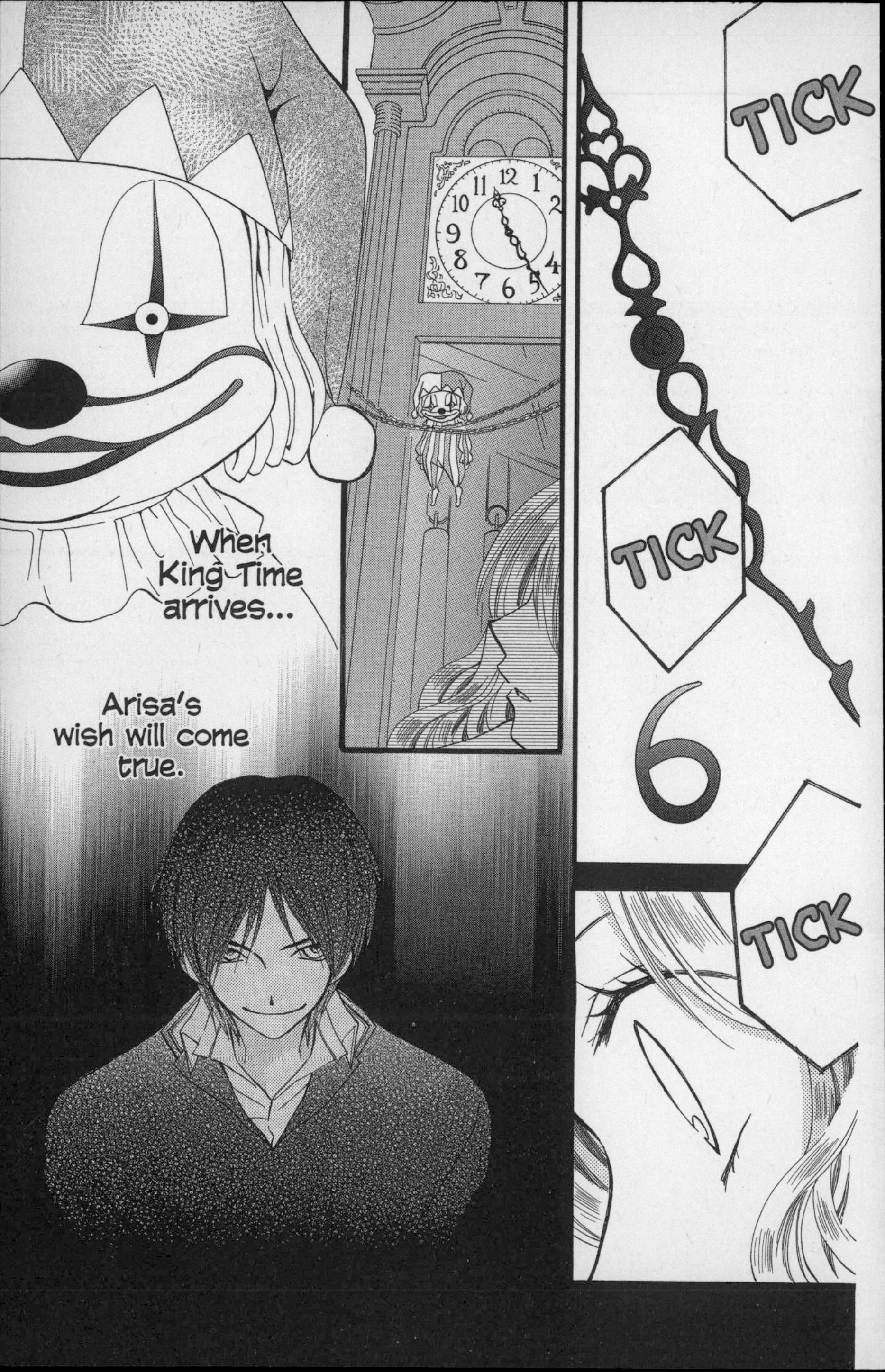
TICK
TICK
6
TICK
When King Time arrives...
Arisa's wish will come true.

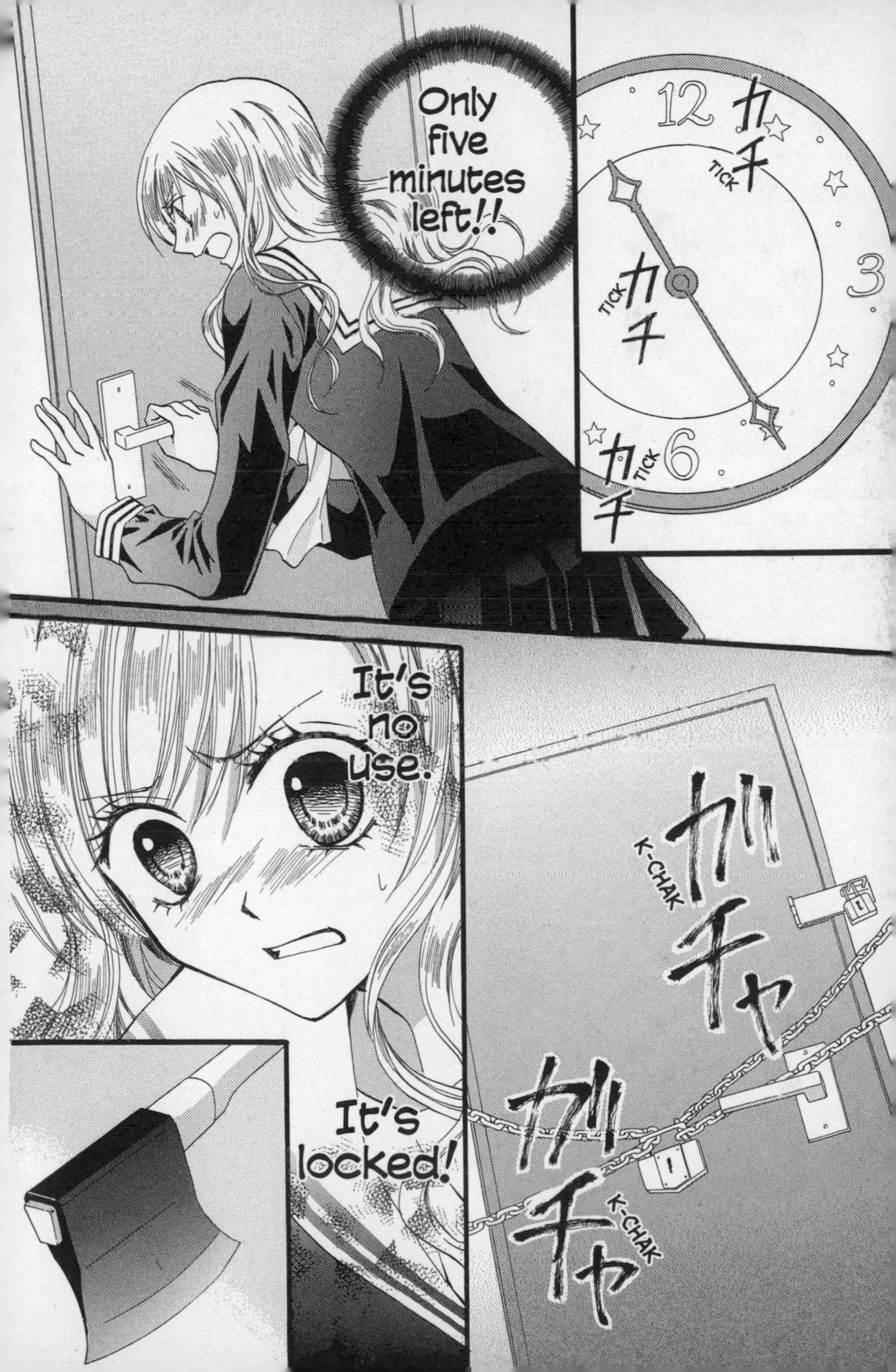
カチ
TICK
カチ
TICK
カチ
TICK
Only five minutes left!!
ガチャ
K-CHAK
ガチャ
K-CHAK
It's no use.
It's locked!

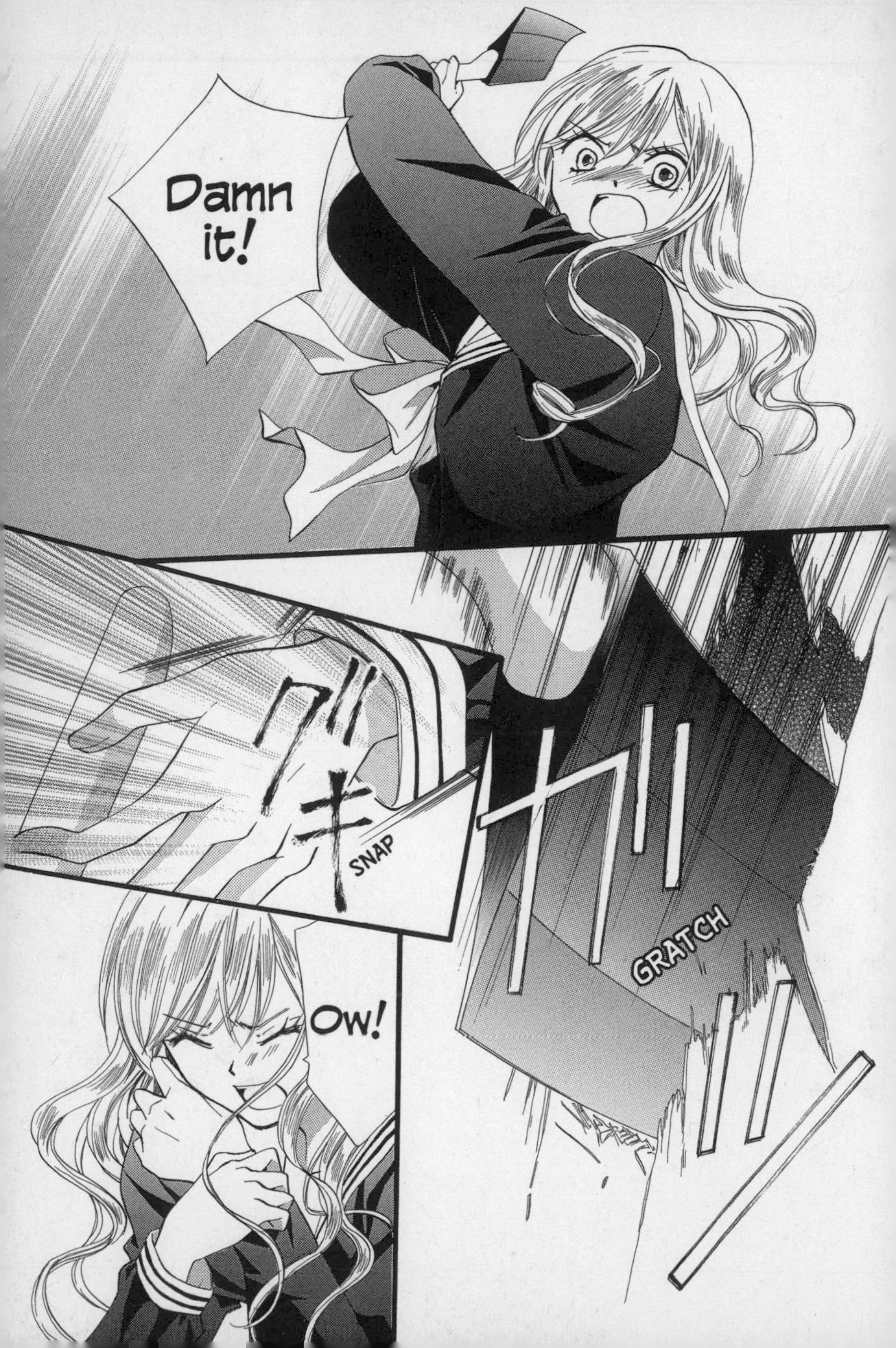
Damn it!
ガリ
GRATCH
グキ
SNAP
Ow!

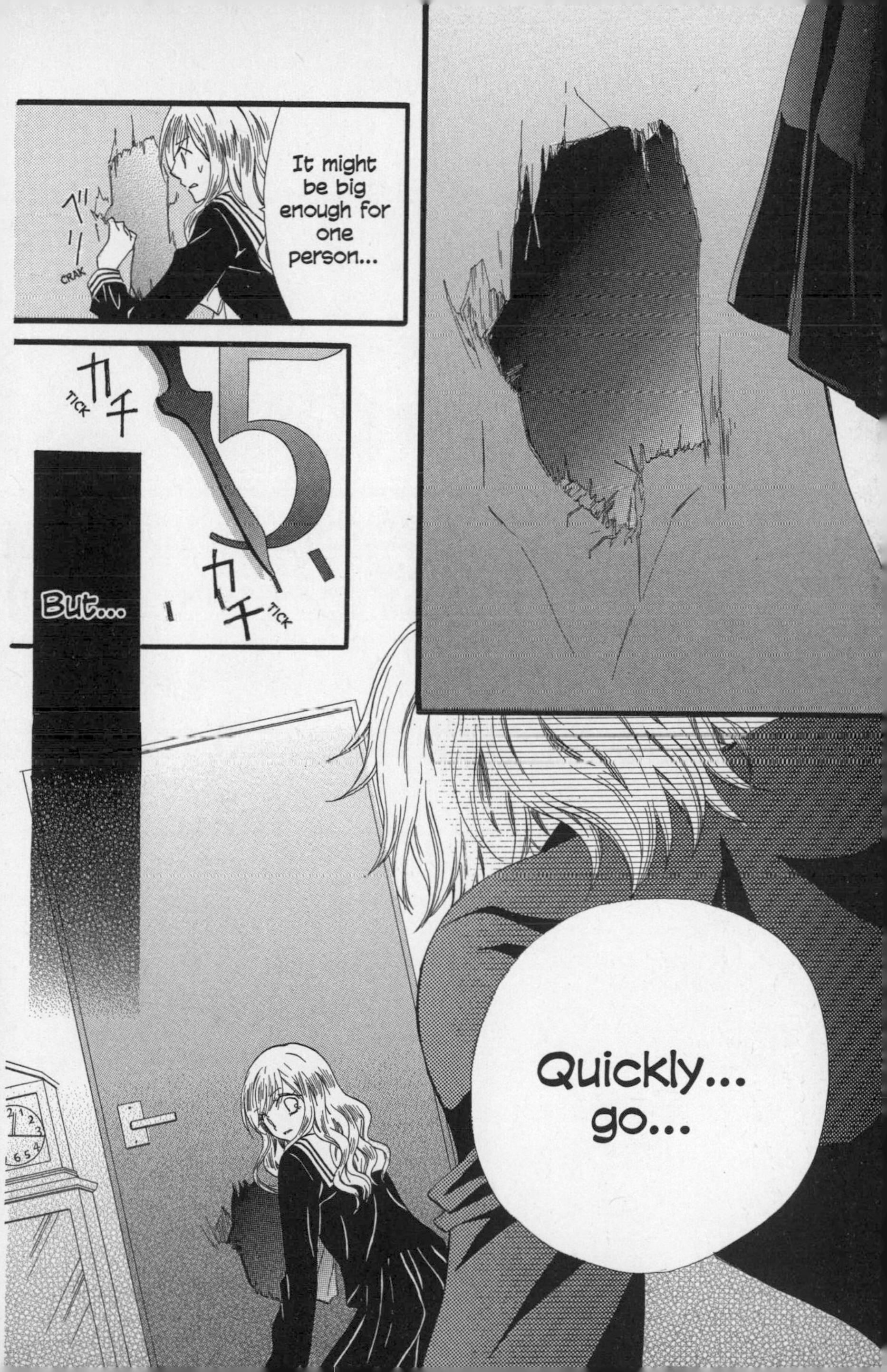
It might be big enough for one person...
ベリ
CRAK
カチ
TICK
カチ
TICK
But...
Quickly... go...

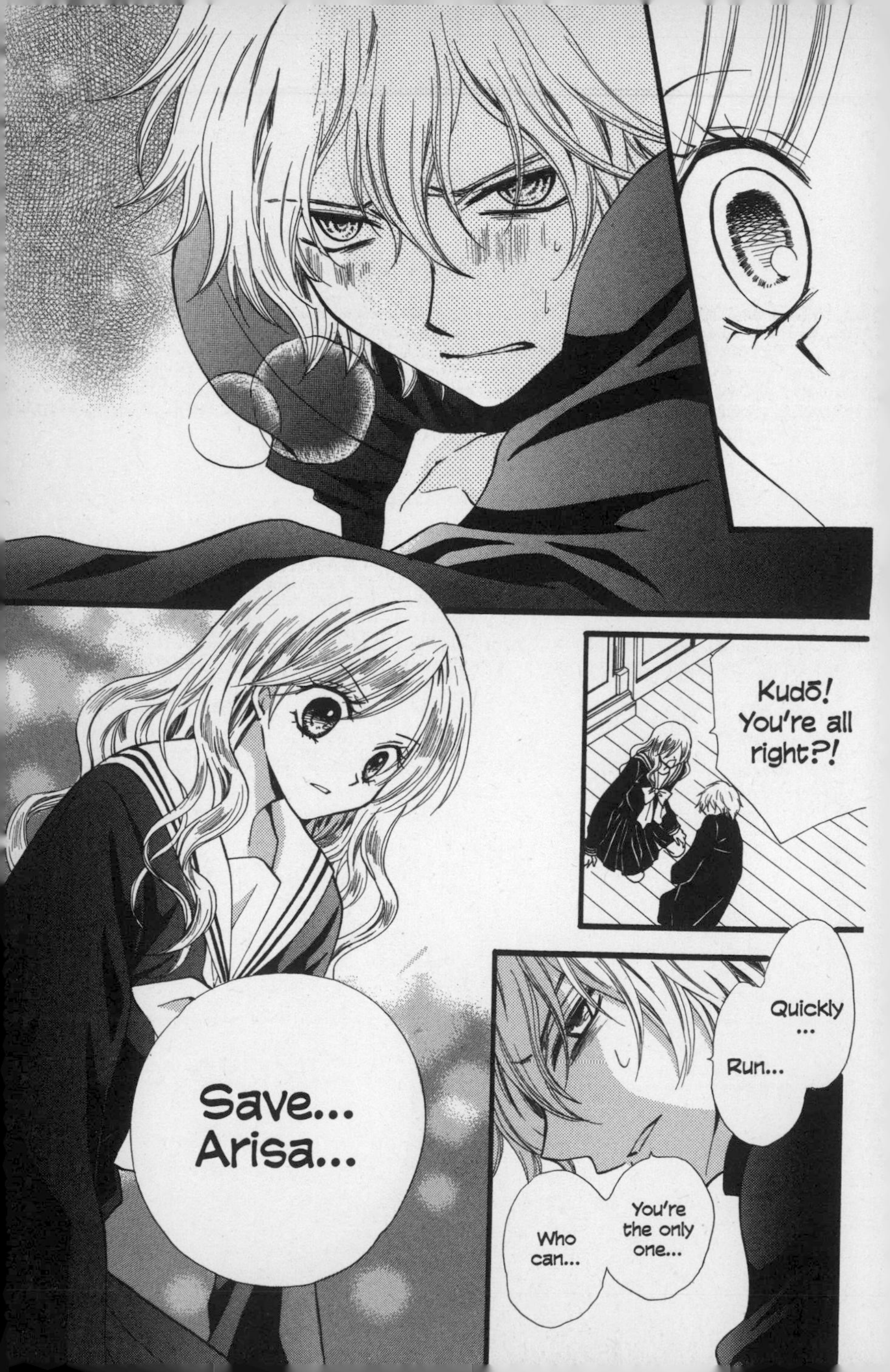

Kudō! You're all right?!
Quickly...
Run...
You're the only one...
Who can...
Save... Arisa...

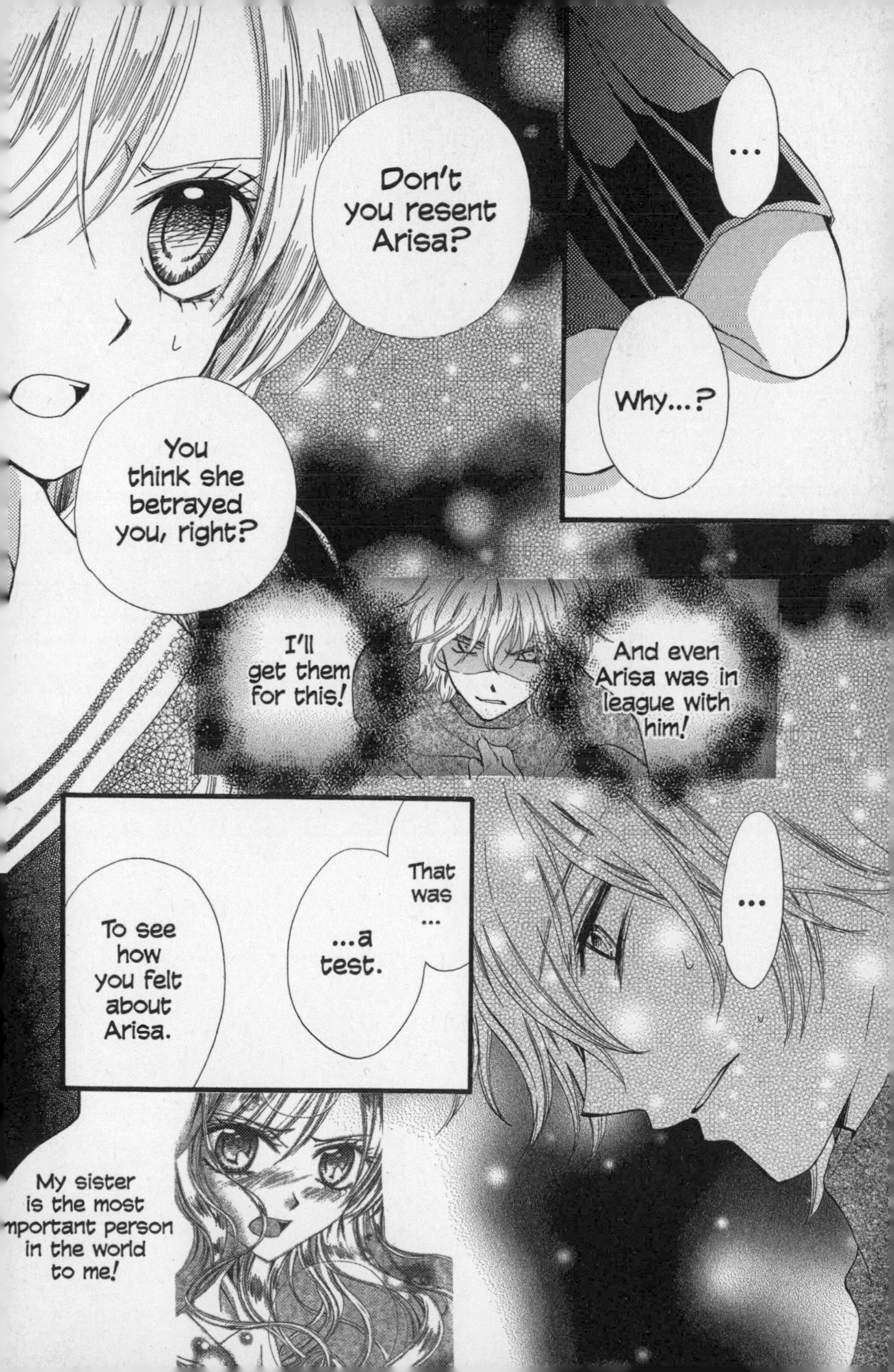
...
Why...?
Don't you resent Arisa?
You think she betrayed you, right?
And even Arisa was in league with him!
I'll get them for this!
...
That was ...
...a test.
To see how you felt about Arisa.
My sister is the most mportant person in the world to me!

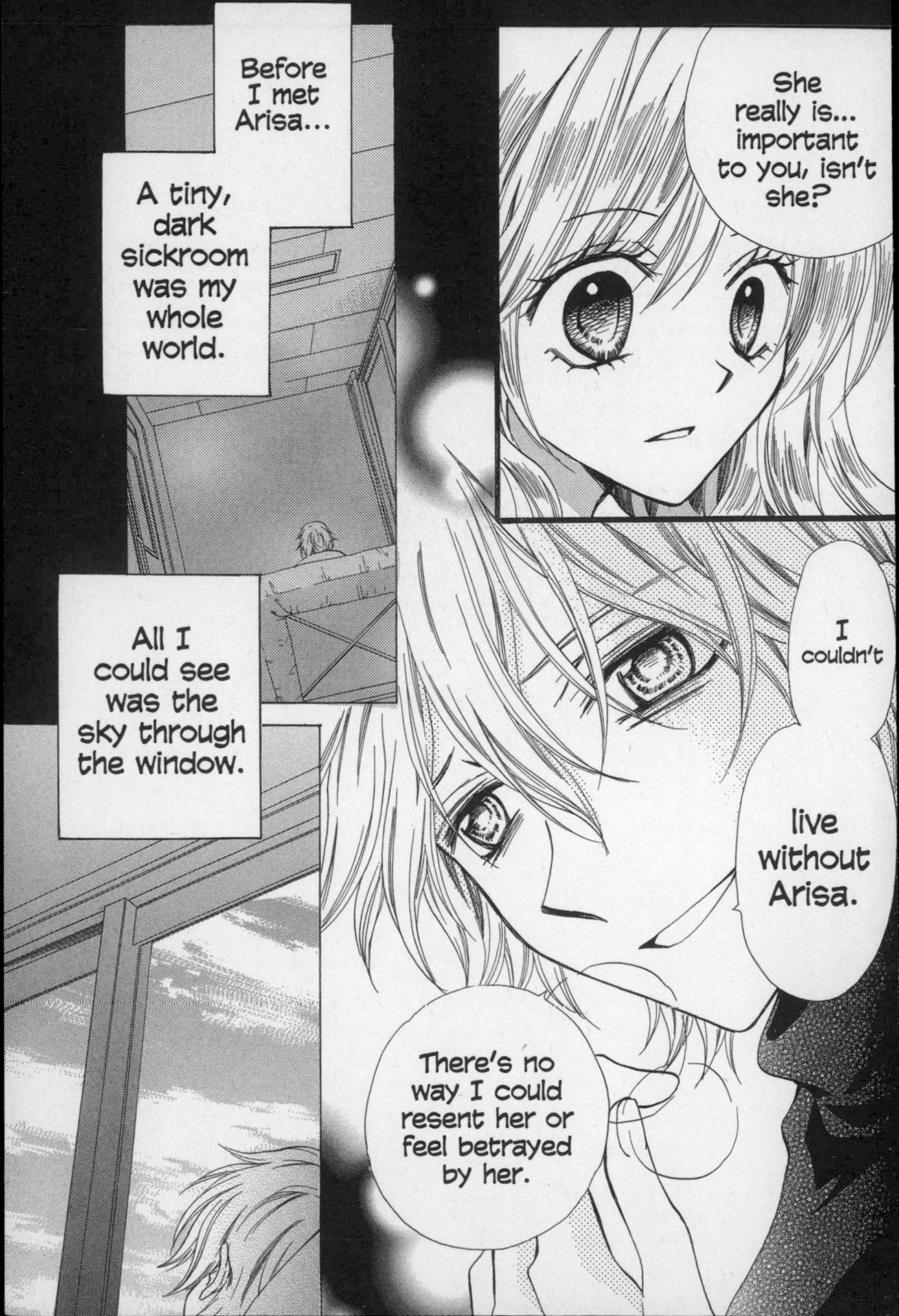
She really is... important to you, isn't she?
I couldn't
live without Arisa.
There's no way I could resent her or feel betrayed by her.
Before I met Arisa...
A tiny, dark sickroom was my whole world.
All I could see was the sky through the window.

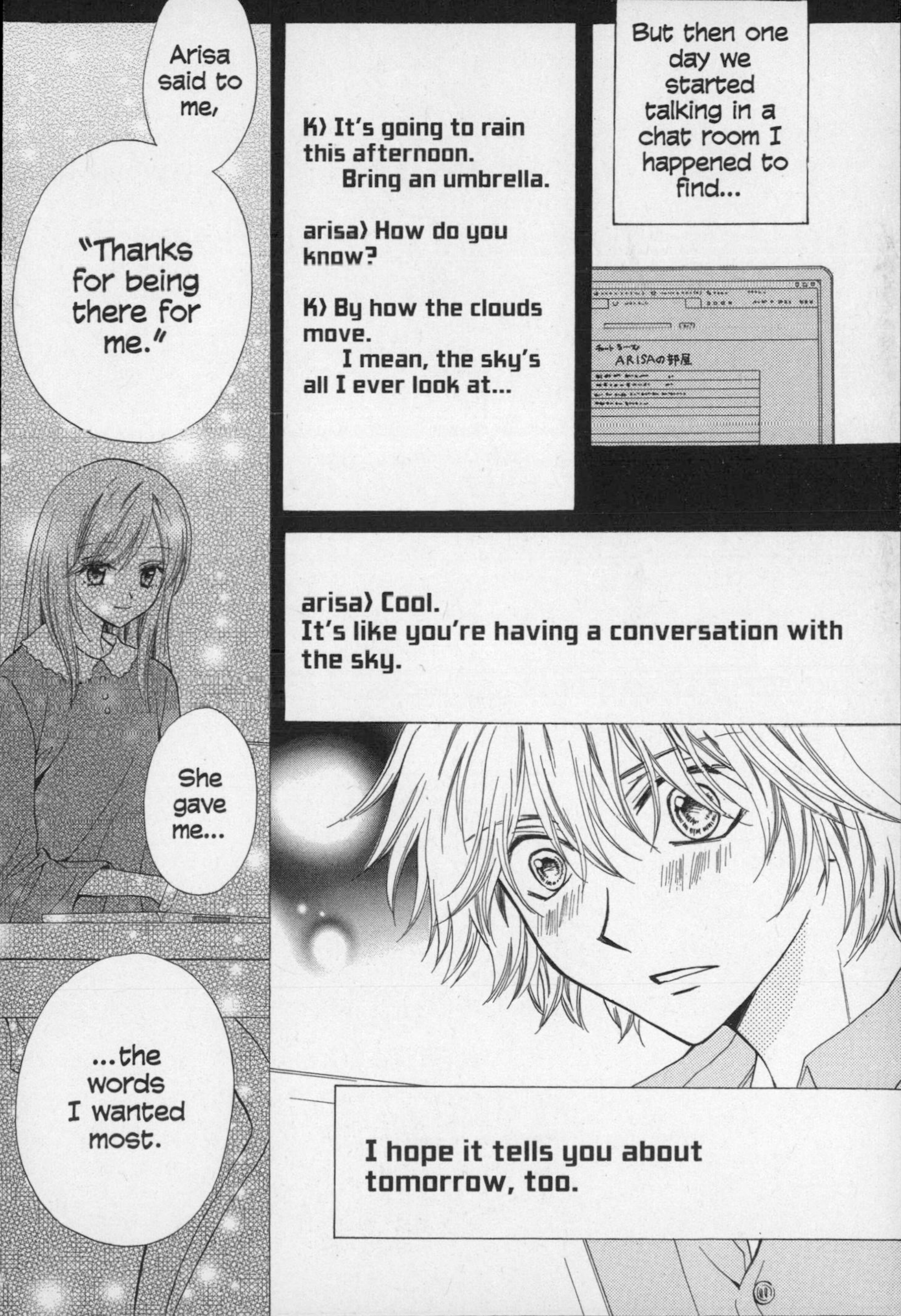
But then one day we started talking in a chat room I happened to find...
ARISAの部屋
K) It's going to rain this afternoon.
Bring an umbrella.
arisa) How do you know?
K) By how the clouds move.
I mean, the sky's all I ever look at...
arisa) Cool.
It's like you're having a conversation with the sky.
I hope it tells you about tomorrow, too.
Arisa said to me,
"Thanks for being there for me."
She gave me...
...the words I wanted most.

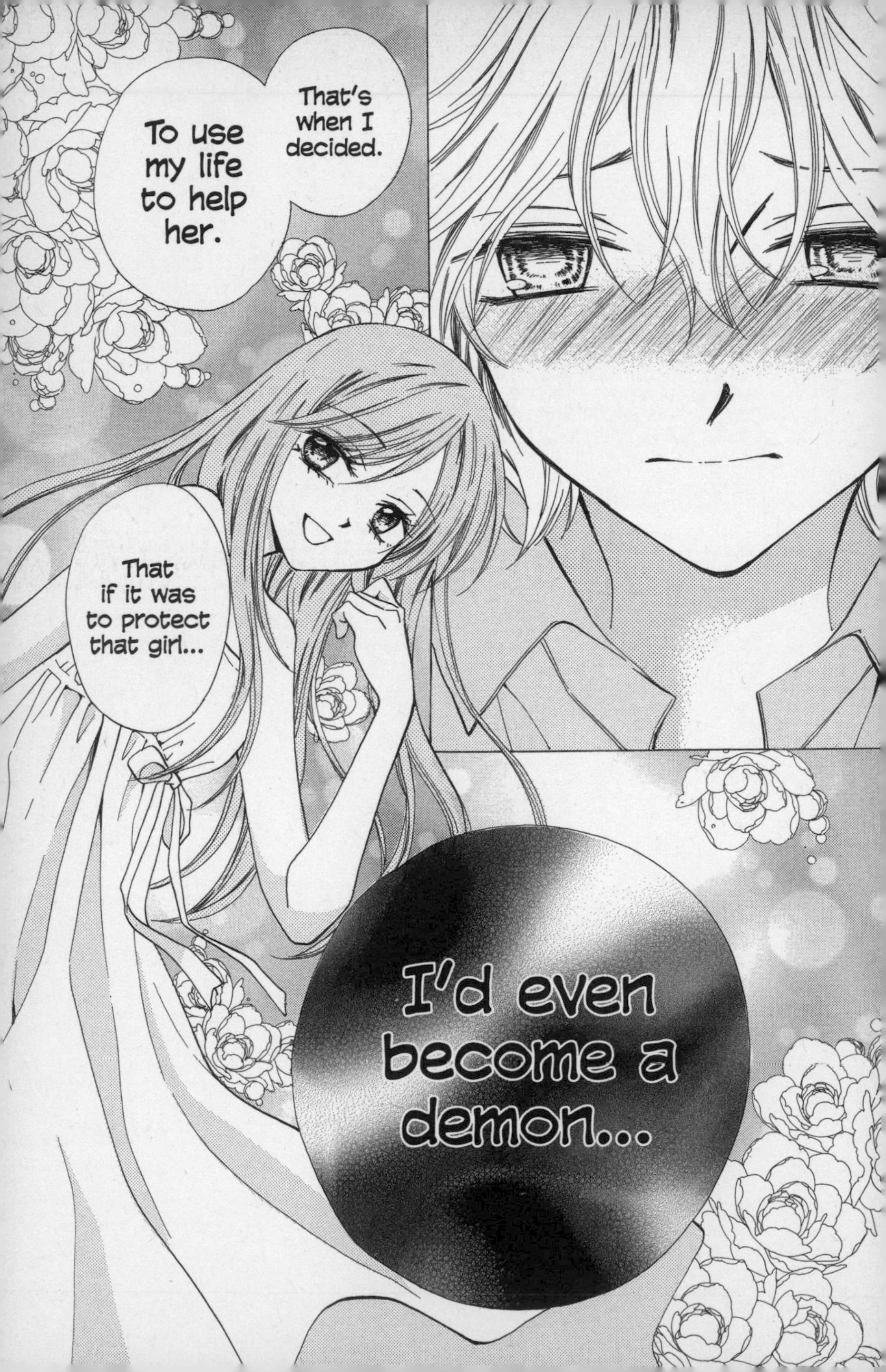
That's when I decided.
To use my life to help her.
That if it was to protect that girl...
I'd even become a demon...

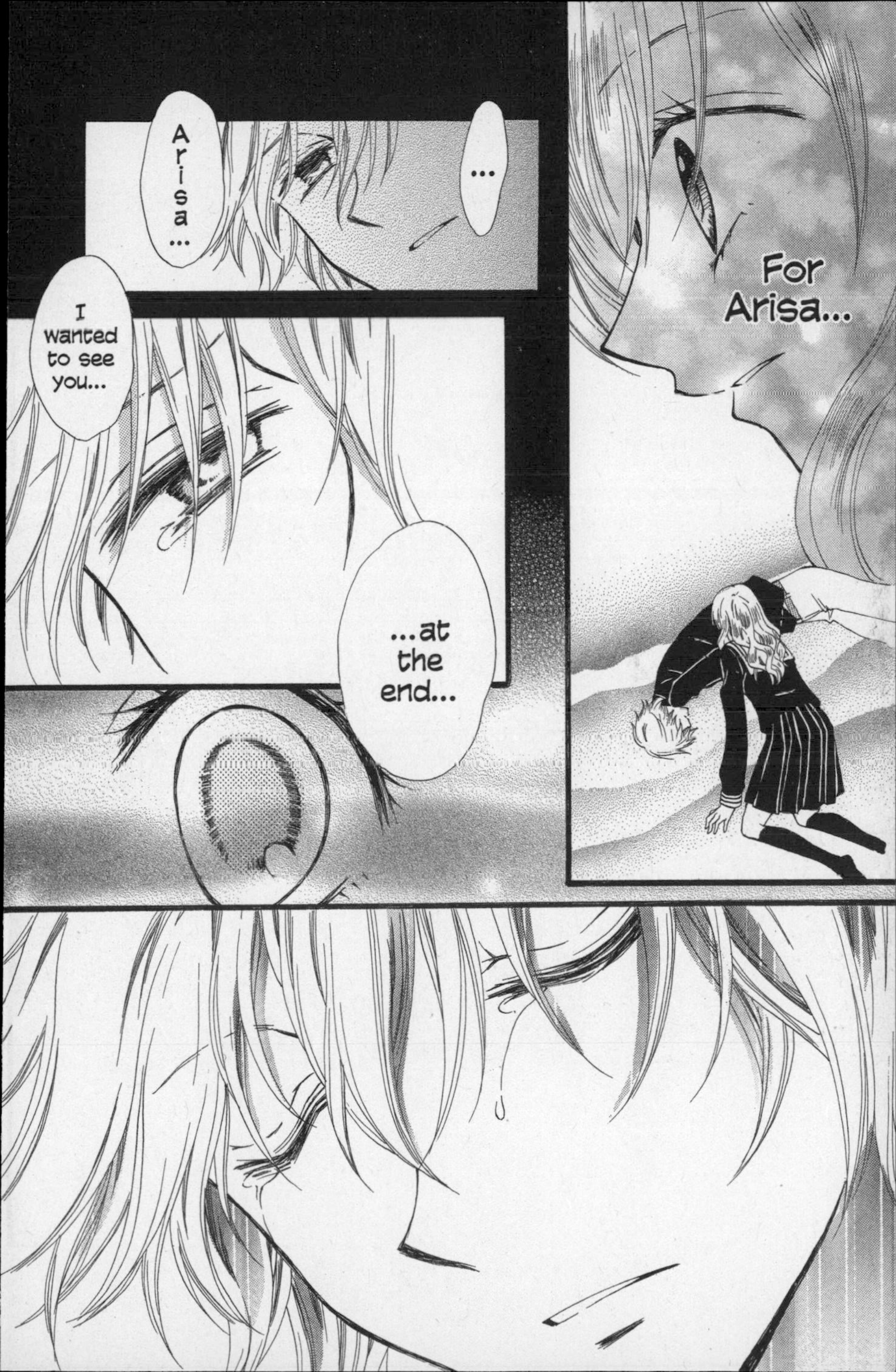
For Arisa...
...
Arisa...
I wanted to see you...
...at the end...

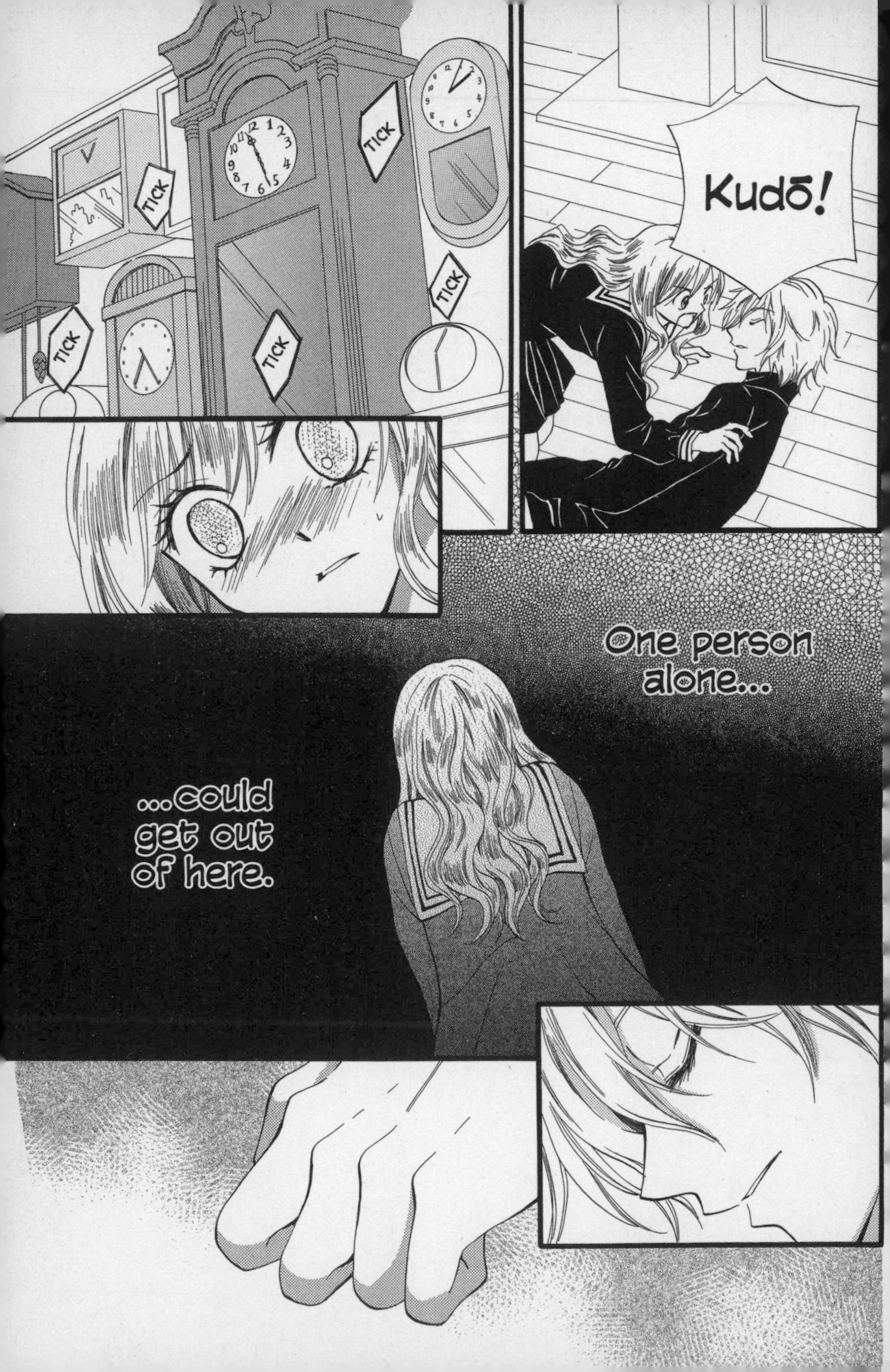
Kudō!
TICK
TICK
TICK
TICK
TICK
One person alone...
...could get out of here.

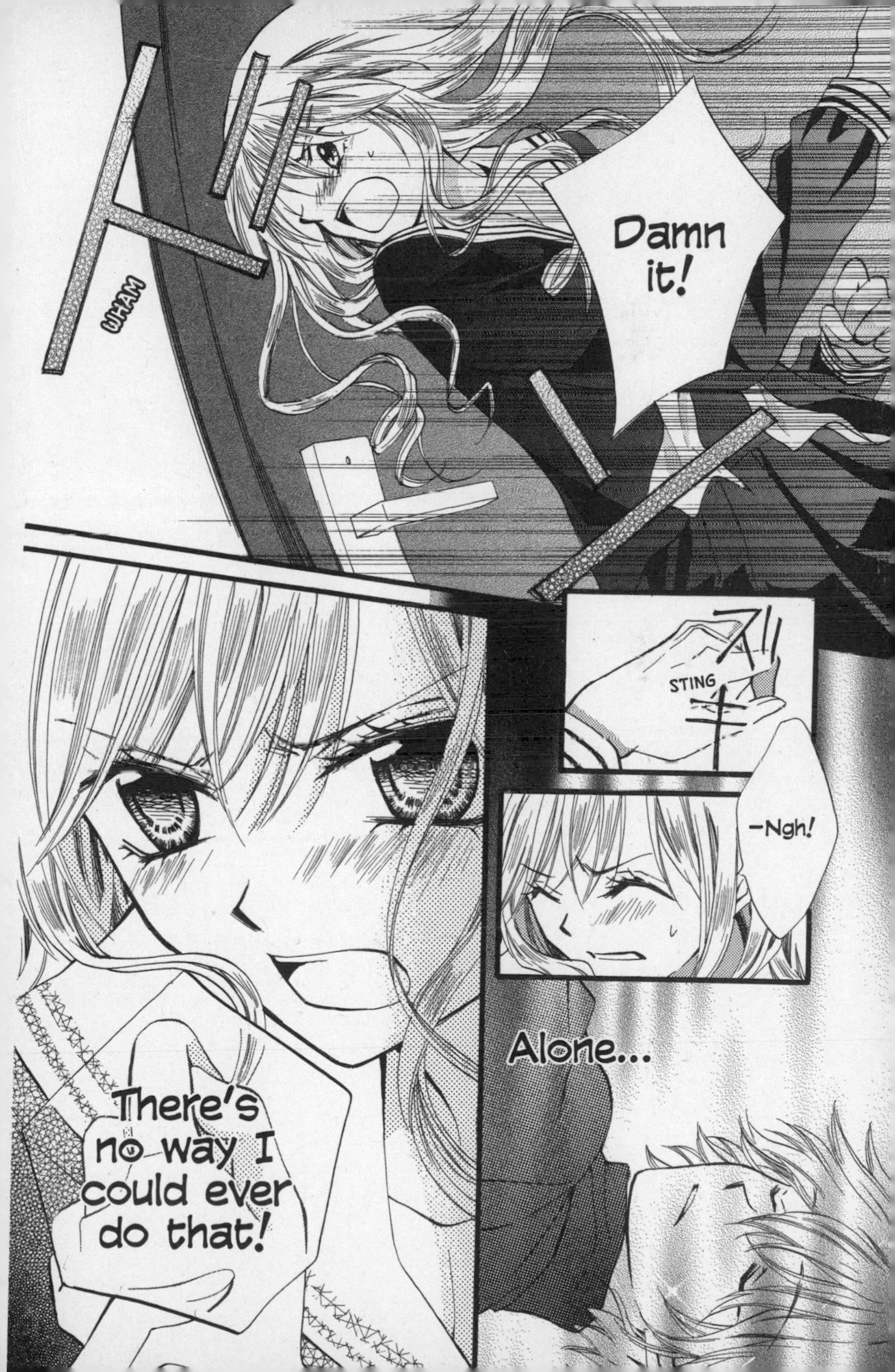
Damn it!
WHAM
STING
–Ngh!
Alone...
There's no way I could ever do that!

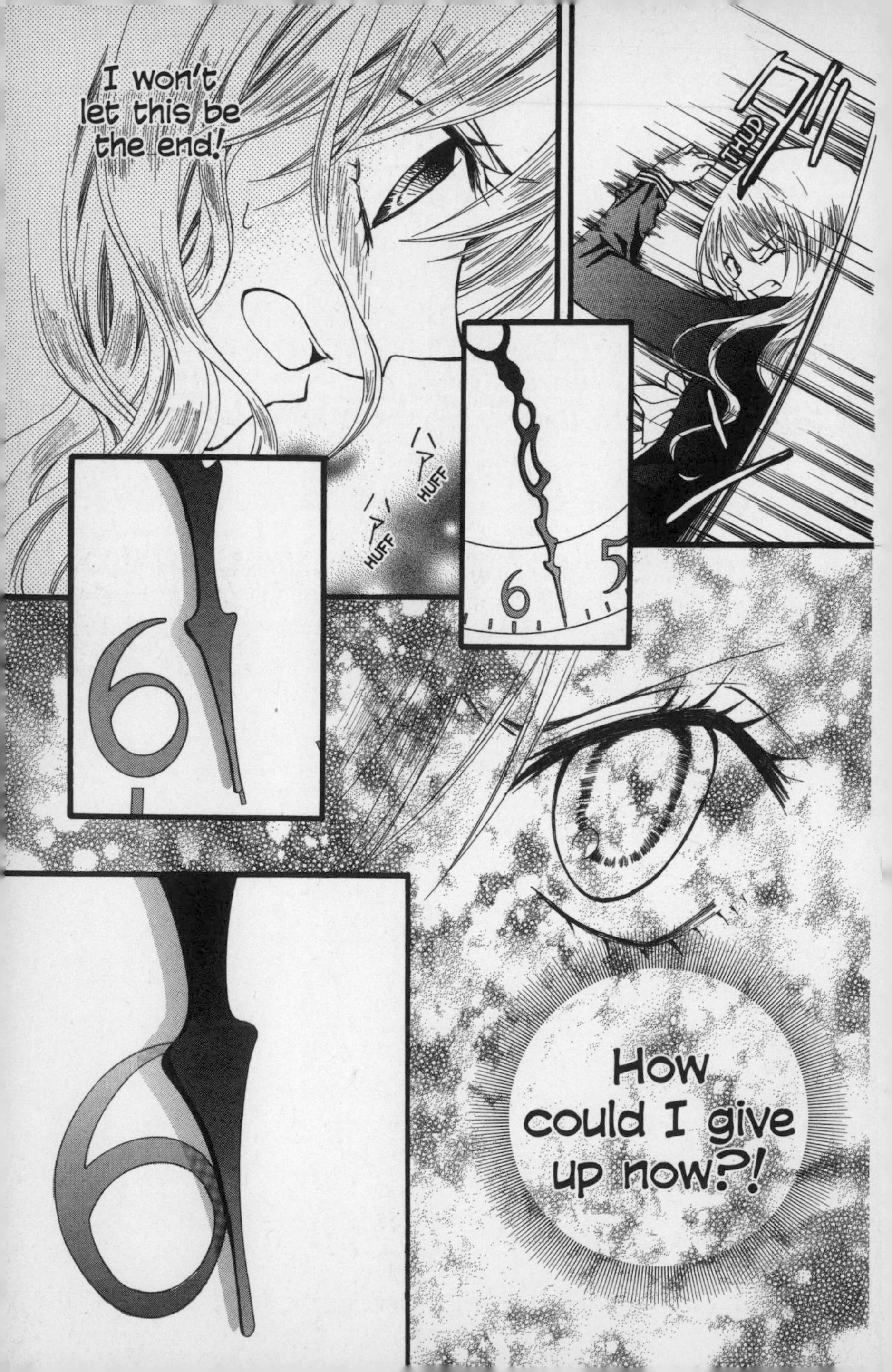
THUD
I won't let this be the end!
ハァ
HUFF
ハァ
HUFF
How could I give up now?!

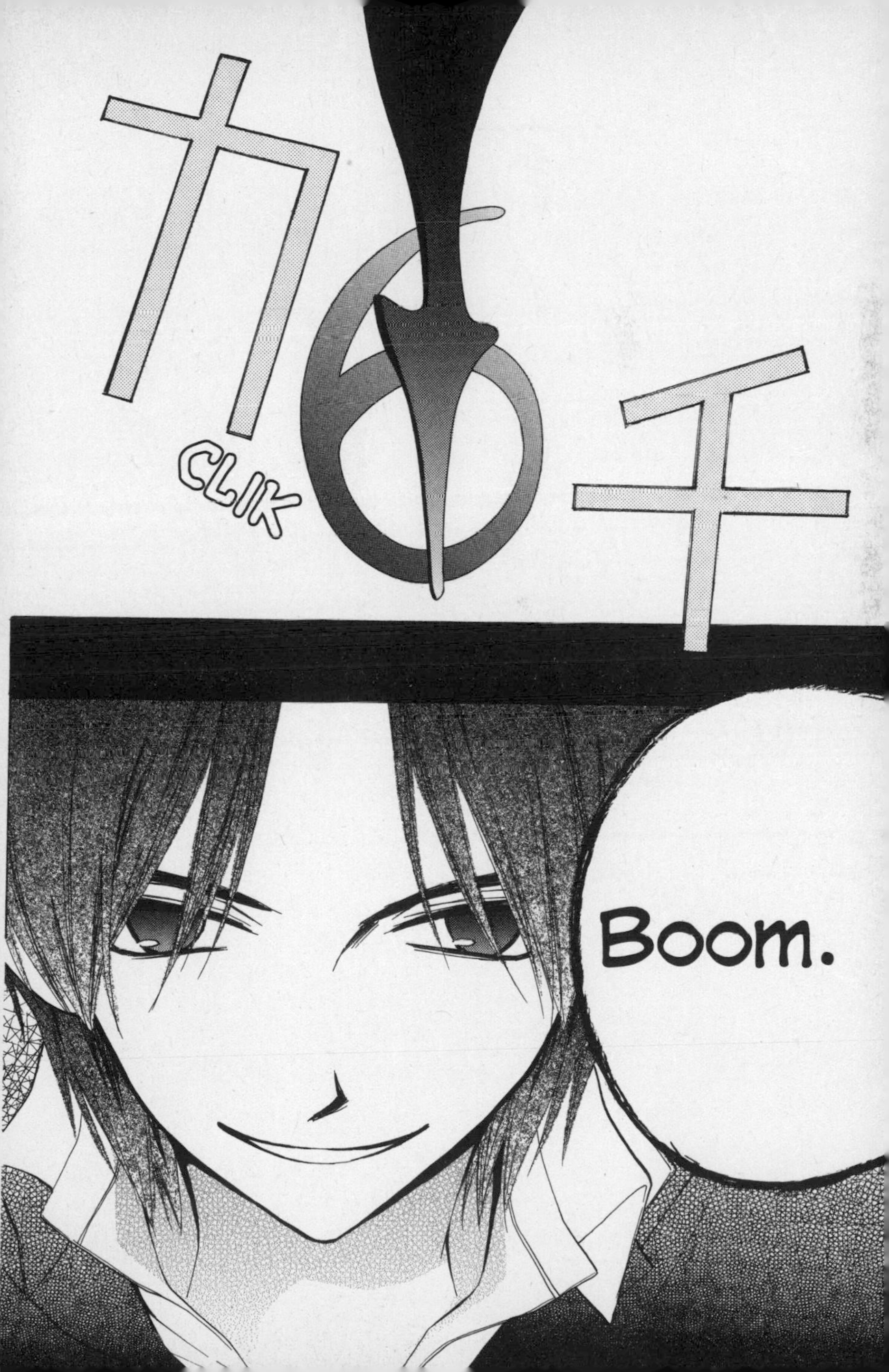
カチ
CLIK
Boom.

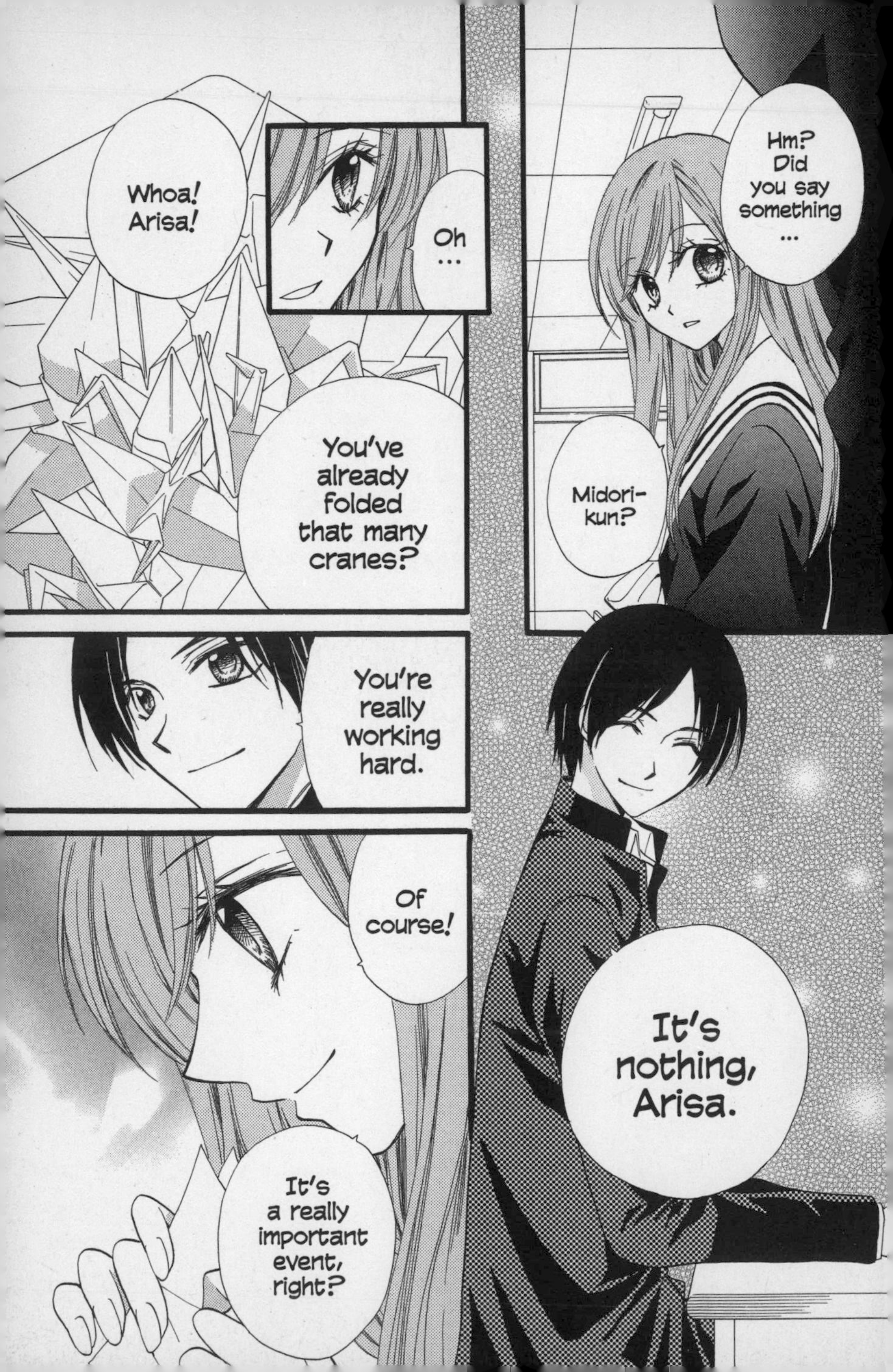
Hm? Did you say something ...
Midori-kun?
Whoa! Arisa!
Oh ...
You've already folded that many cranes?
It's nothing, Arisa.
You're really working hard.
Of course!
It's a really important event, right?

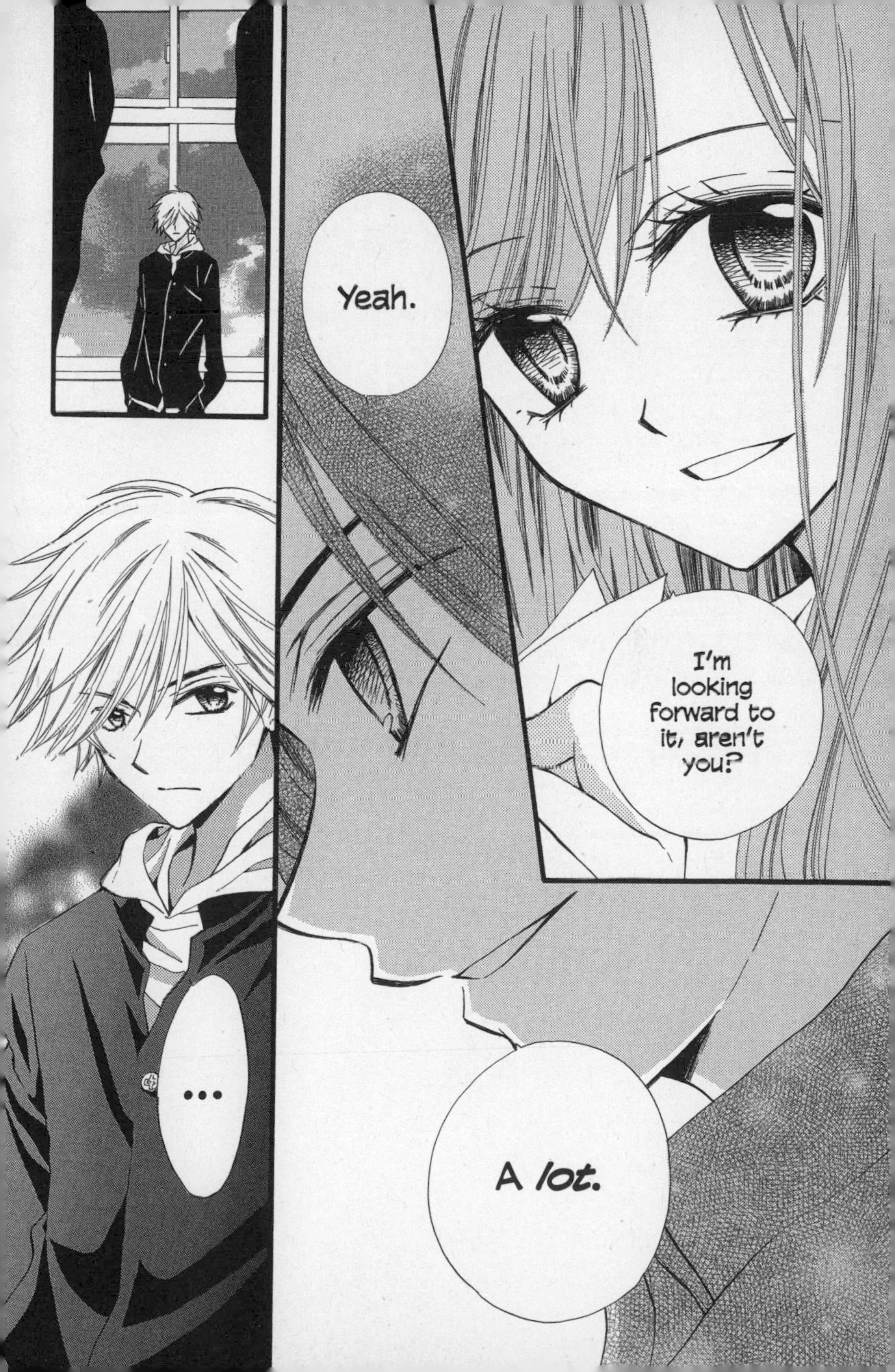

I'm looking forward to it, aren't you?
Yeah.
A lot.
...

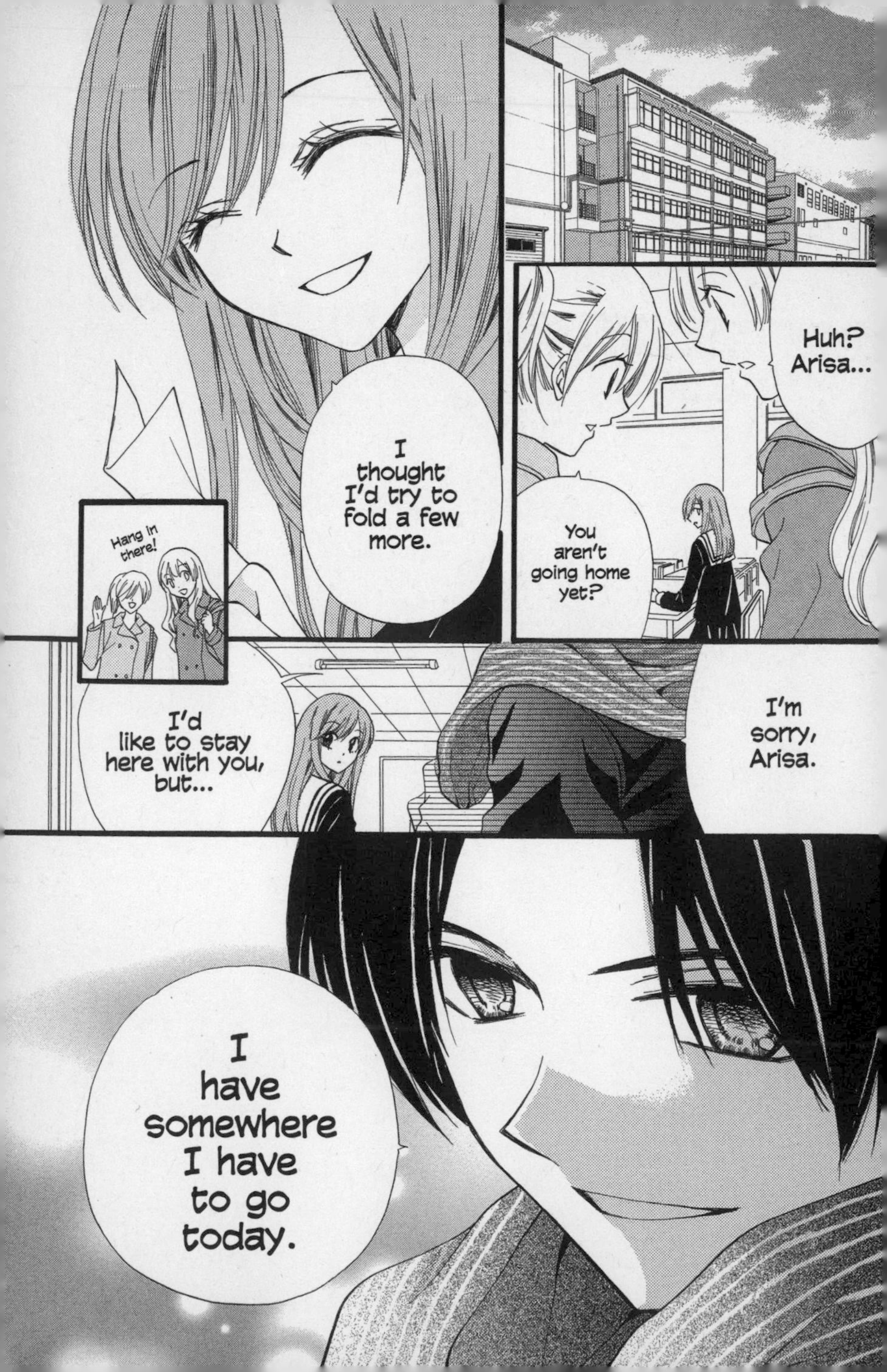
Huh? Arisa...
You aren't going home yet?
I thought I'd try to fold a few more.
I'm sorry, Arisa.
I'd like to stay here with you, but...
Hang in there!
I have somewhere I have to go today.

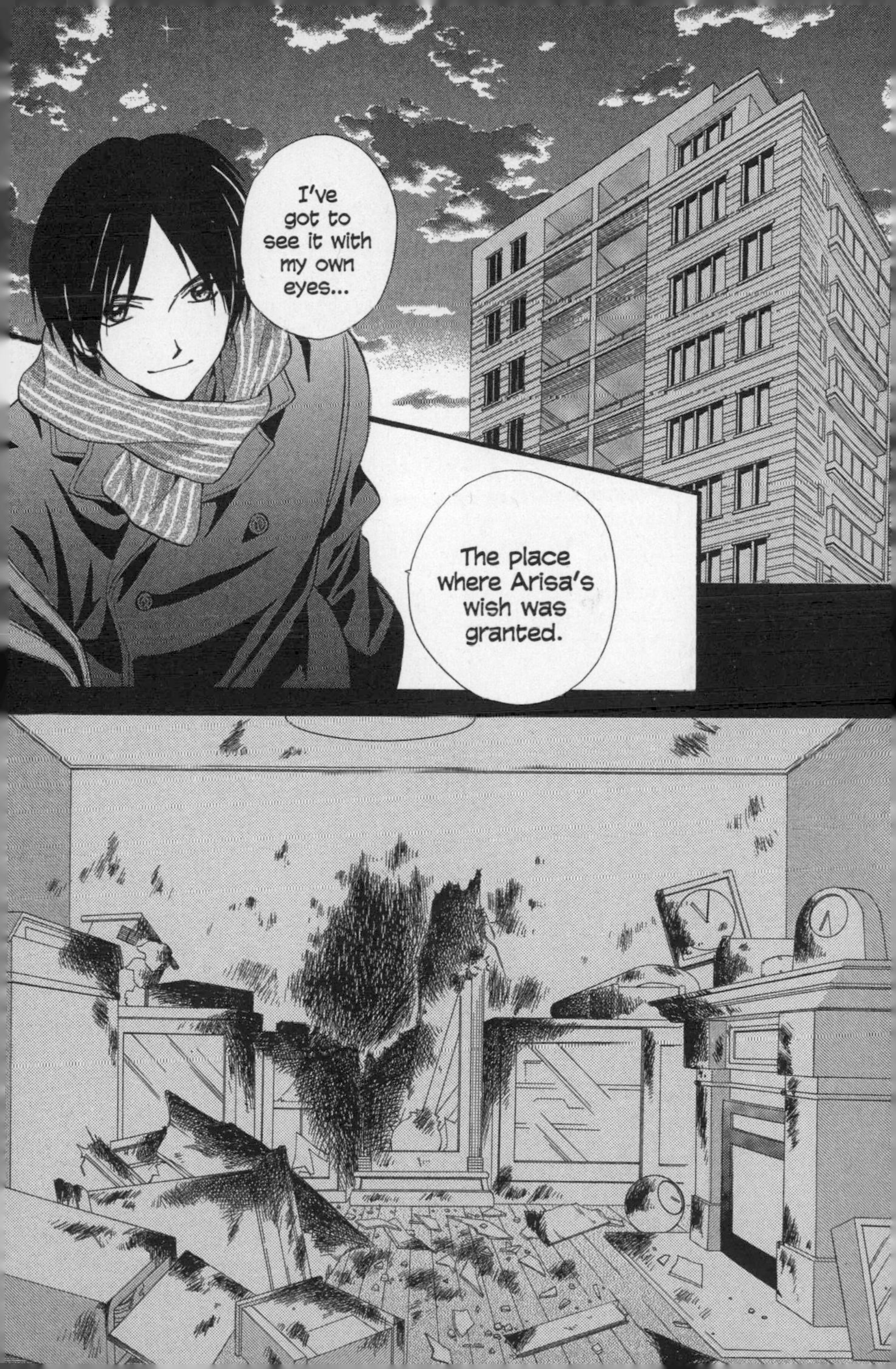
I've got to see it with my own eyes...
The place where Arisa's wish was granted.

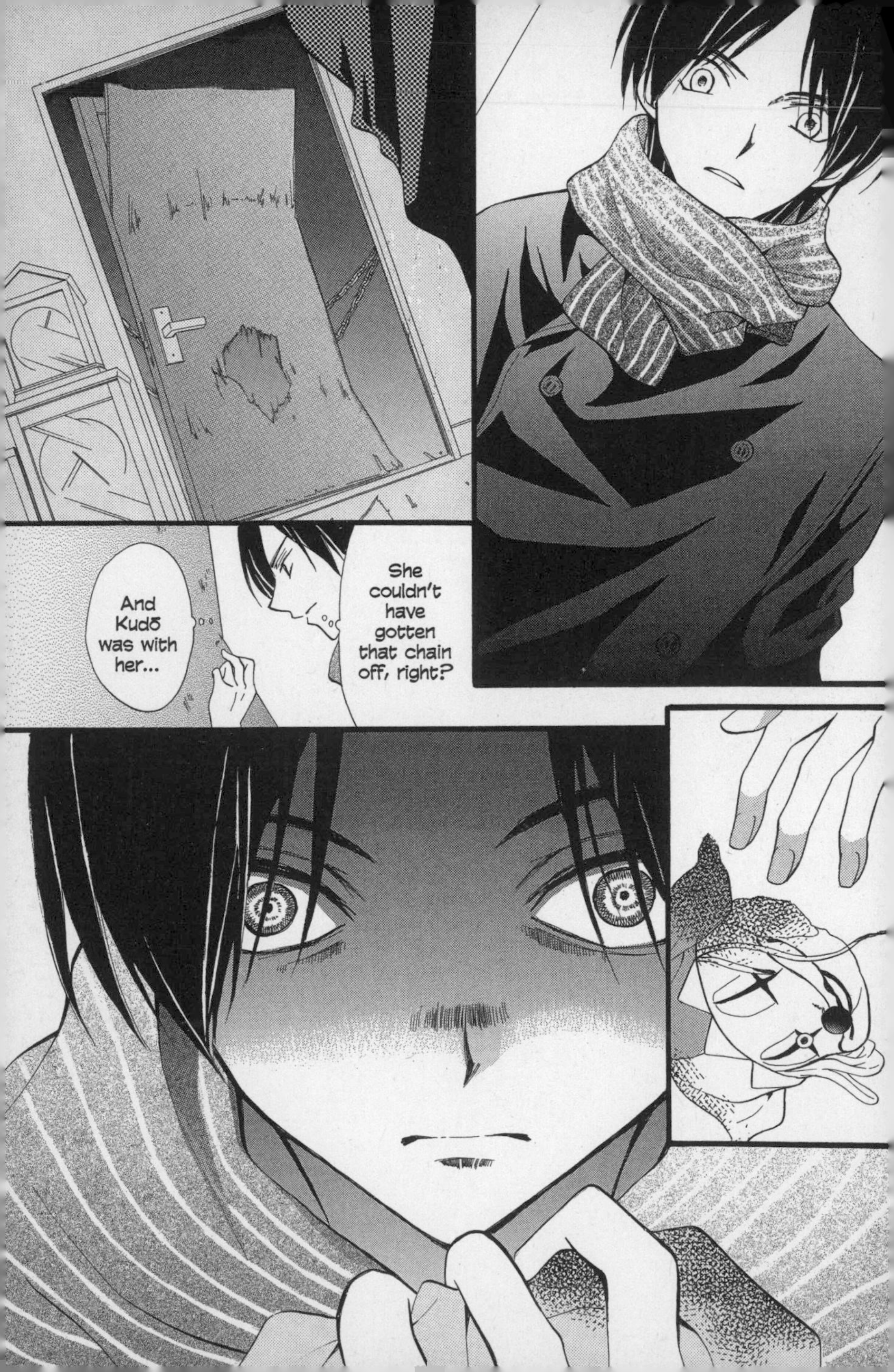
She couldn't have gotten that chain off, right?
And Kudō was with her...

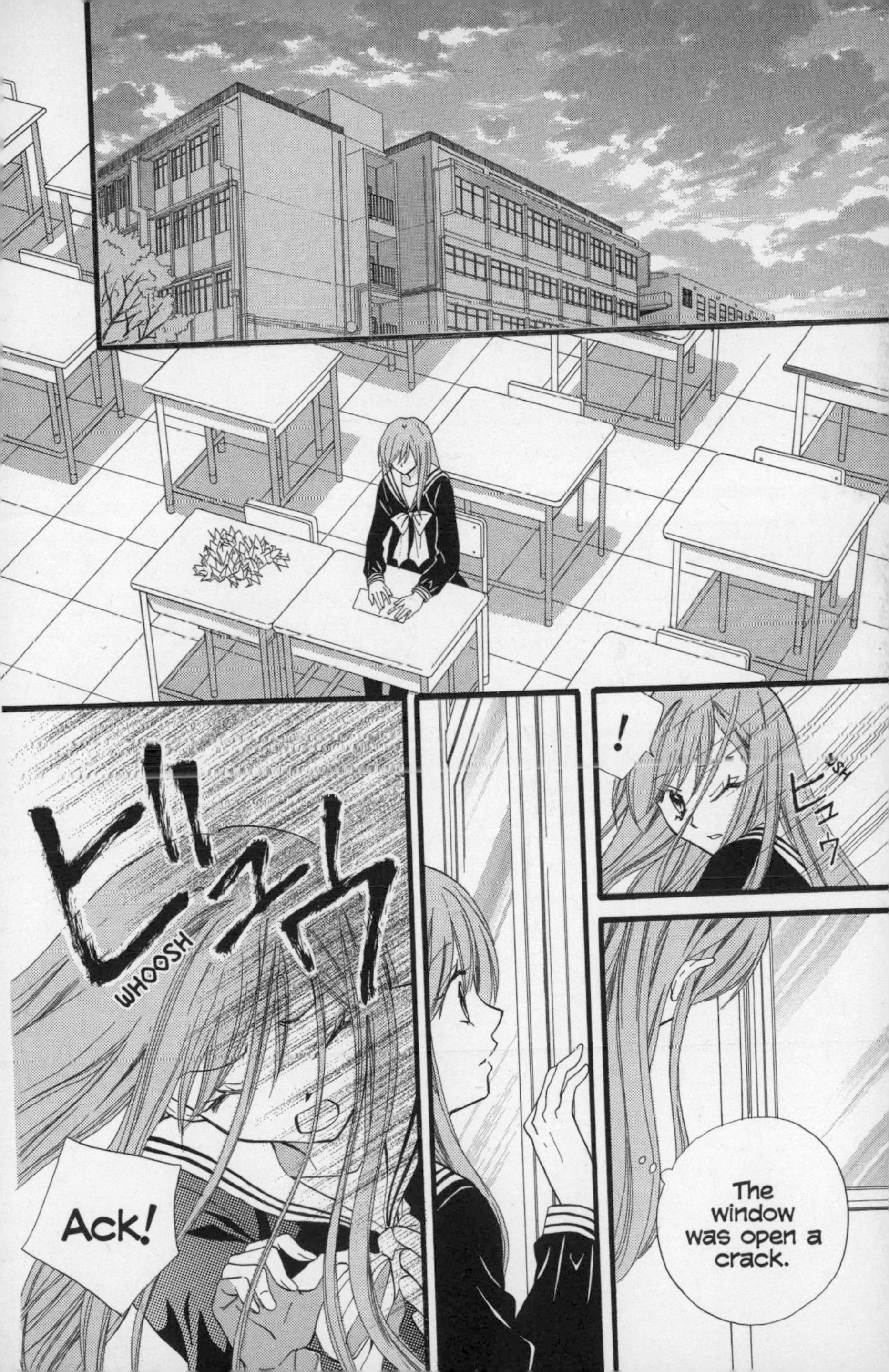
!
ヒュウ
SH
The window was open a crack.
ヒュウ
WHOOSH
Ack!

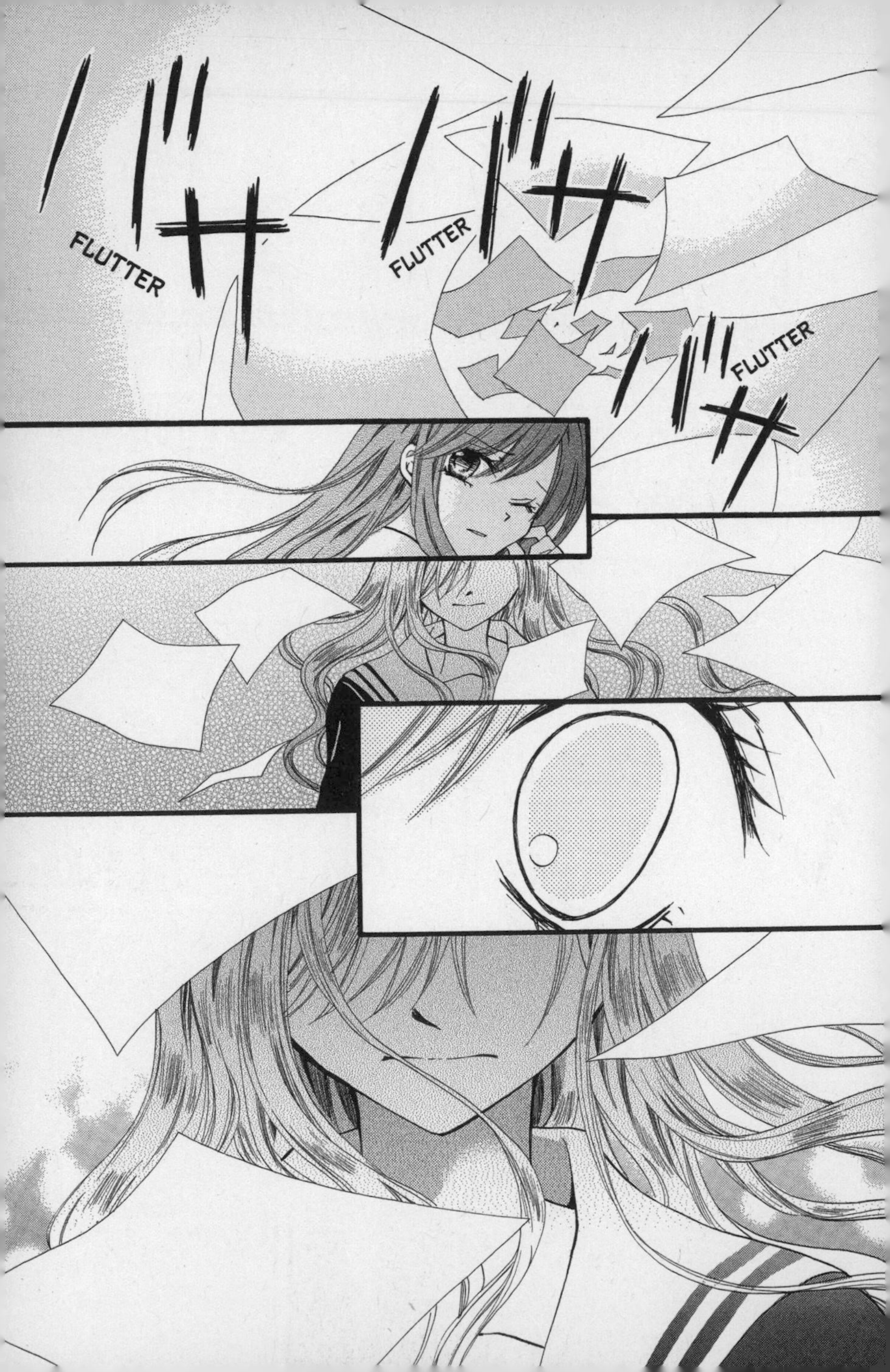

FLUTTER
FLUTTER
FLUTTER

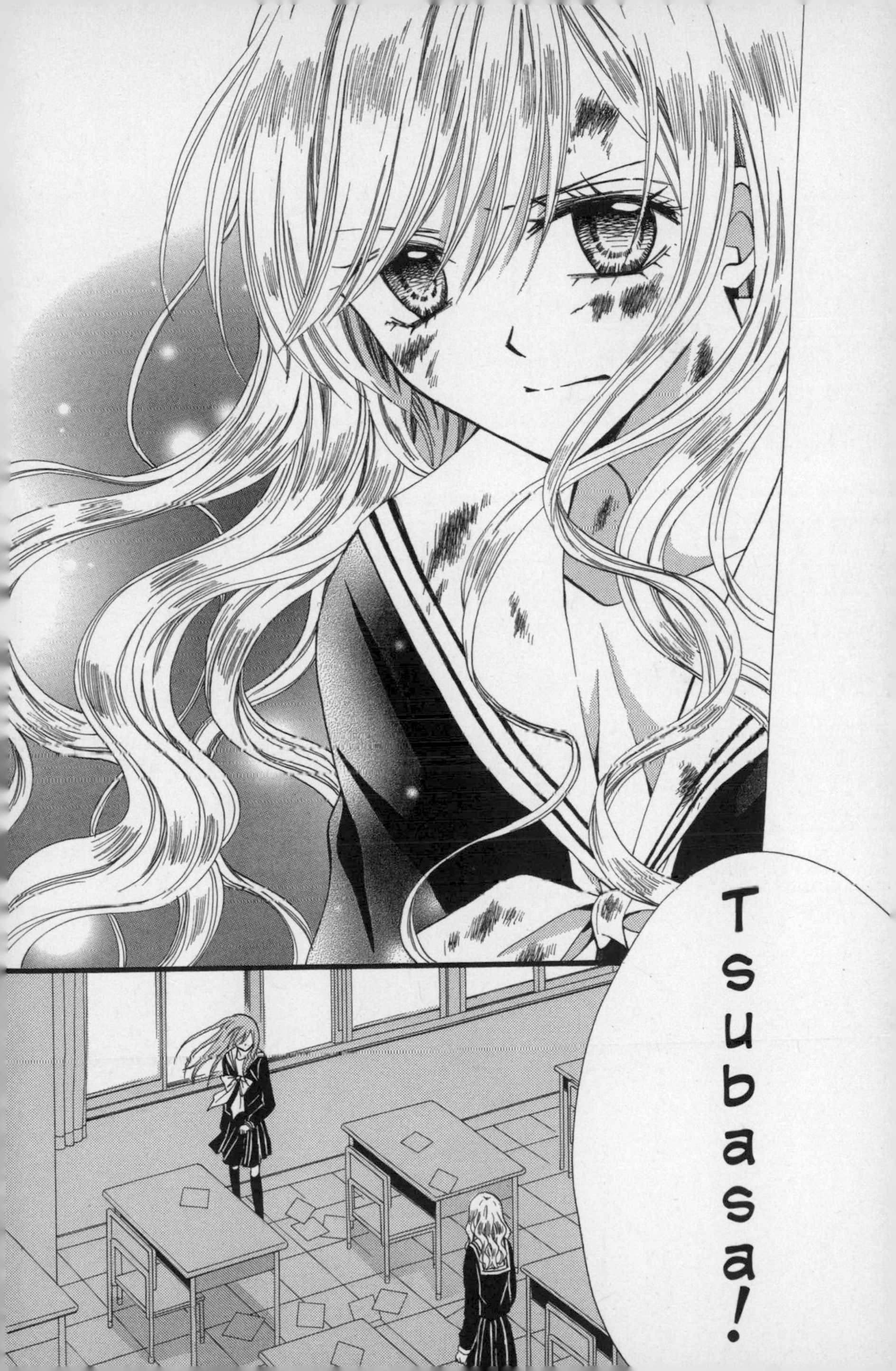
Tsubasa!

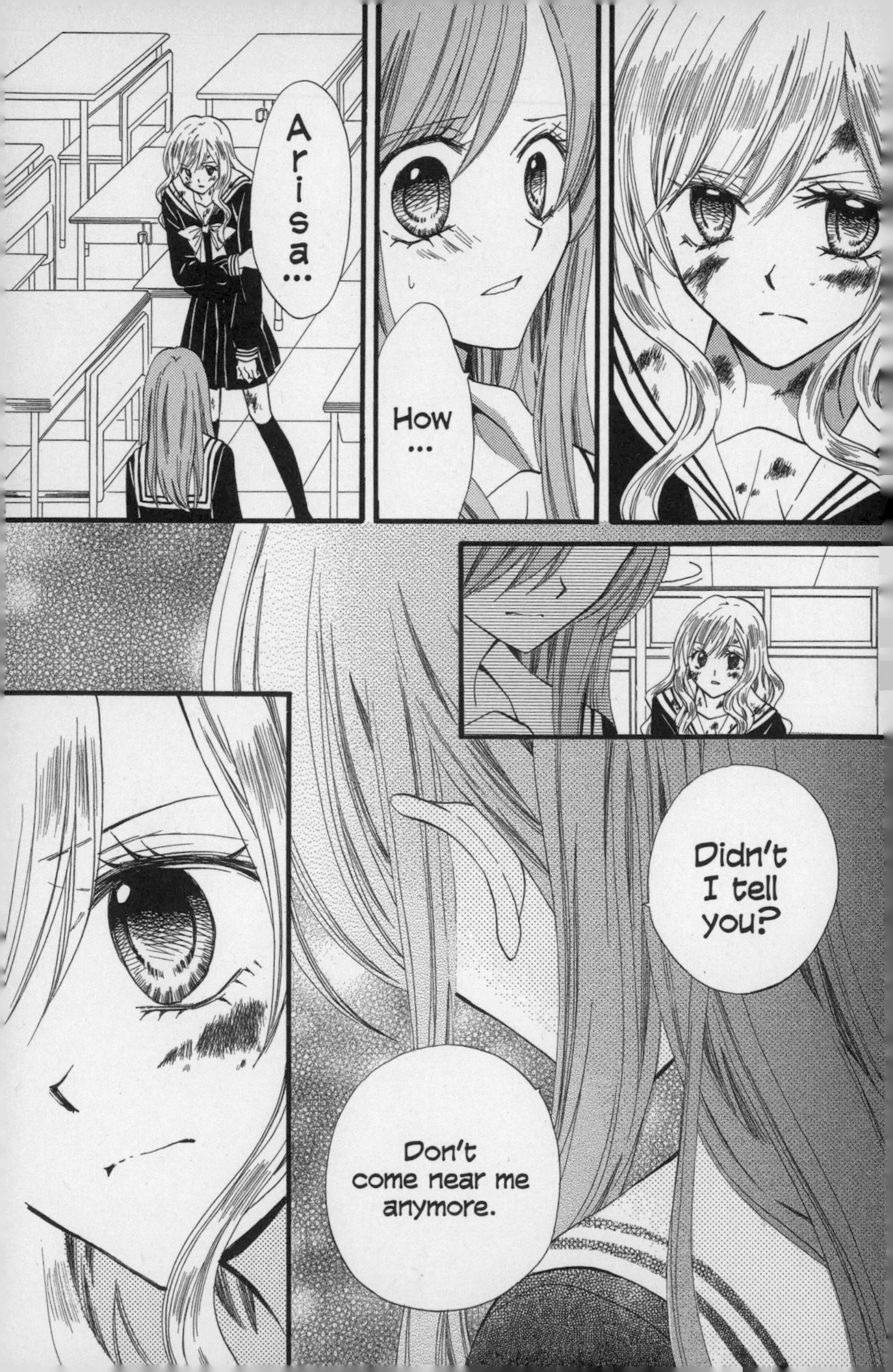
How...
Arisa...
Didn't I tell you?
Don't come near me anymore.

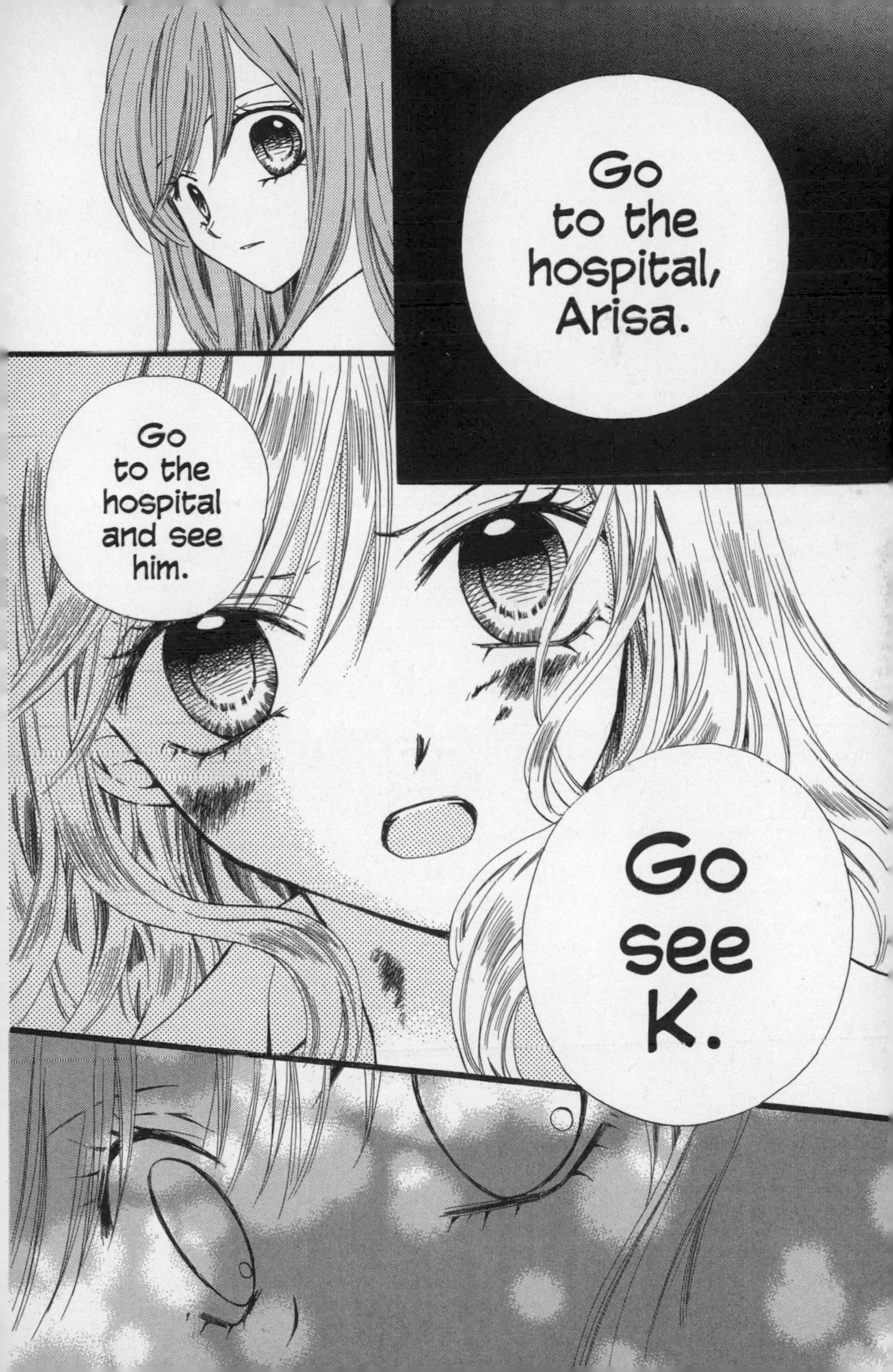
Go to the hospital, Arisa.
Go to the hospital and see him.
Go see K.

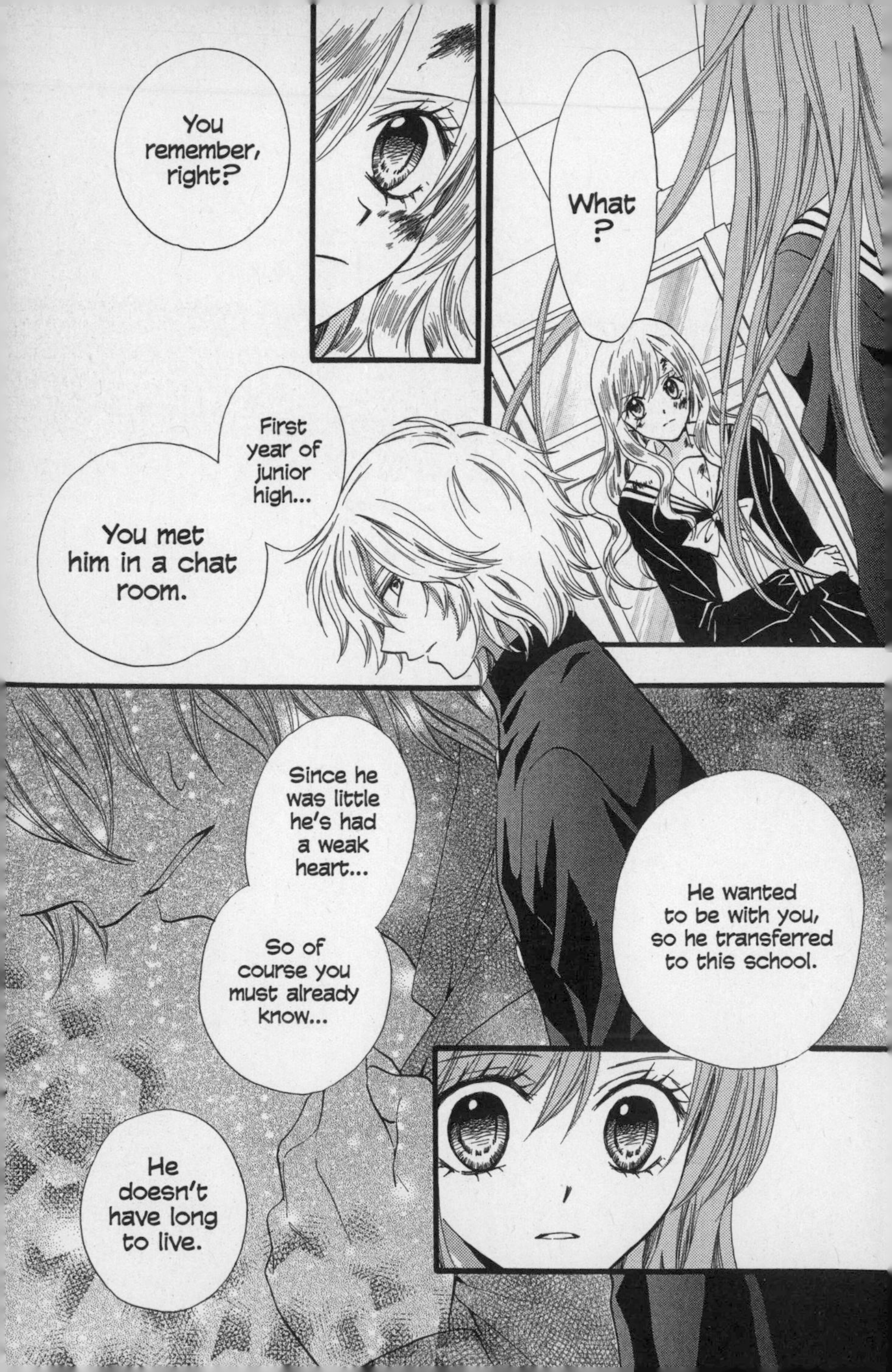
What?
You remember, right?
First year of junior high...
You met him in a chat room.
He wanted to be with you, so he transferred to this school.
Since he was little he's had a weak heart...
So of course you must already know...
He doesn't have long to live.

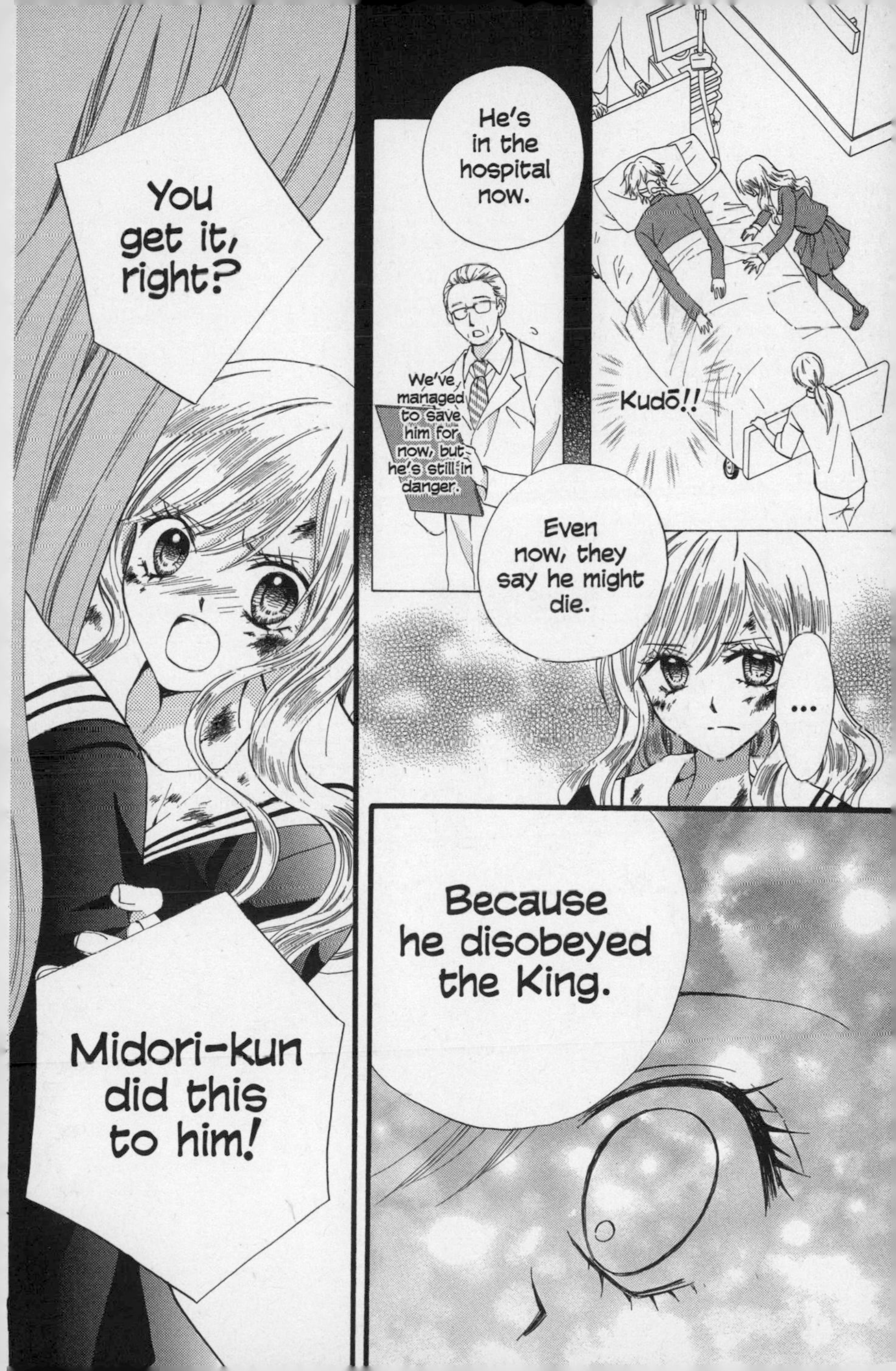
Kudō!!
He's in the hospital now.
We've managed to save him for now, but he's still in danger.
Even now, they say he might die.
...
Because he disobeyed the King.
You get it, right?
Midori-kun did this to him!

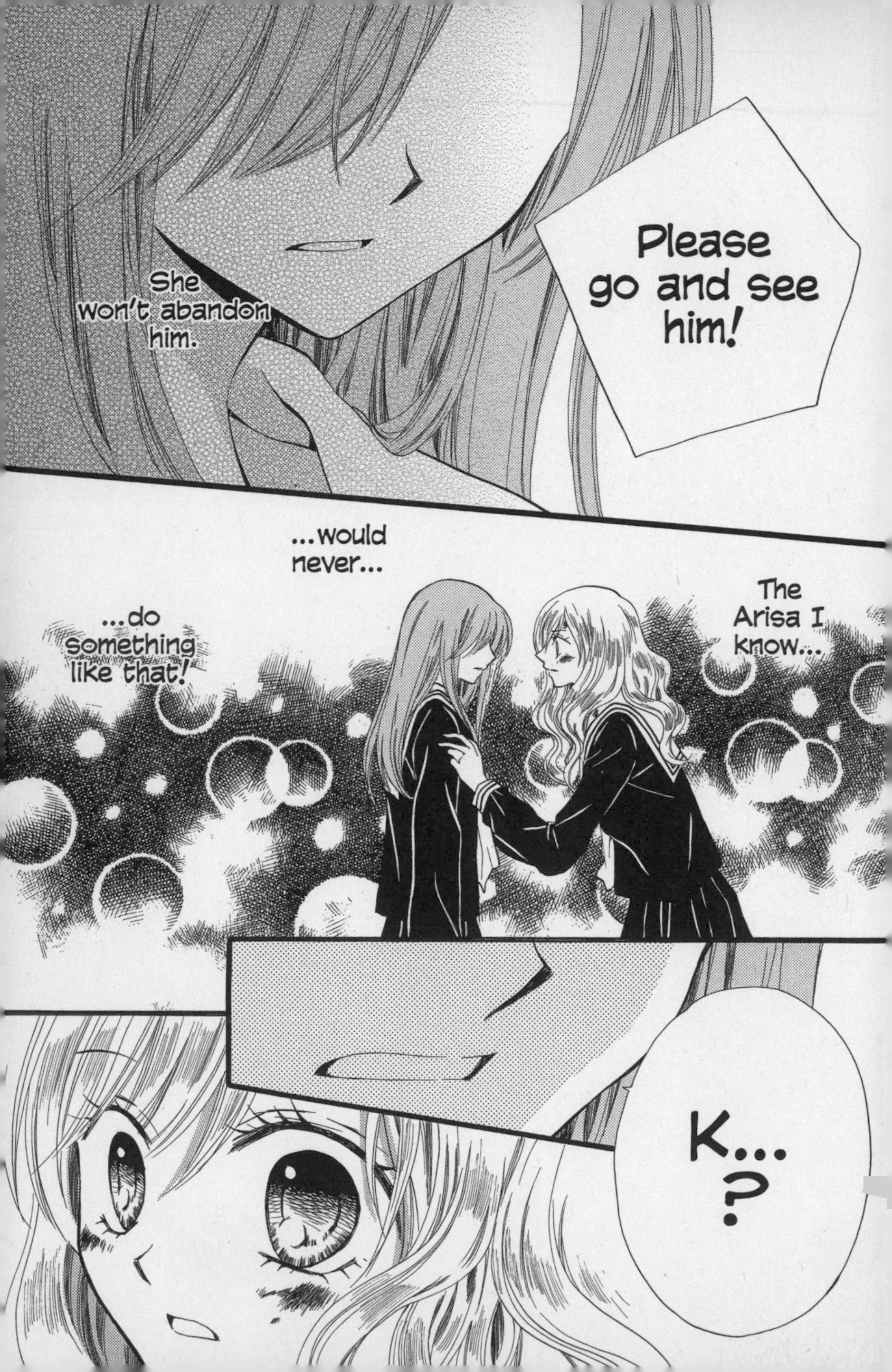

Please go and see him!
She won't abandon him.
The Arisa I know...
...would never...
...do something like that!
K...?

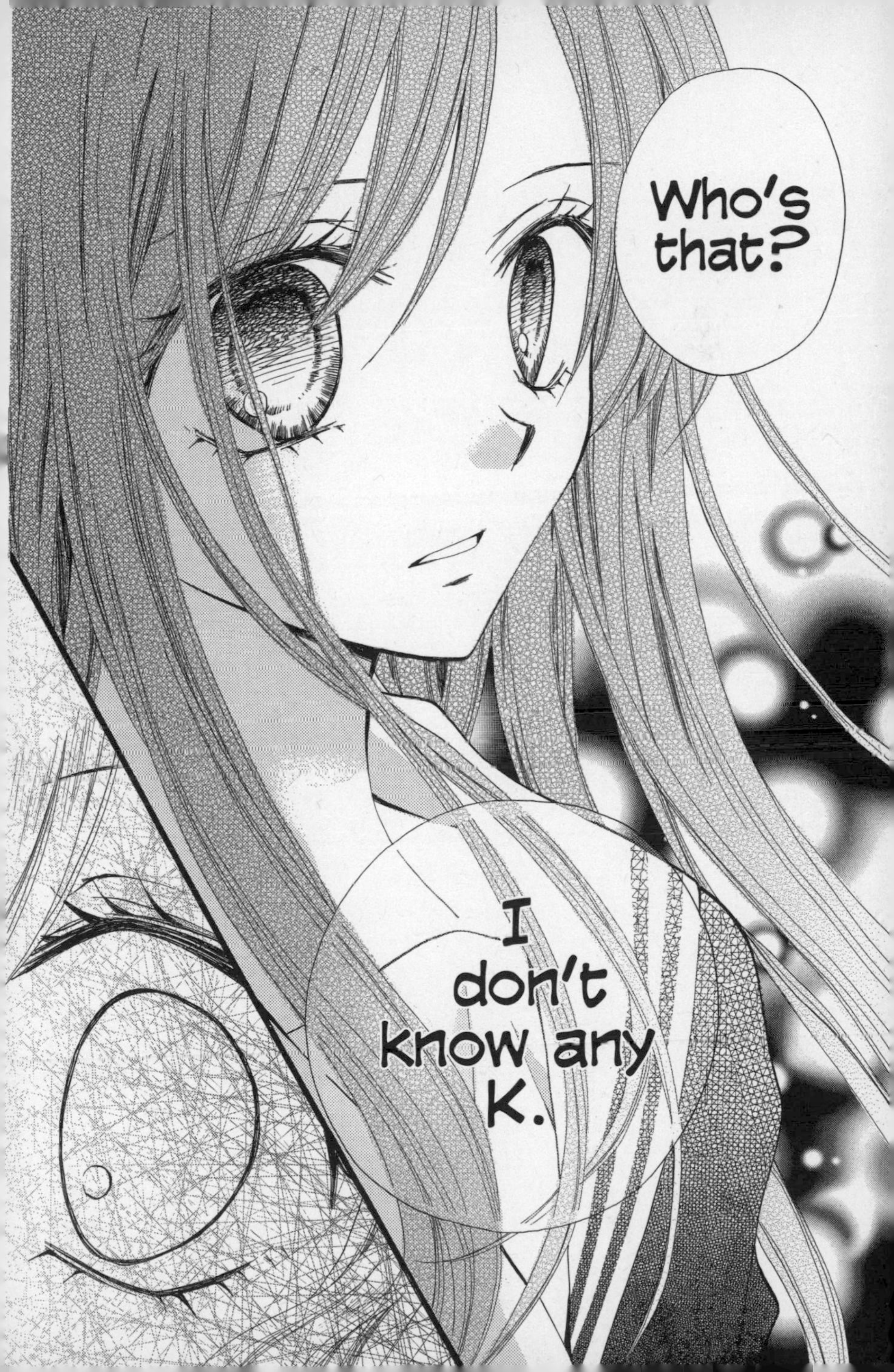
Who's that?
I don't know any K.

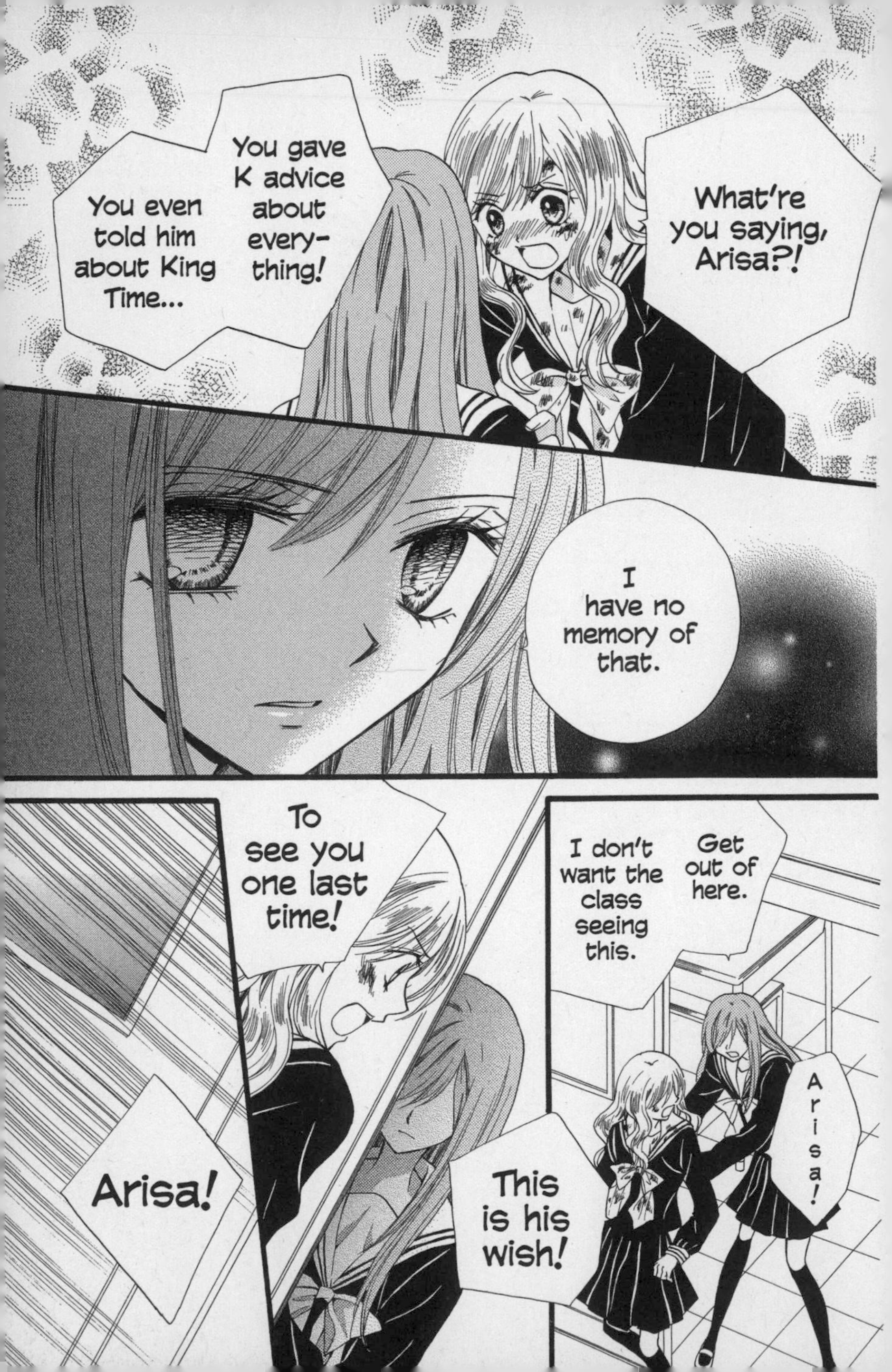
What're you saying, Arisa?!
You gave K advice about every-thing!
You even told him about King Time...
I have no memory of that.
Get out of here.
I don't want the class seeing this.
Arisa!
This is his wish!
To see you one last time!
Arisa!

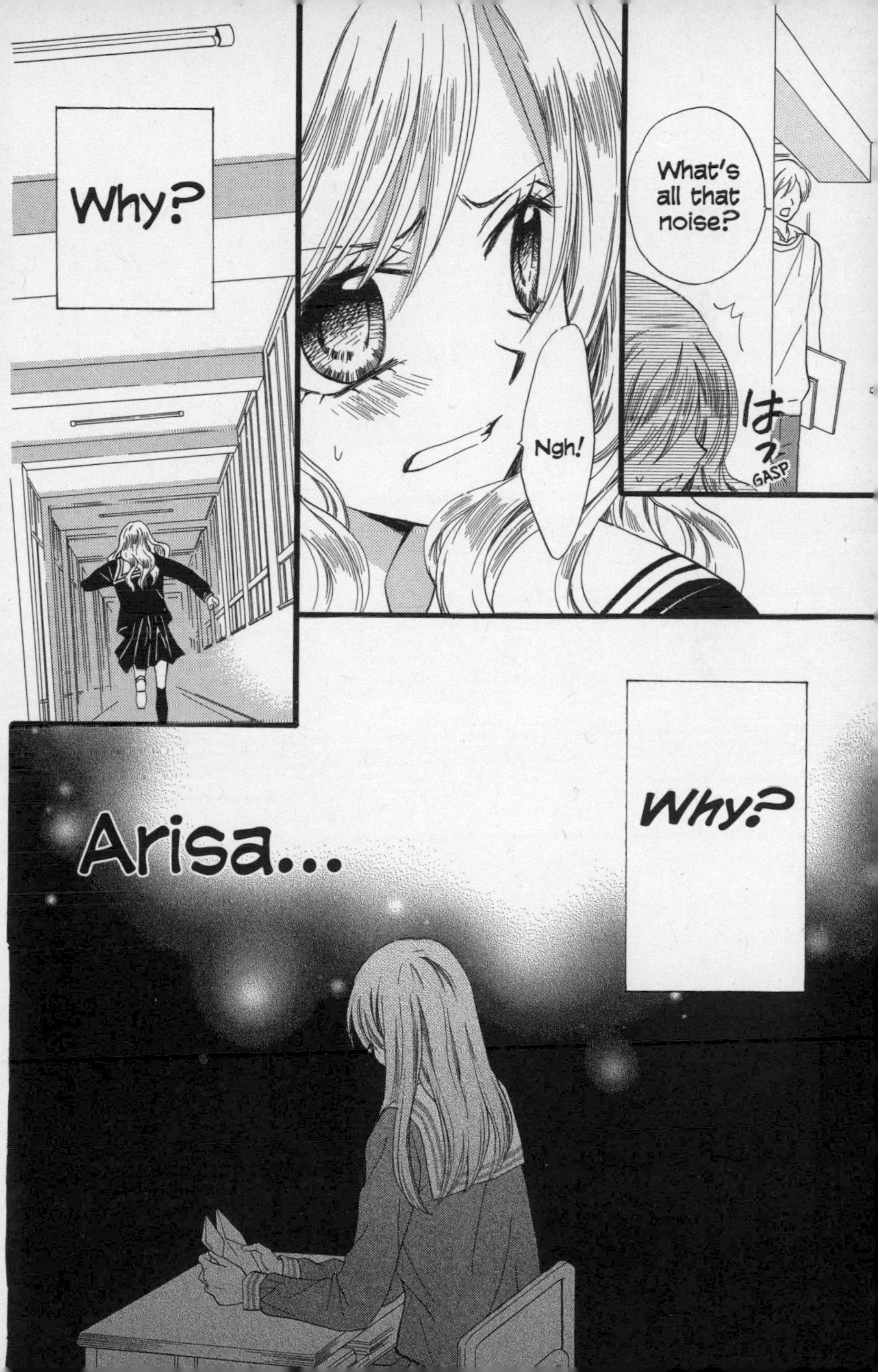
What's all that noise?
は
GASP
Ngh!
Why?
Why?
Arisa...

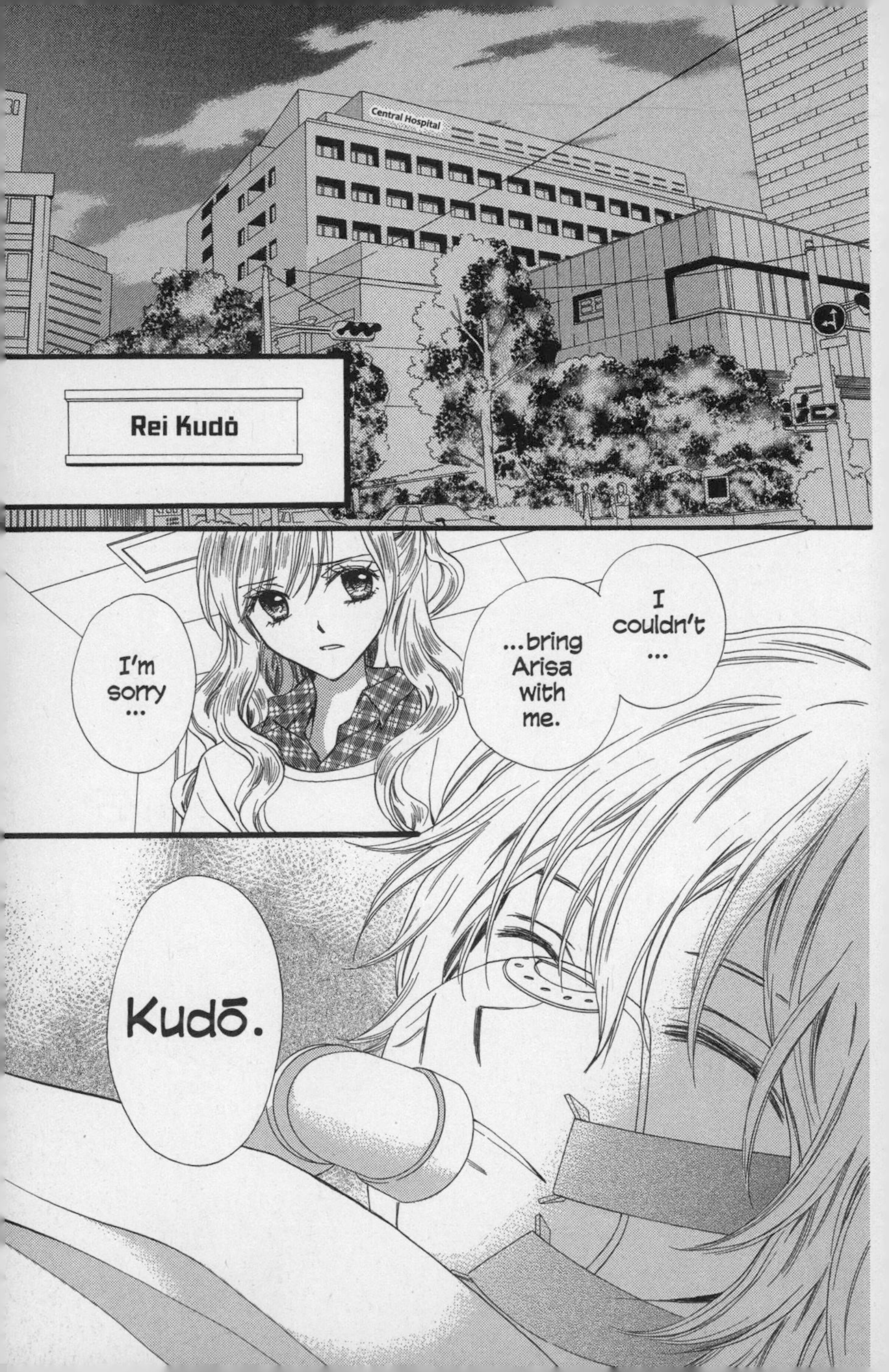
Central Hospital
Rei Kudō
I couldn't ...
...bring Arisa with me.
I'm sorry ...
Kudō.

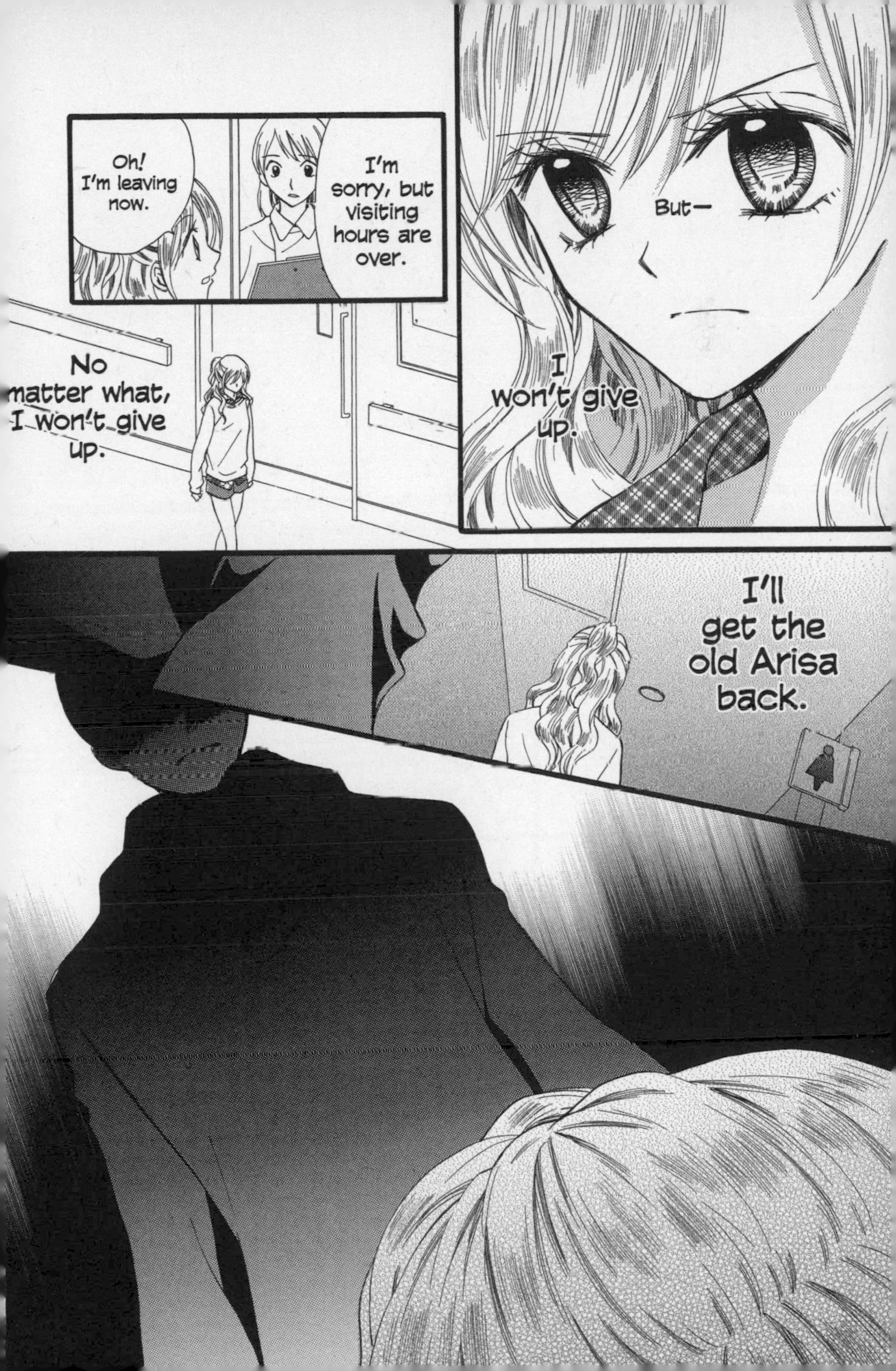
But—
I won't give up.
I'm sorry, but visiting hours are over.
Oh! I'm leaving now.
No matter what, I won't give up.
I'll get the old Arisa back.

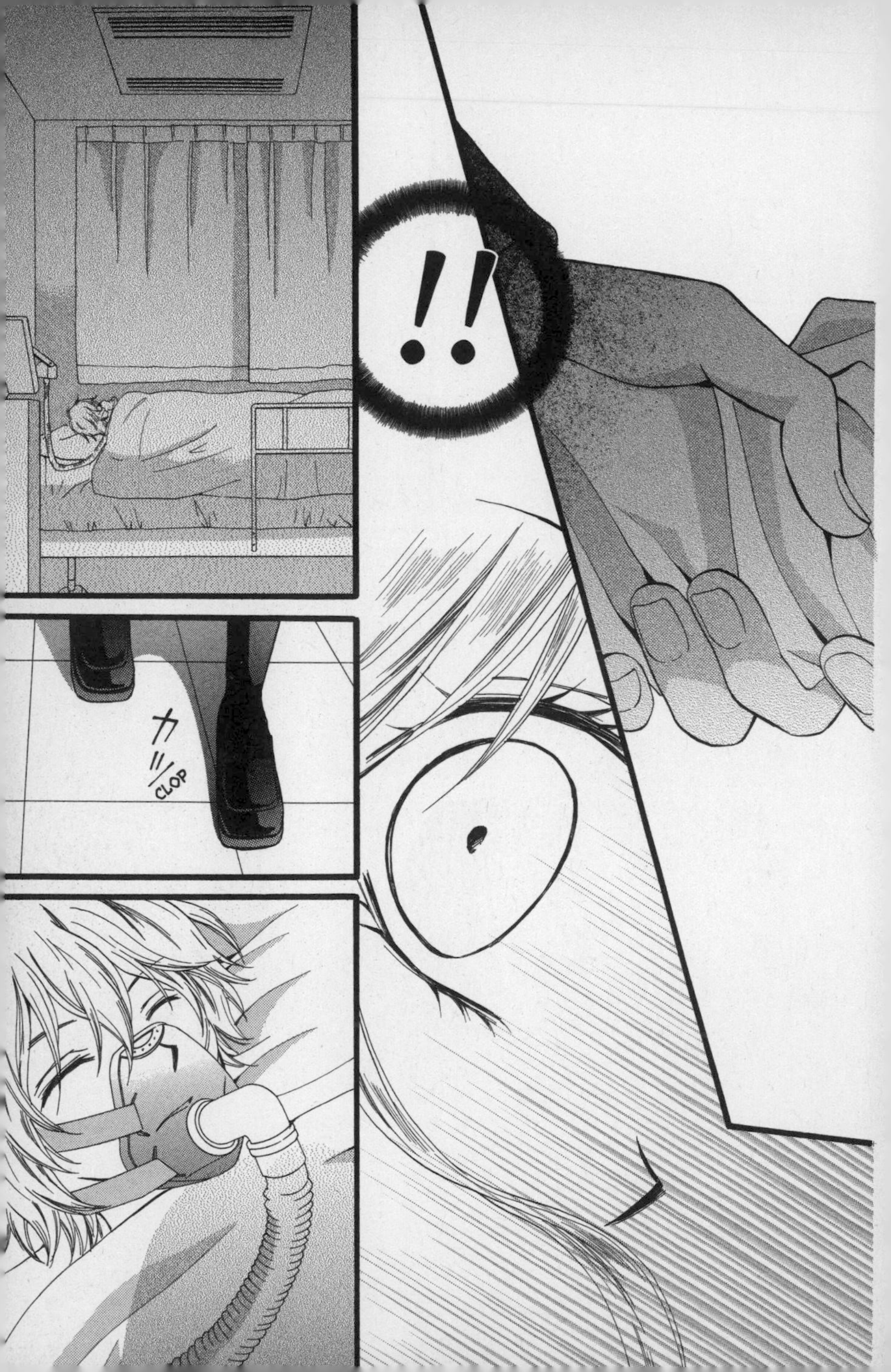
!!
カッ
CLOP

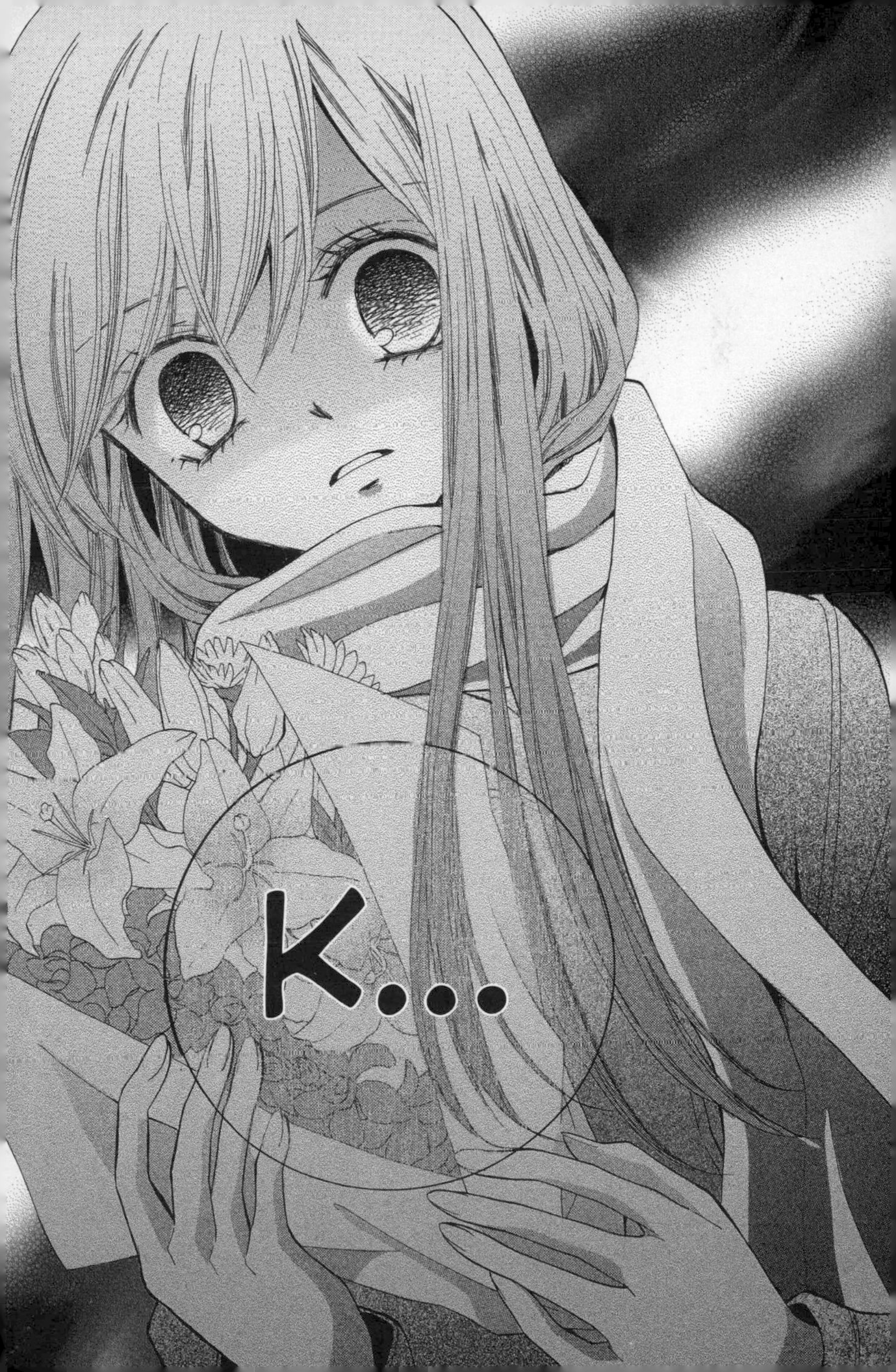
K...

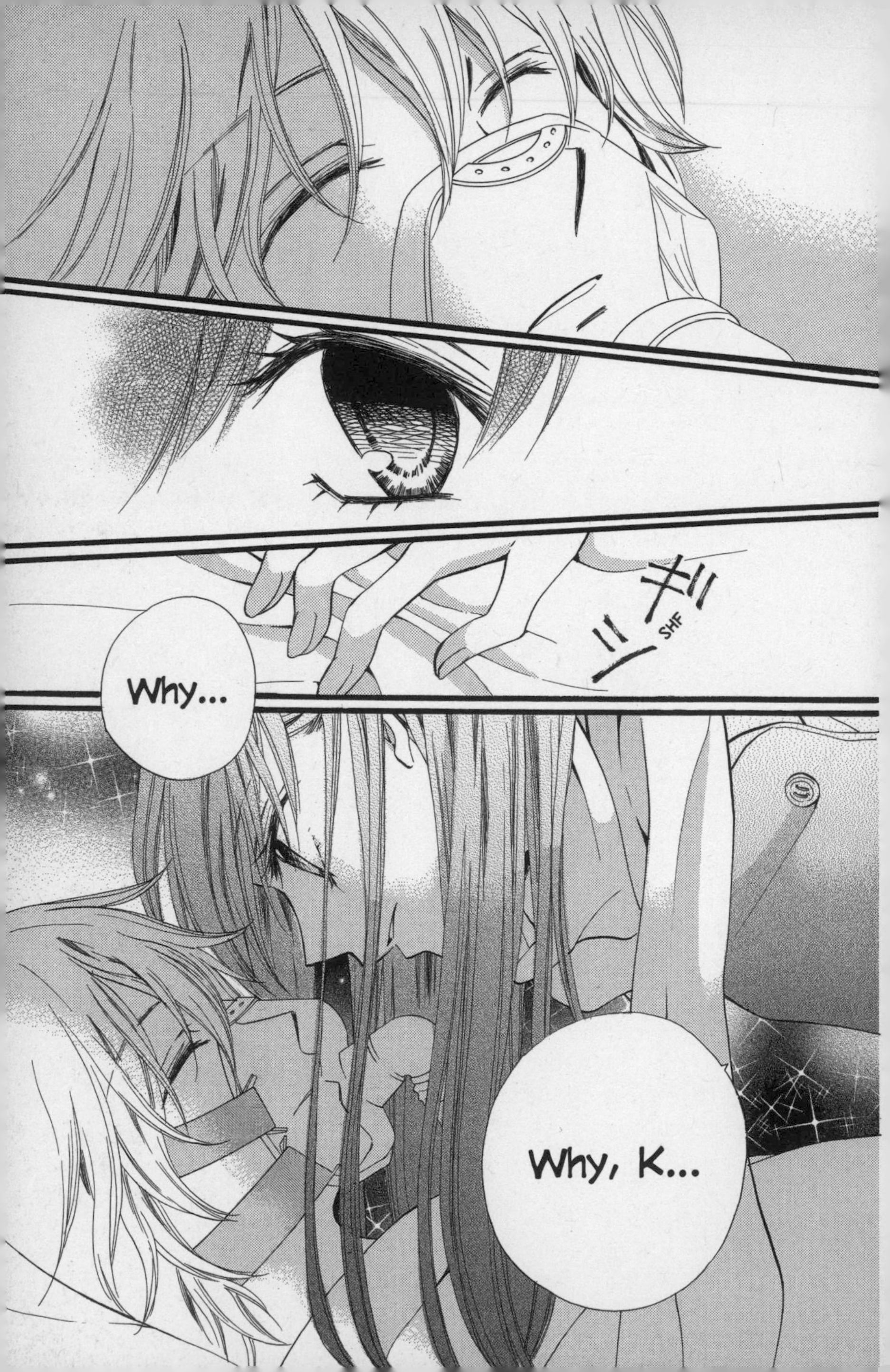
SHF
Why...
Why, K...

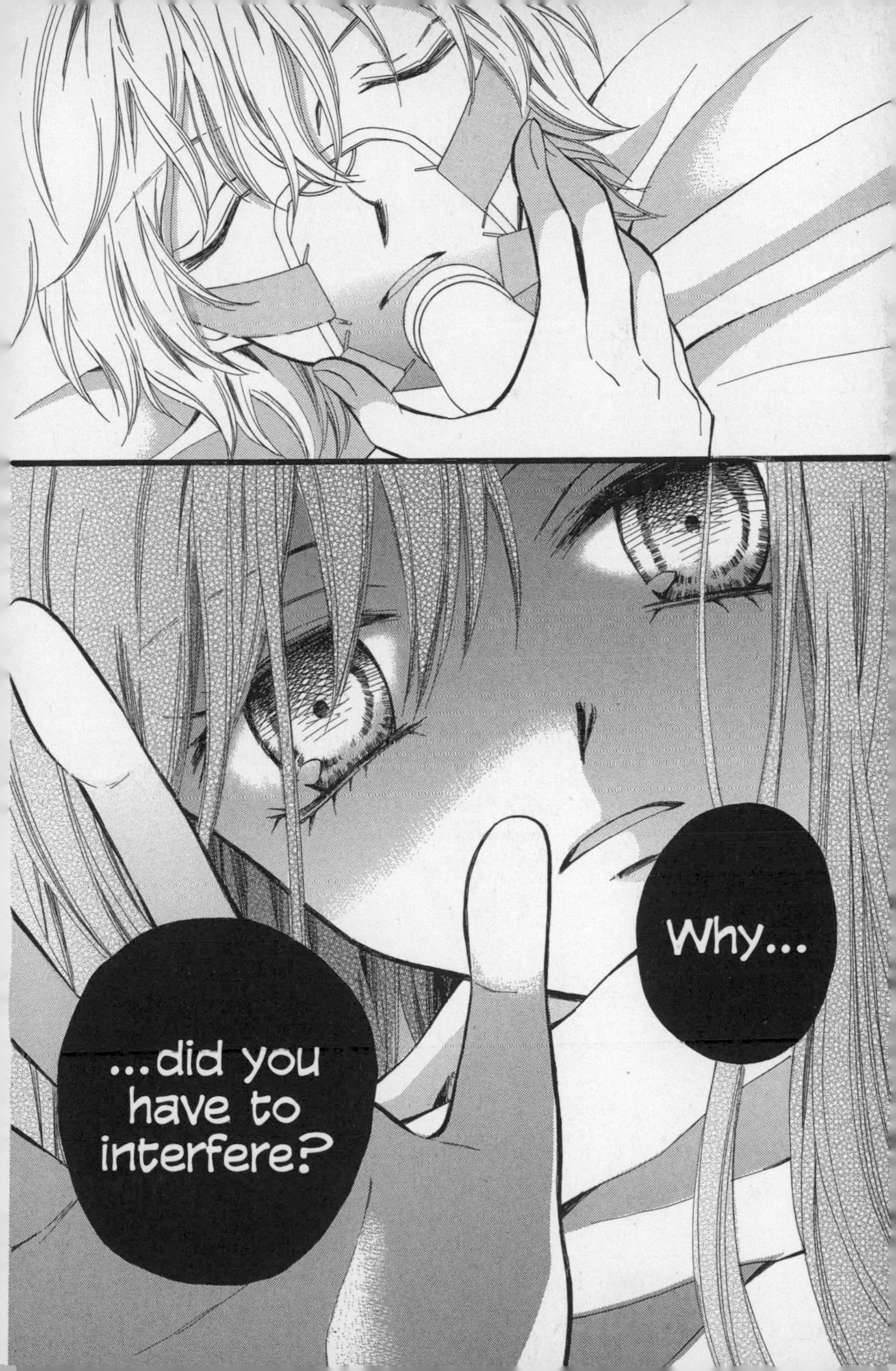
Why...
...did you have to interfere?

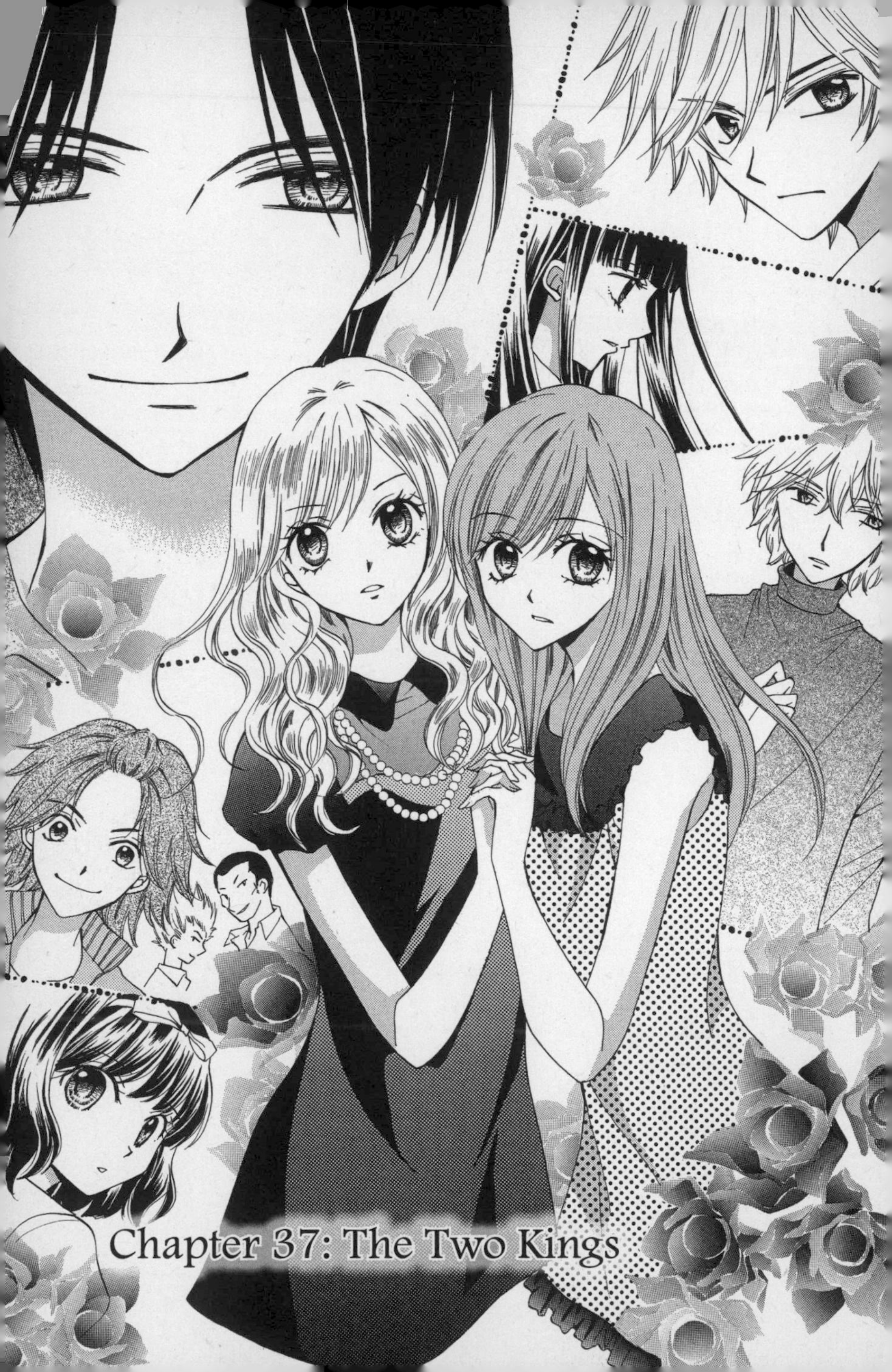

Chapter 37: The Two Kings

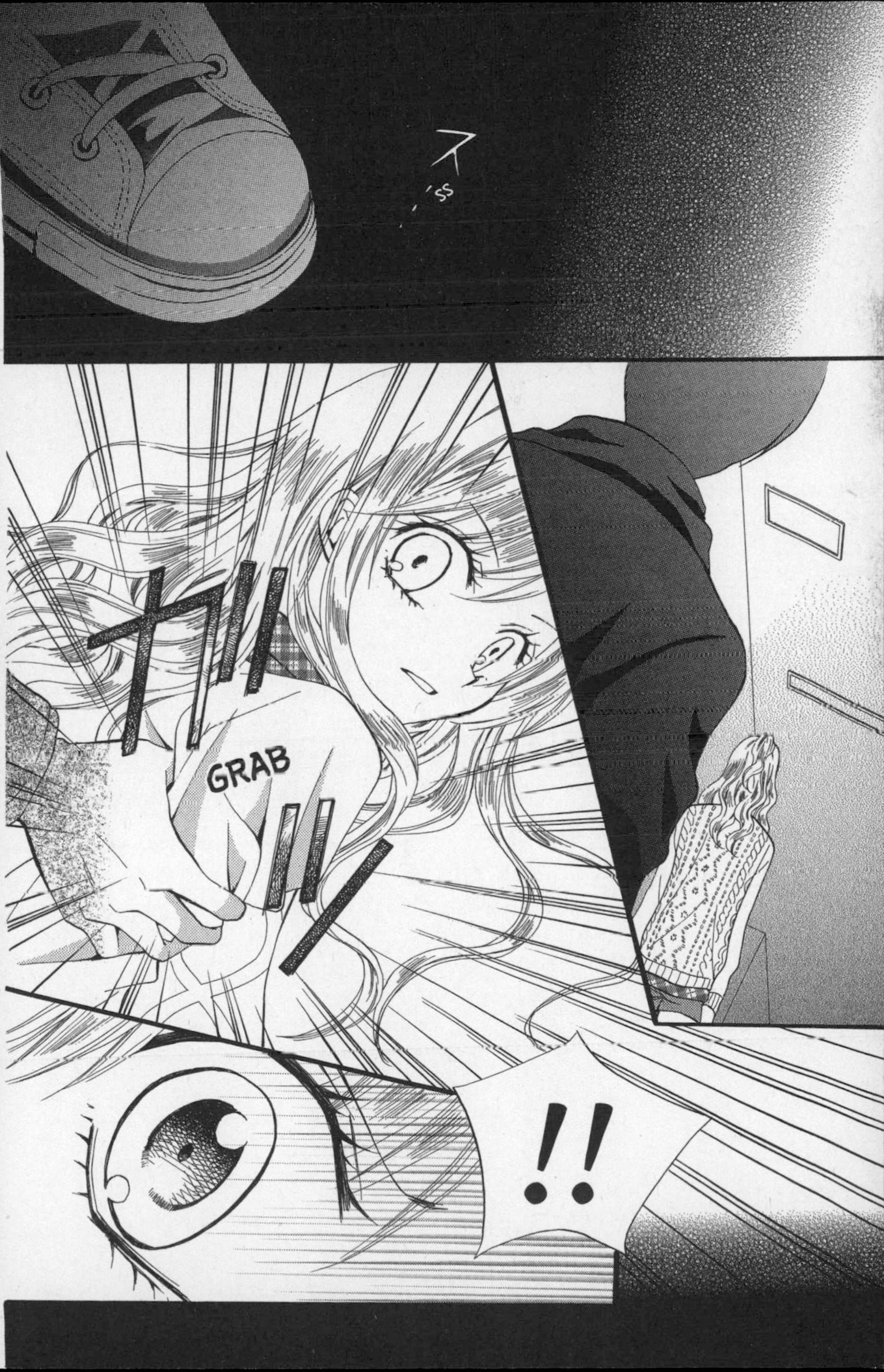
ス
'SS
GRAB
!!

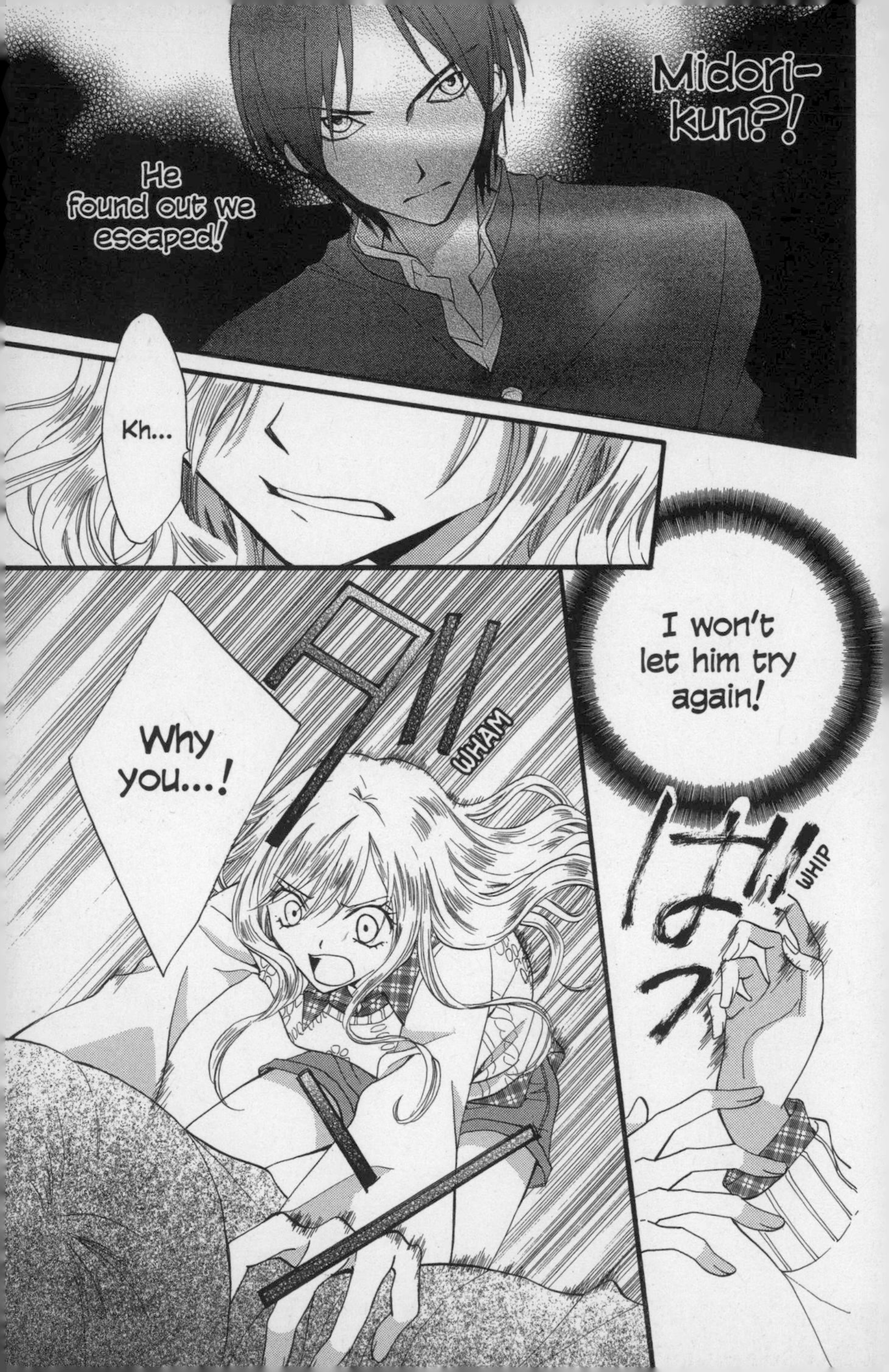
Midori-kun?!
He found out we escaped!
Kh...
I won't let him try again!
はっ
WHIP
WHAM
Why you...!

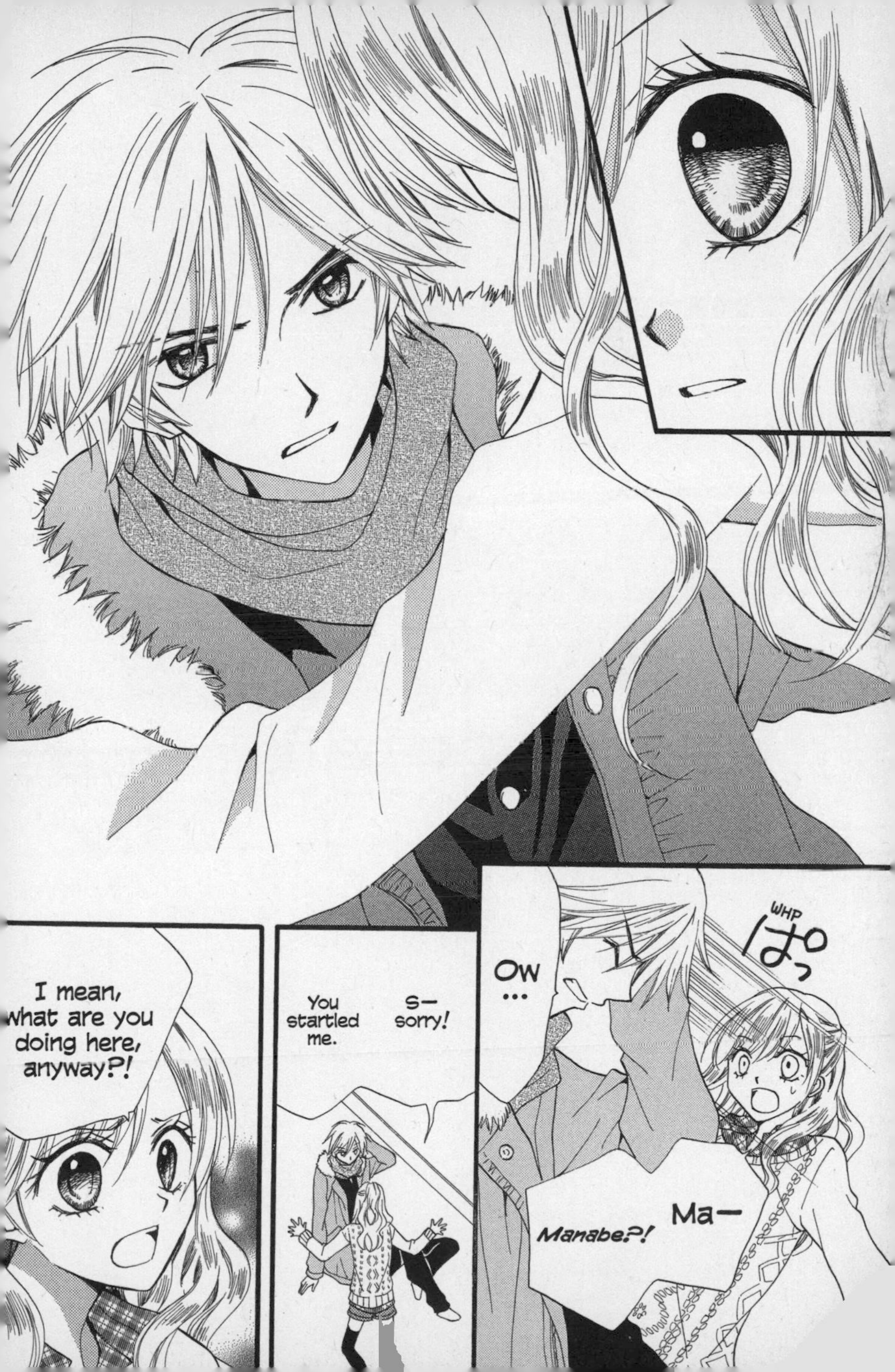
WHP
ぱっ
Ow ...
Ma—
Manabe?!
S—sorry!
You startled me.
I mean, what are you doing here, anyway?!

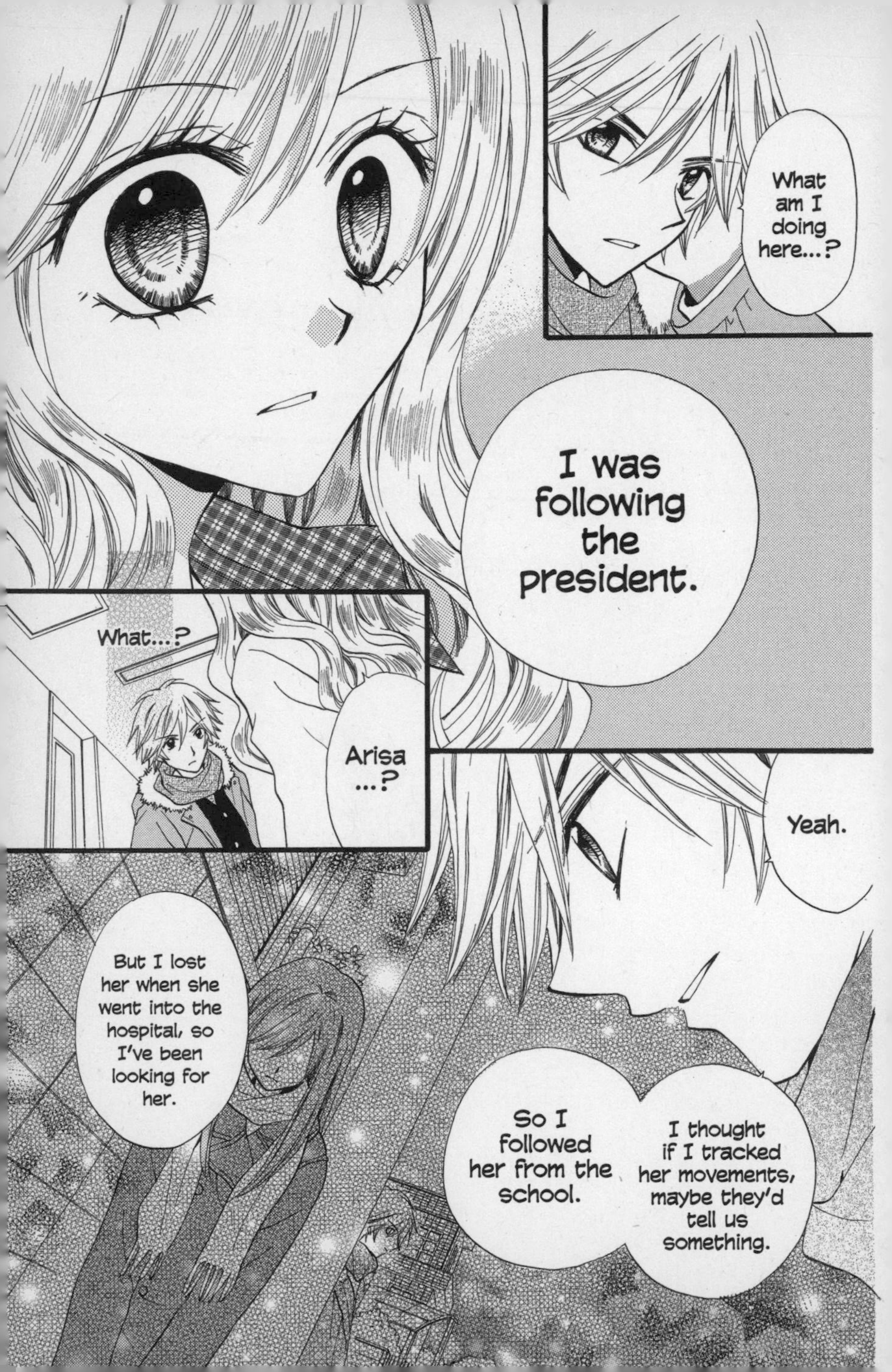

What am I doing here...?
I was following the president.
What...?
Arisa ...?
Yeah.
I thought if I tracked her movements, maybe they'd tell us something.
So I followed her from the school.
But I lost her when she went into the hospital, so I've been looking for her.

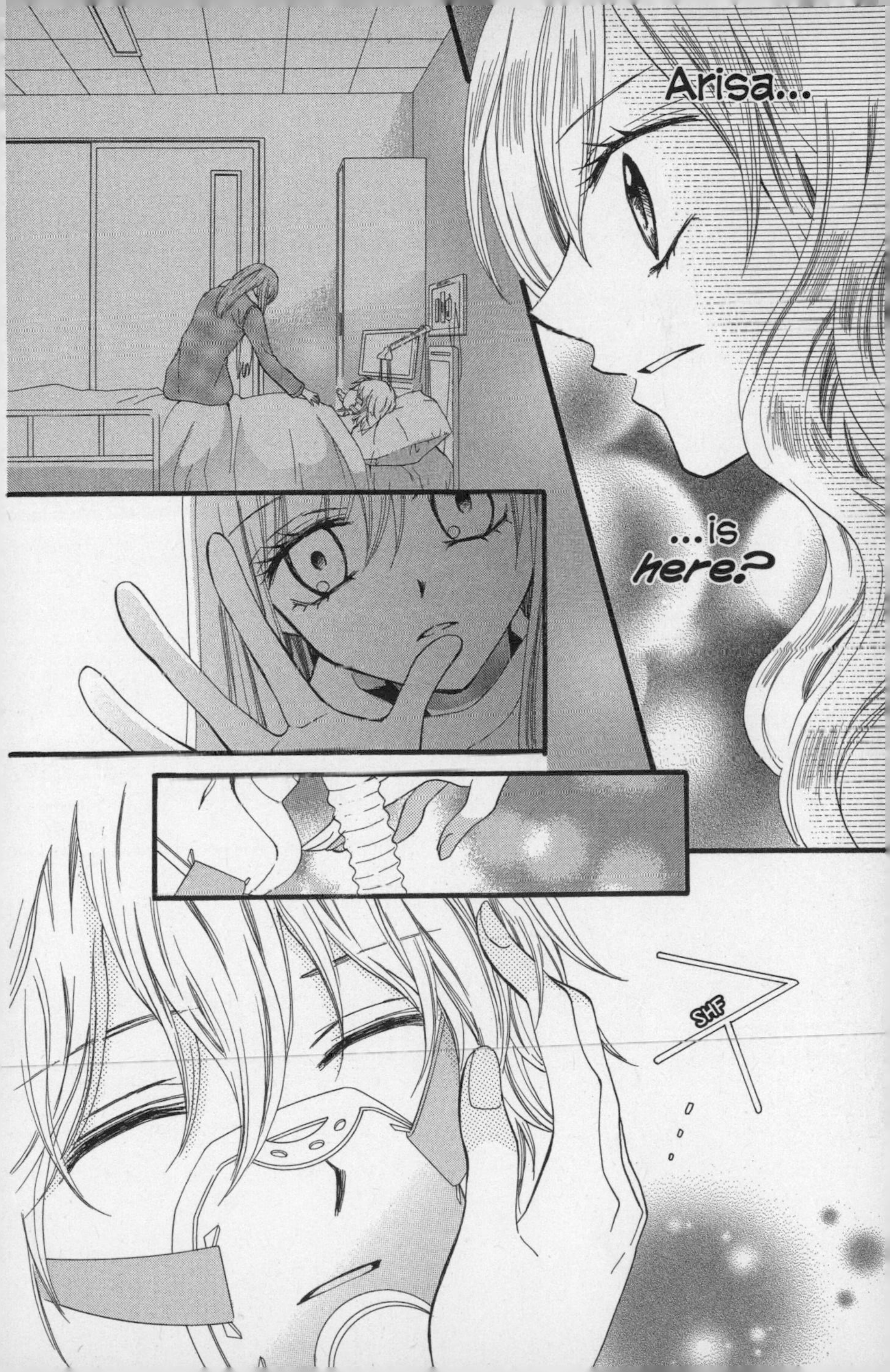
Arisa...
...is here?
SHF

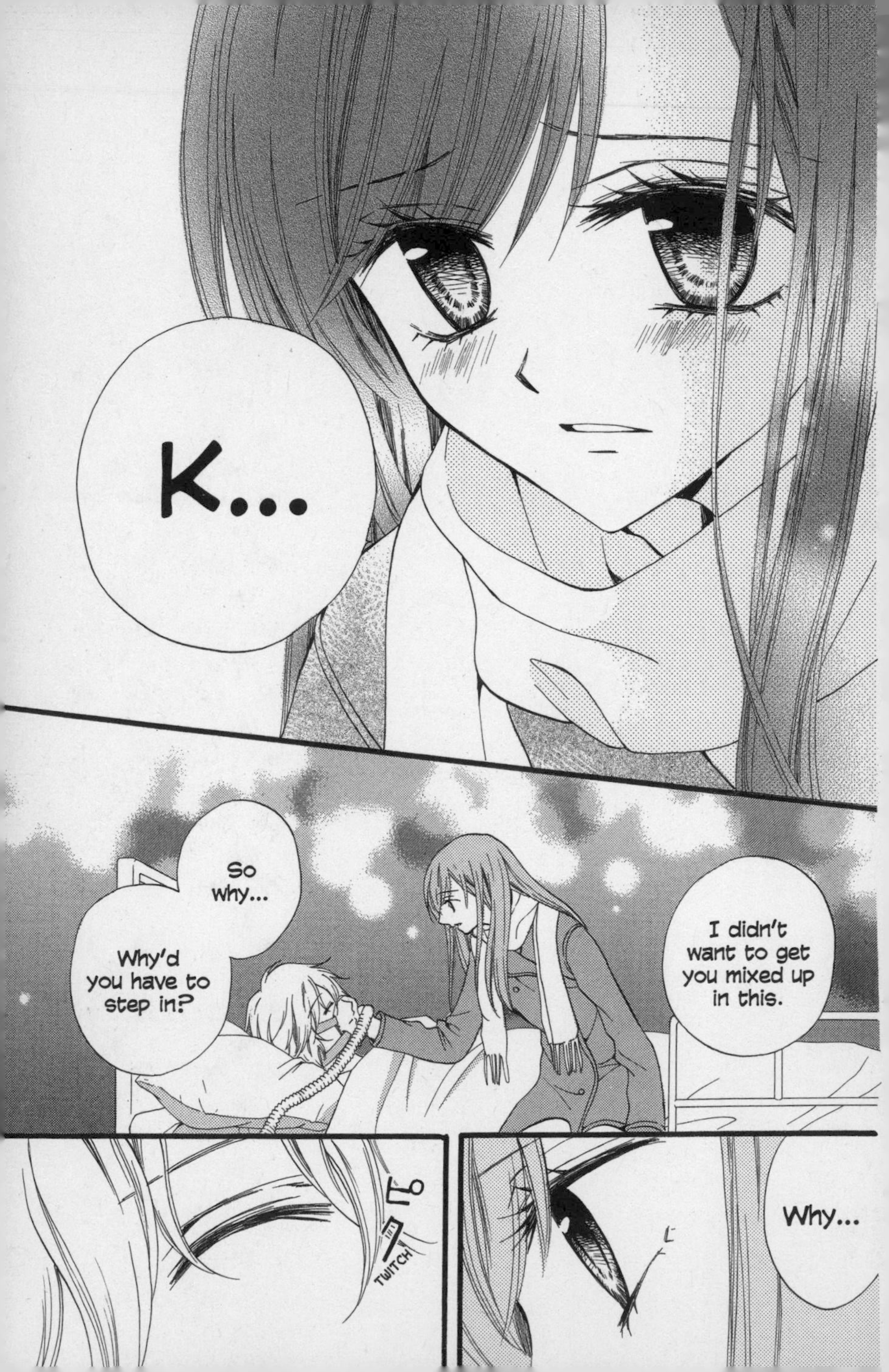
K...
I didn't want to get you mixed up in this.
So why...
Why'd you have to step in?
Why...
TWITCH

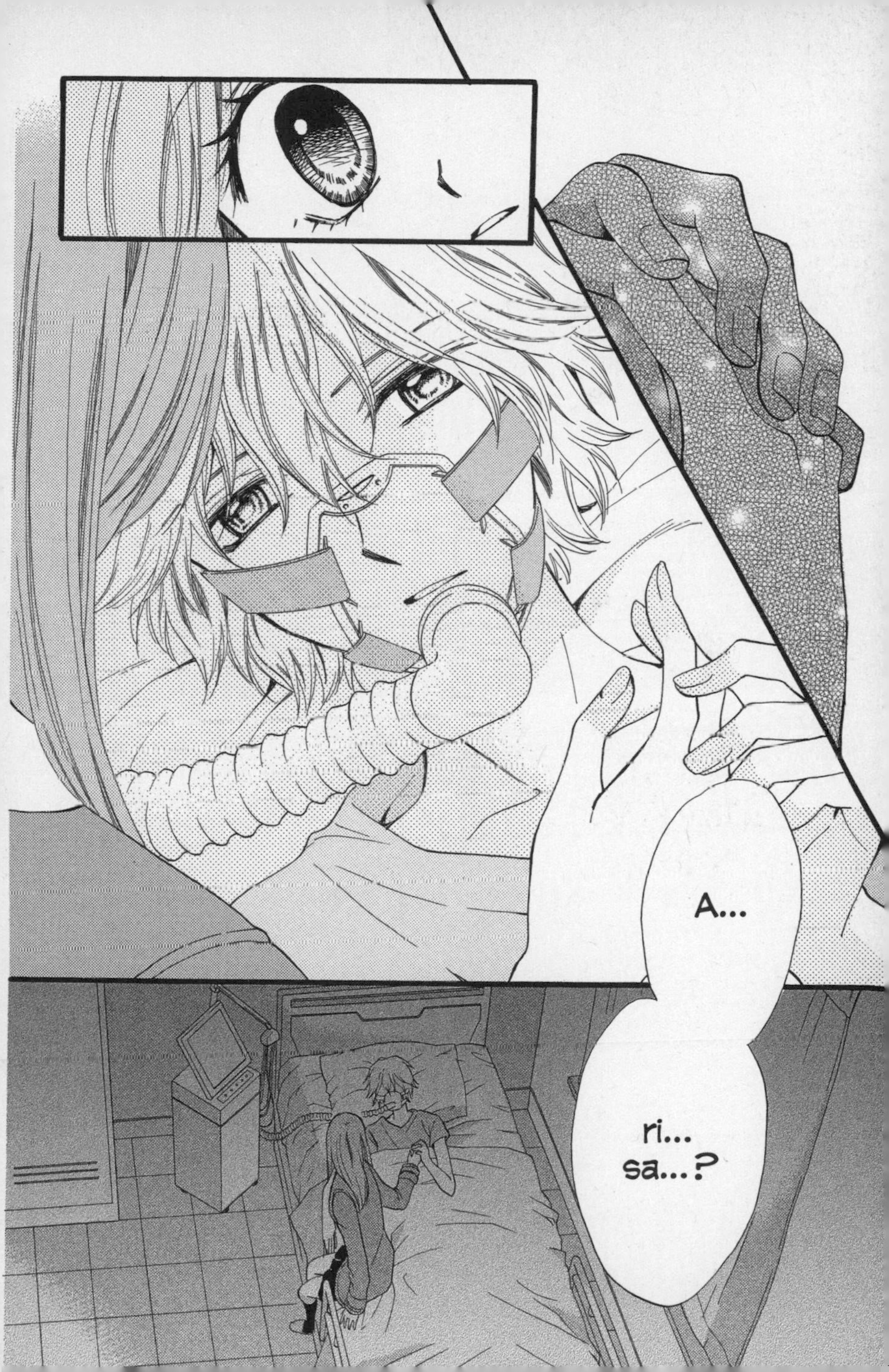
A...
ri... sa...?

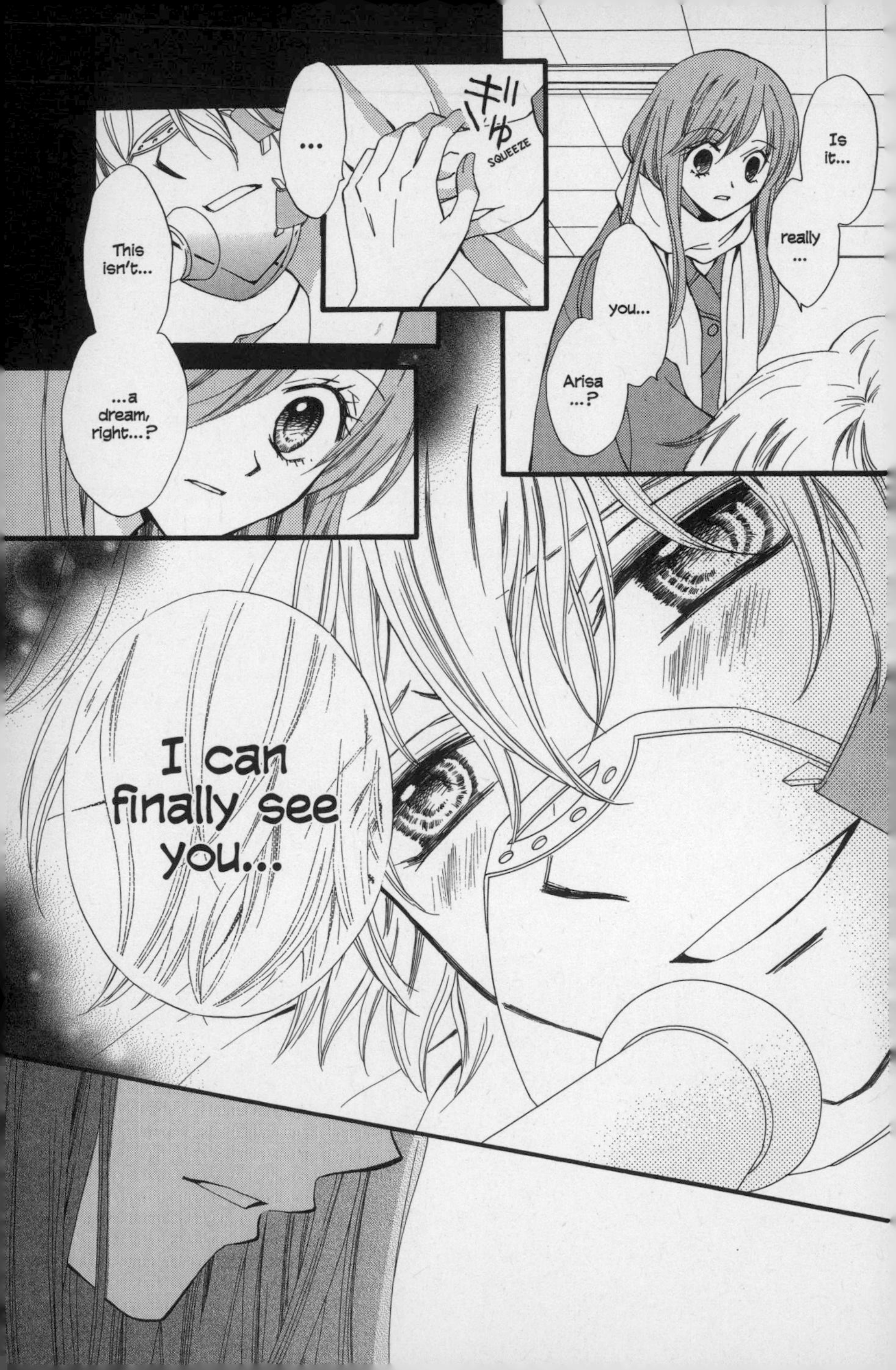
Is it... really... you... Arisa...?
...
ぎゅ
SQUEEZE
This isn't...
...a dream, right...?
I can finally see you...

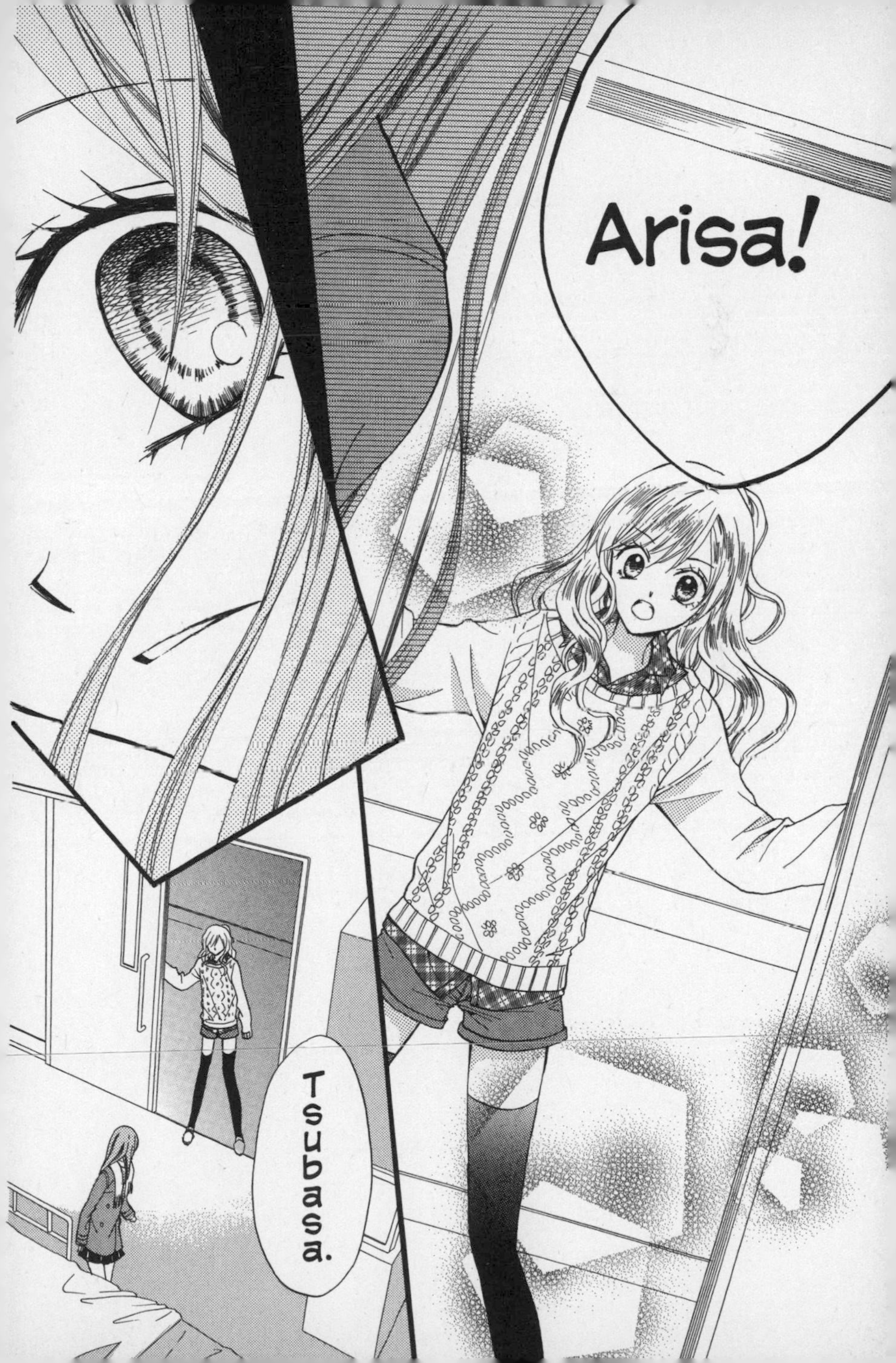
Arisa!
Tsubasa.

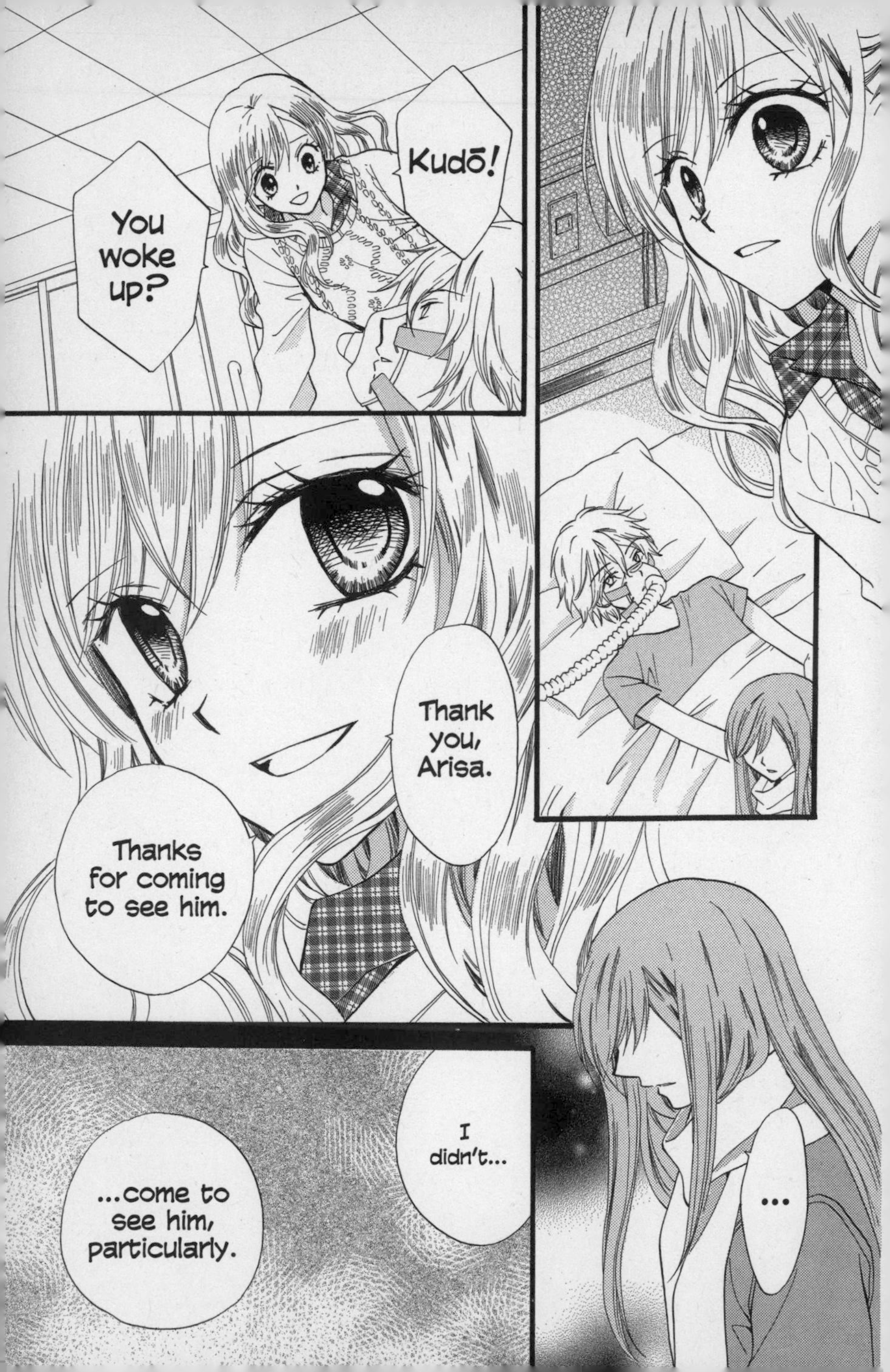
Kudō!
You woke up?
Thank you, Arisa.
Thanks for coming to see him.
...
I didn't...
...come to see him, particularly.

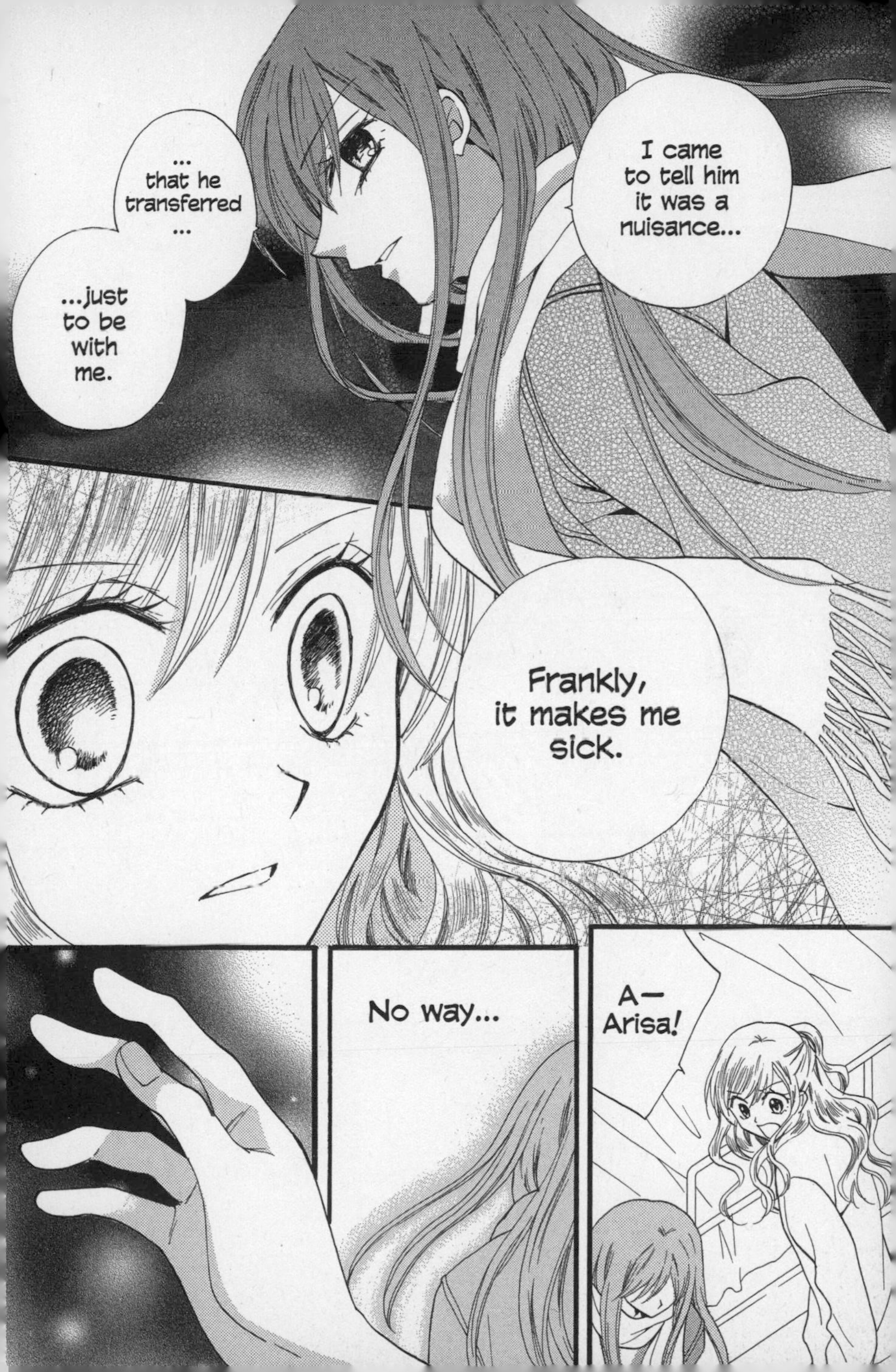
I came to tell him it was a nuisance...
...that he transferred...
...just to be with me.
Frankly, it makes me sick.
A— Arisa!
No way...

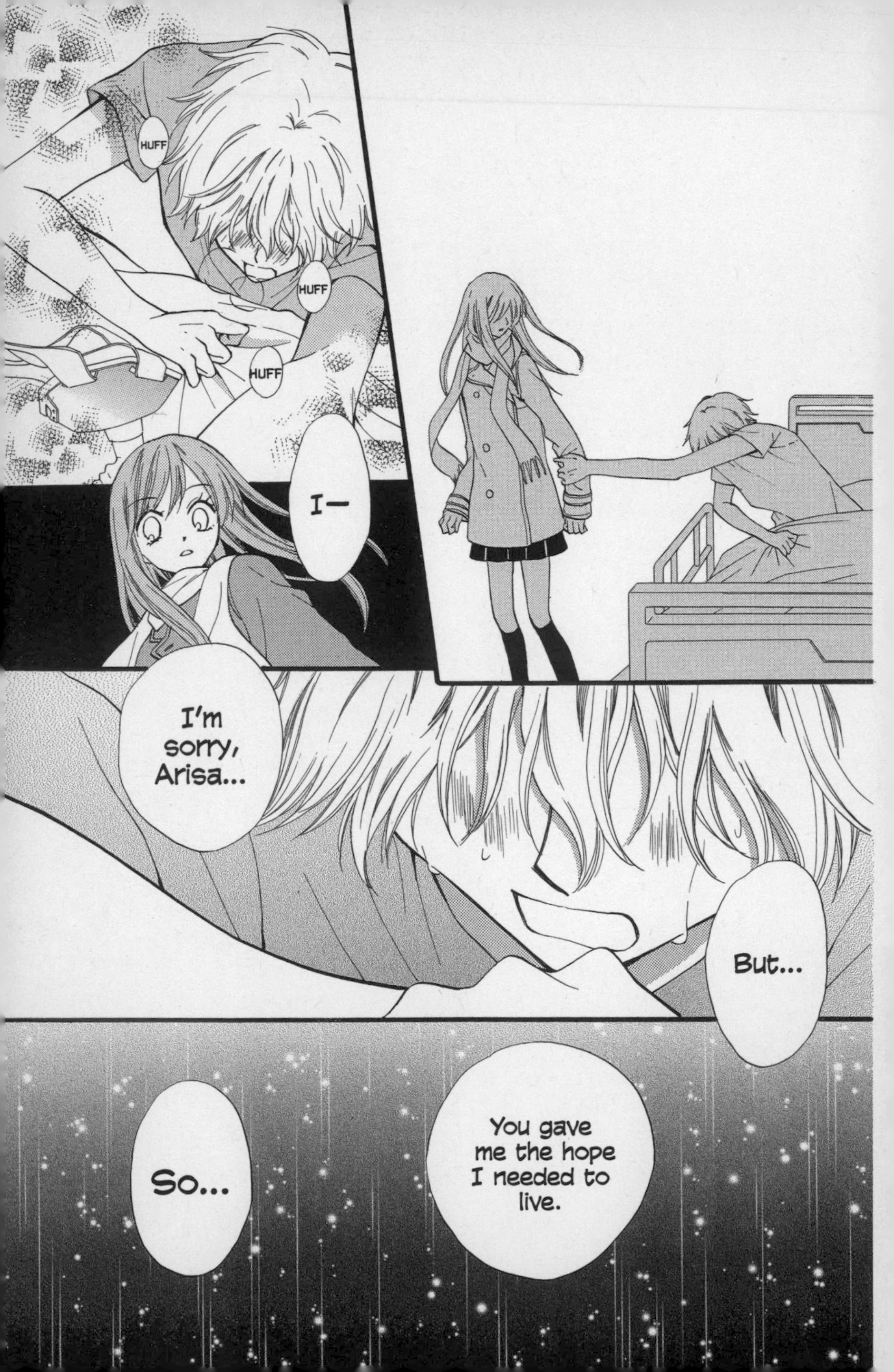
HUFF
HUFF
HUFF
I—
I'm sorry, Arisa...
But...
You gave me the hope I needed to live.
So...

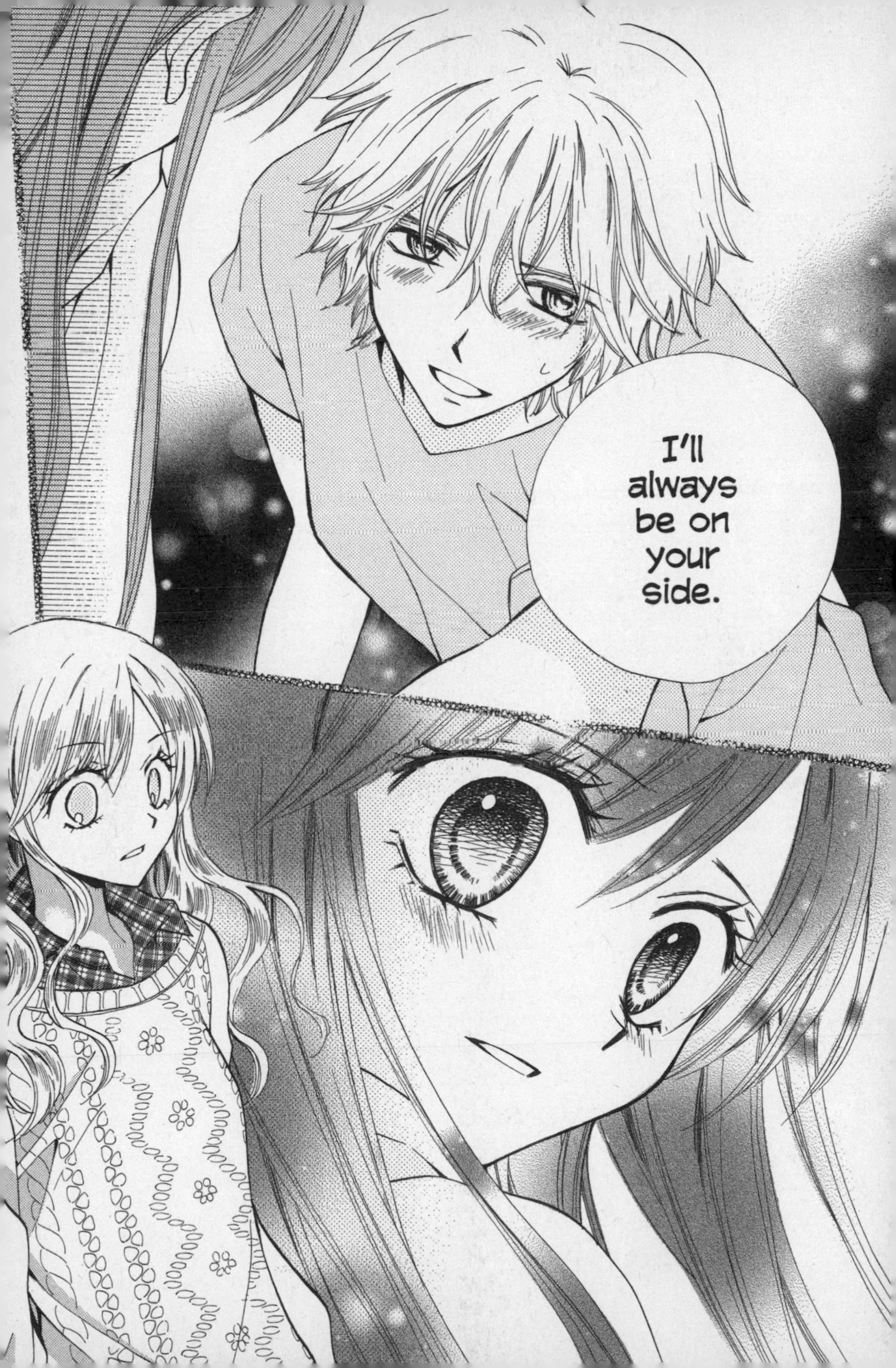
I'll always be on your side.

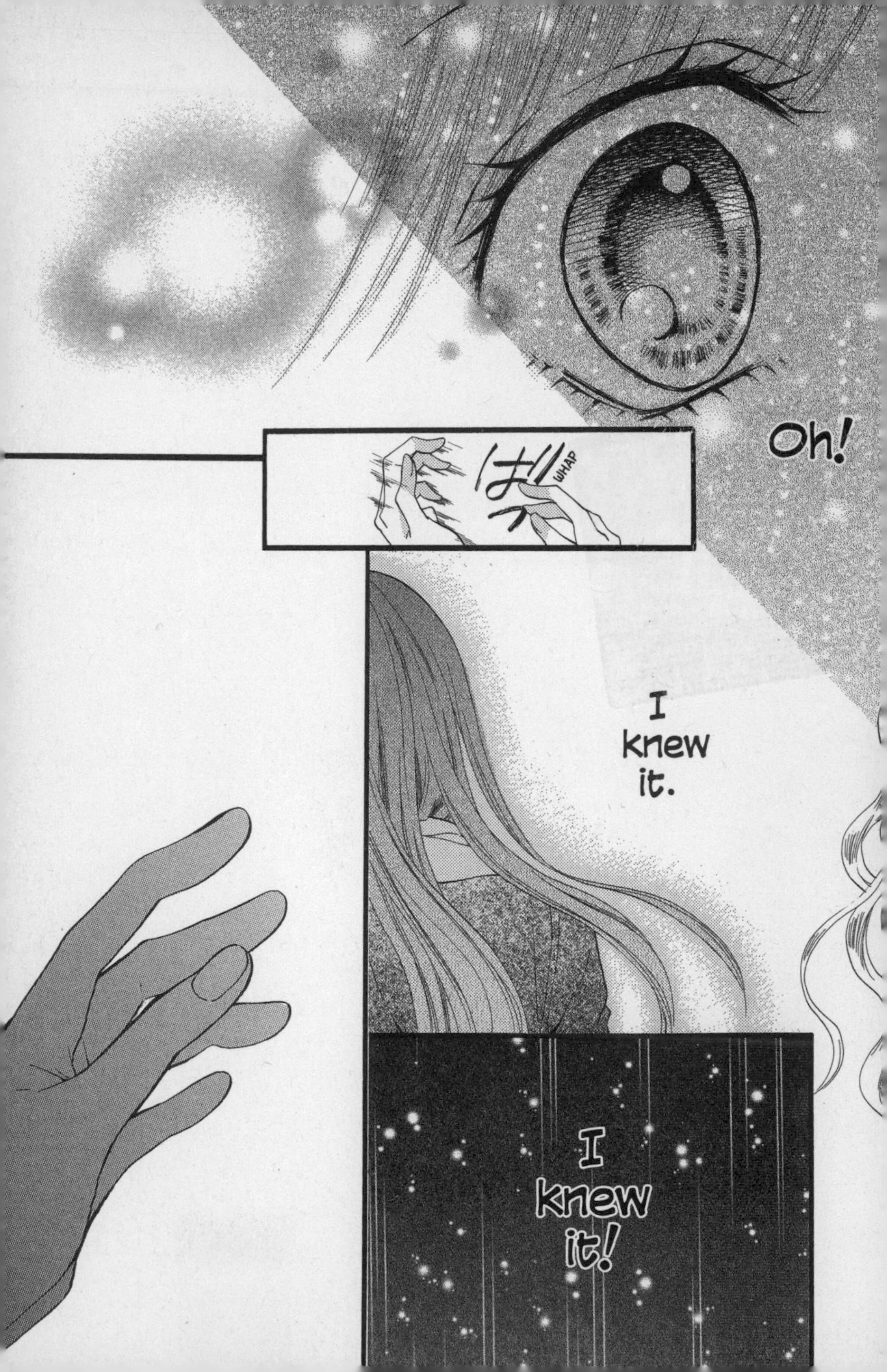
Oh!
はっ
WHAP
I knew it.
I knew it!

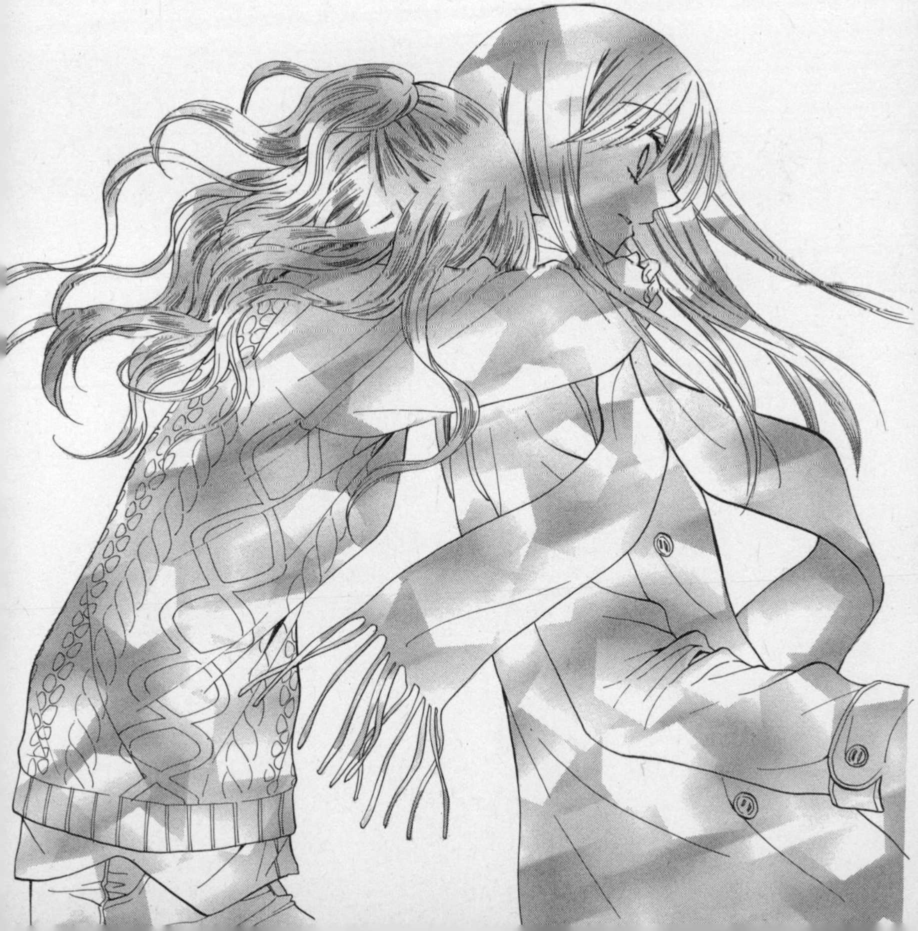

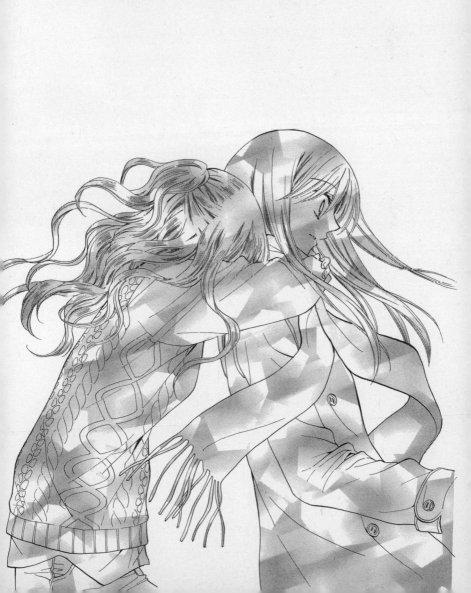

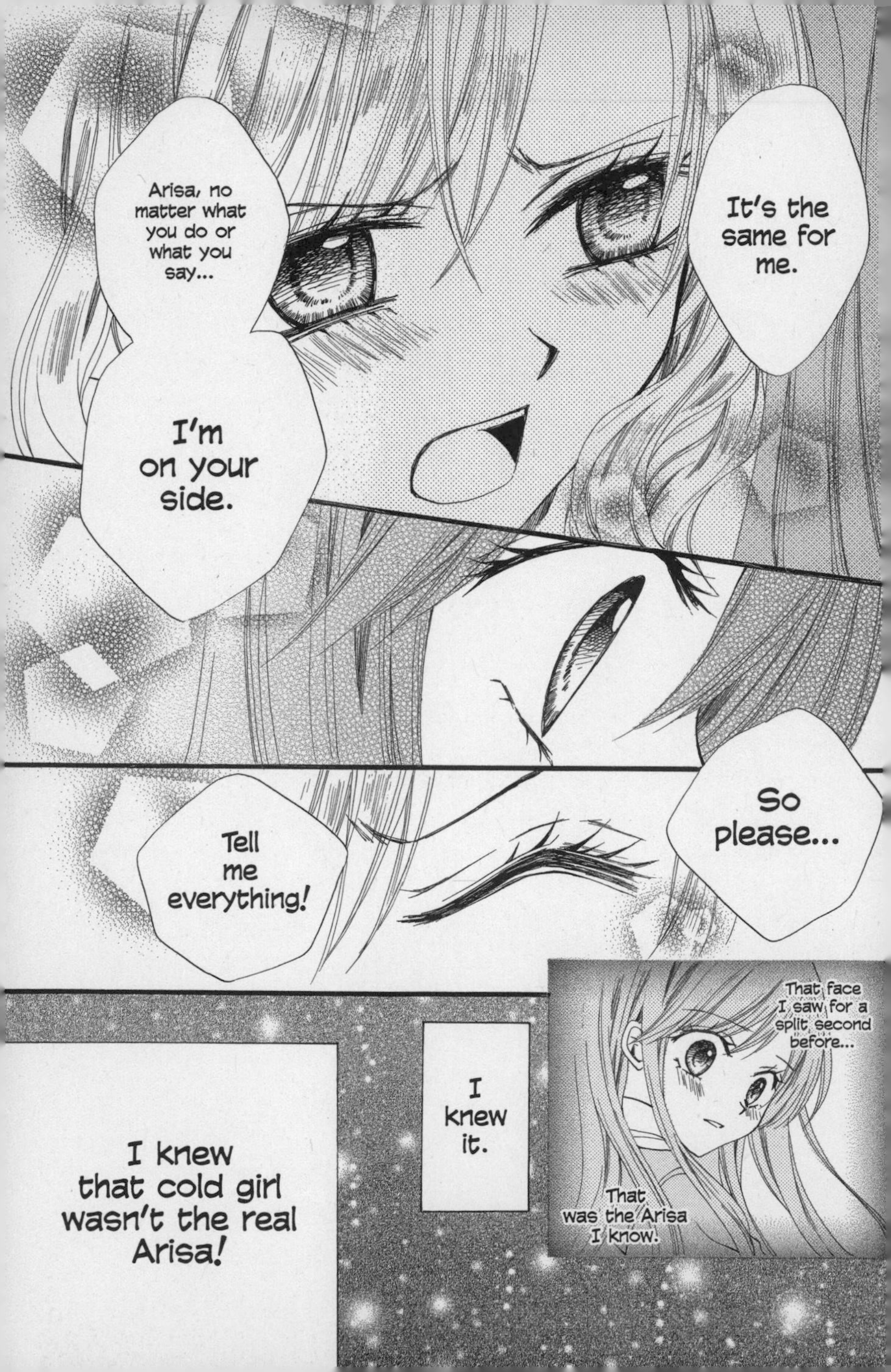
It's the same for me.
Arisa, no matter what you do or what you say...
I'm on your side.
So please...
Tell me everything!
That face I saw for a split second before...
That was the Arisa I know.
I knew it.
I knew that cold girl wasn't the real Arisa!

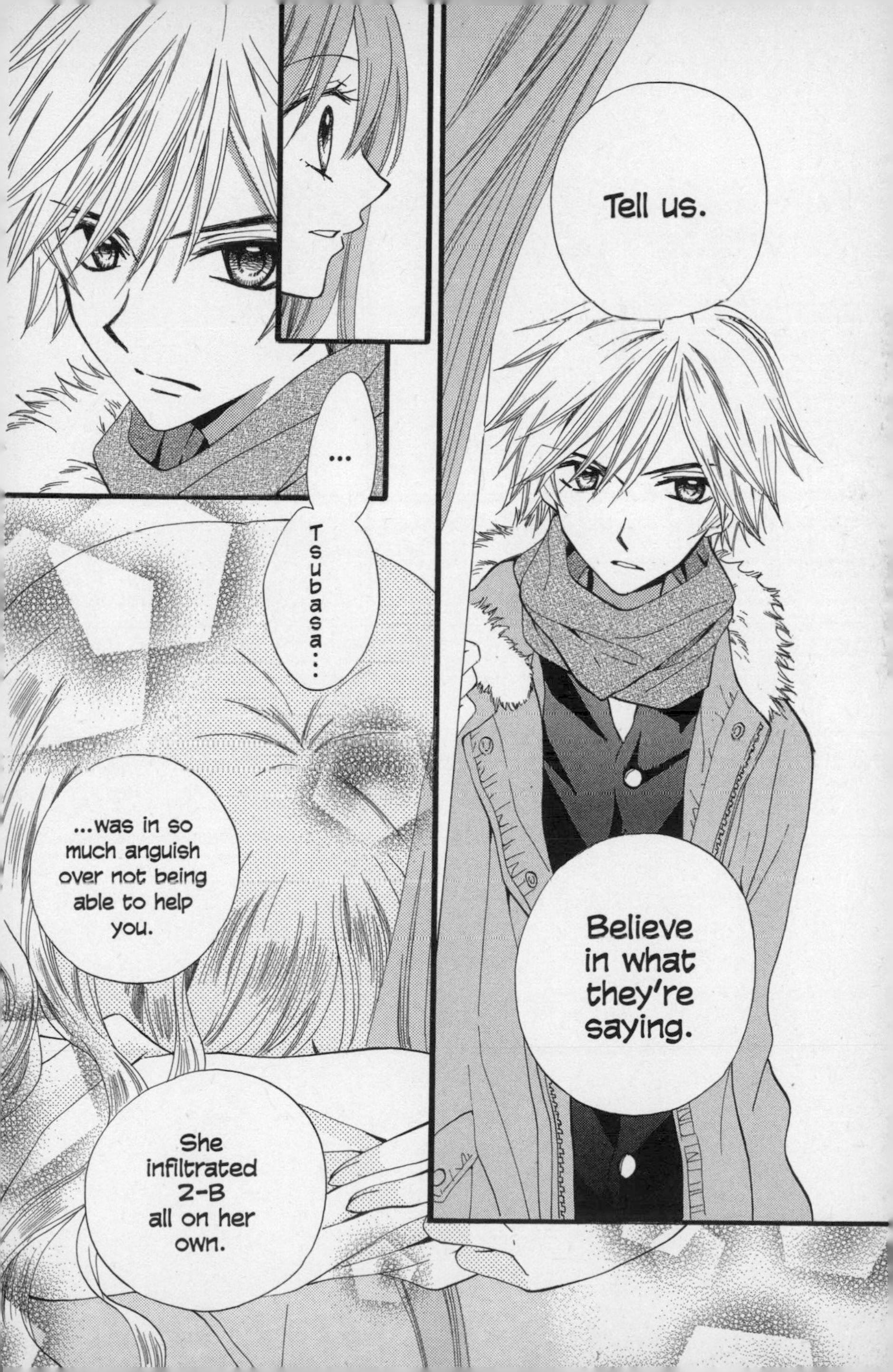
Tell us.
Believe in what they're saying.
...
Tsubasa...
...was in so much anguish over not being able to help you.
She infiltrated 2-B all on her own.

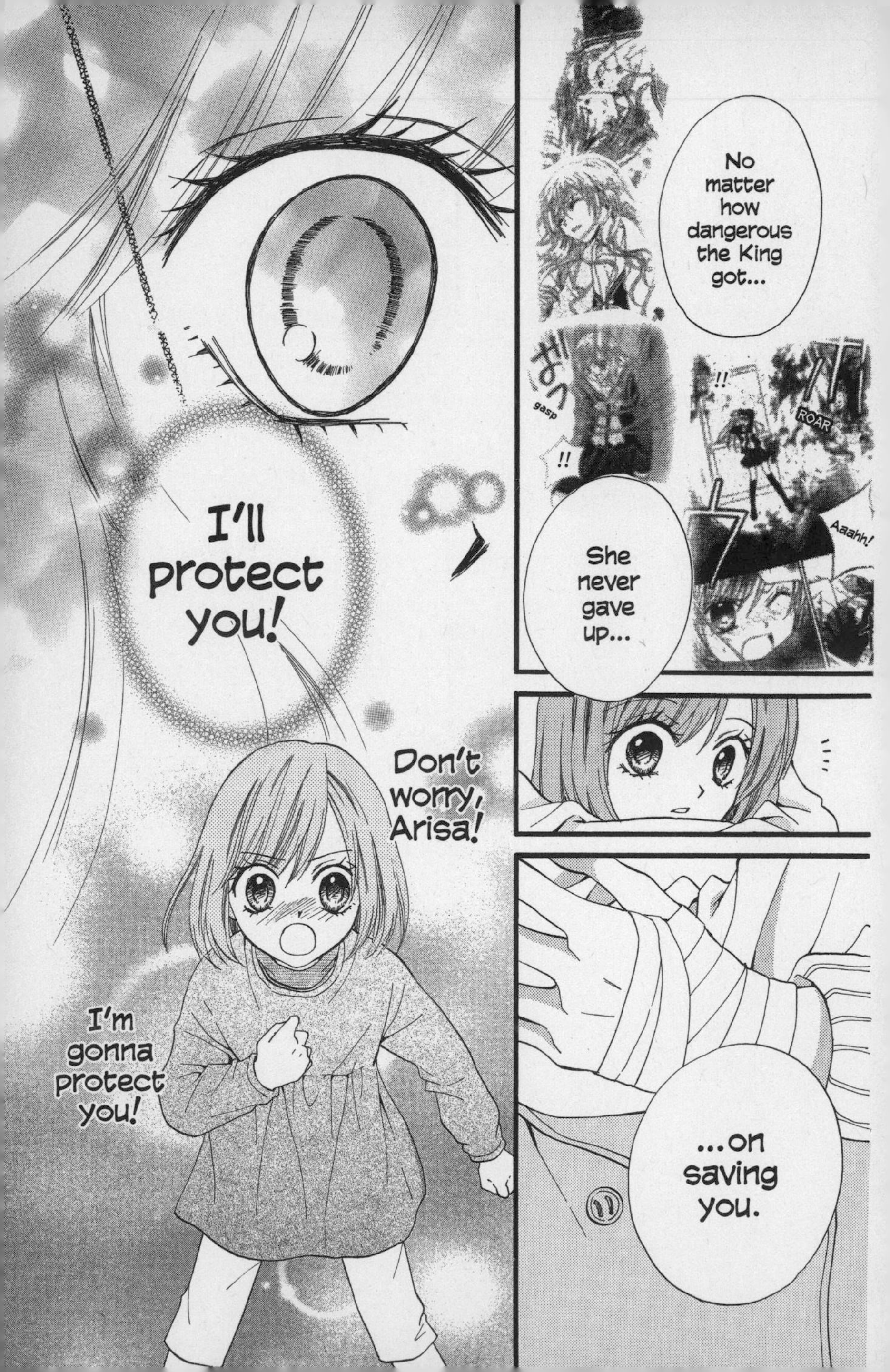
No matter how dangerous the King got...
!!
ROAR
Aaahh!
gasp
!!
She never gave up...
...on saving you.
I'll protect you!
Don't worry, Arisa!
I'm gonna protect you!

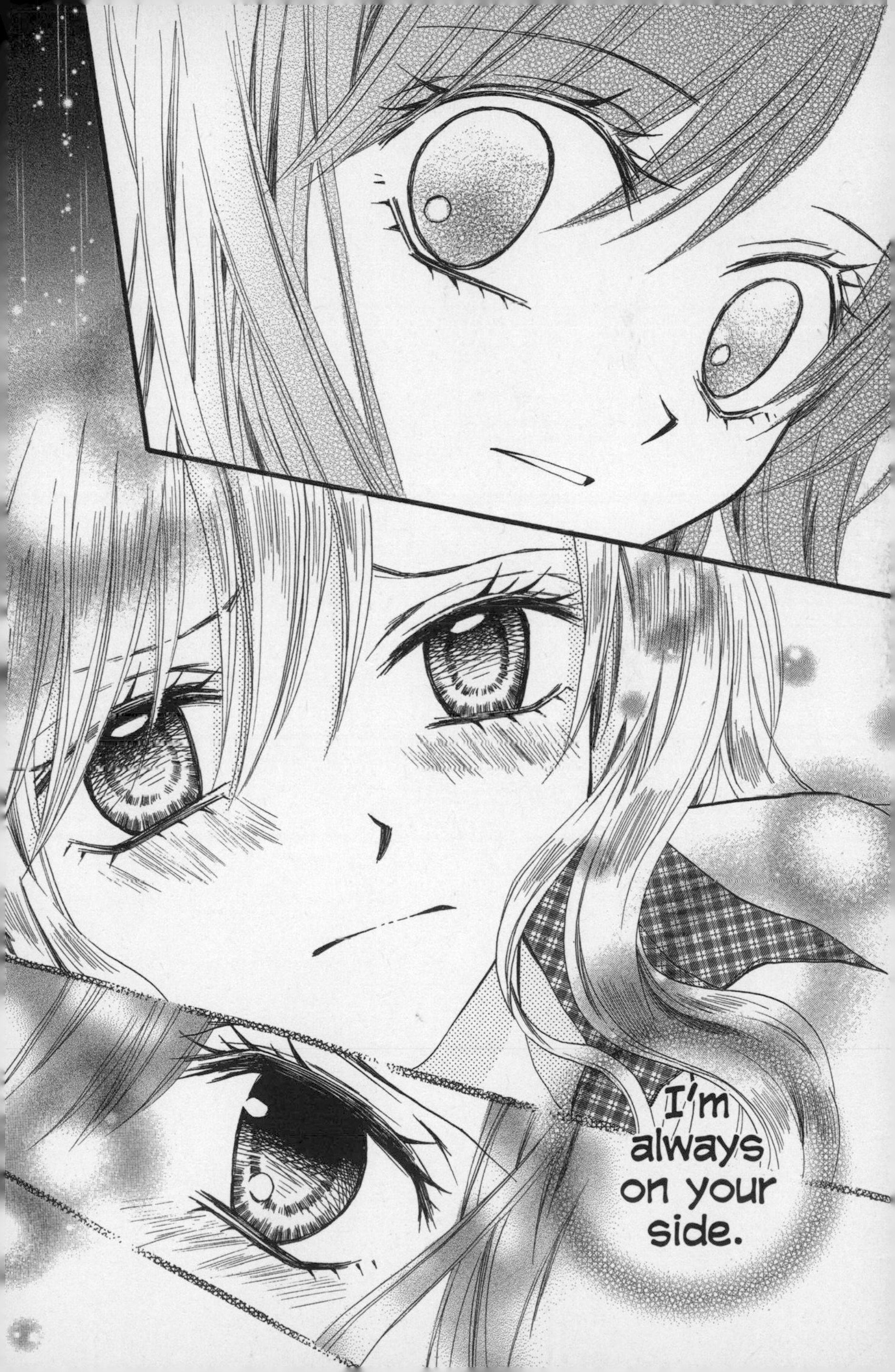
I'm always on your side.

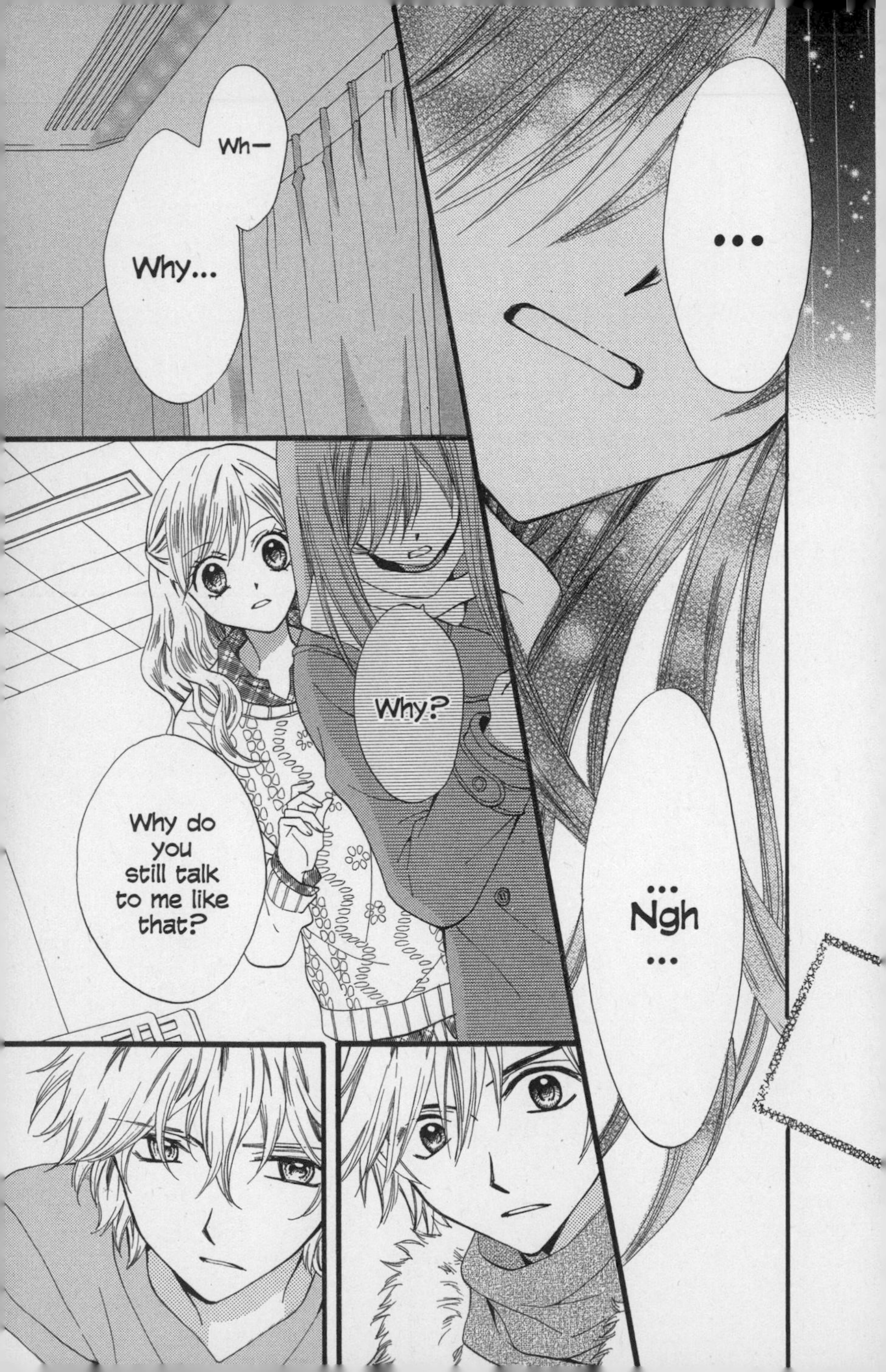
...
... Ngh ...
Wh—
Why...
Why?
Why do you still talk to me like that?

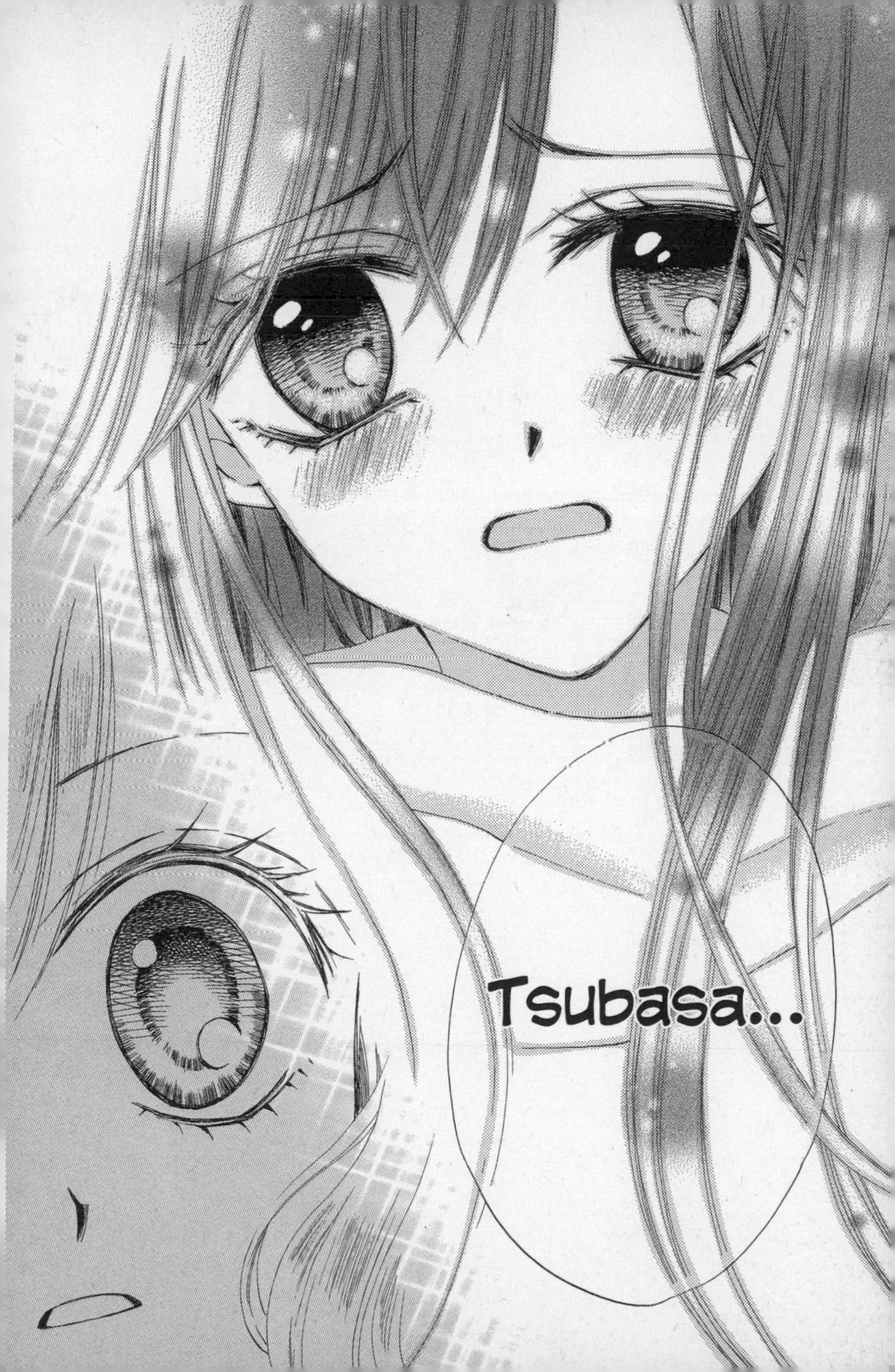
Tsubasa...

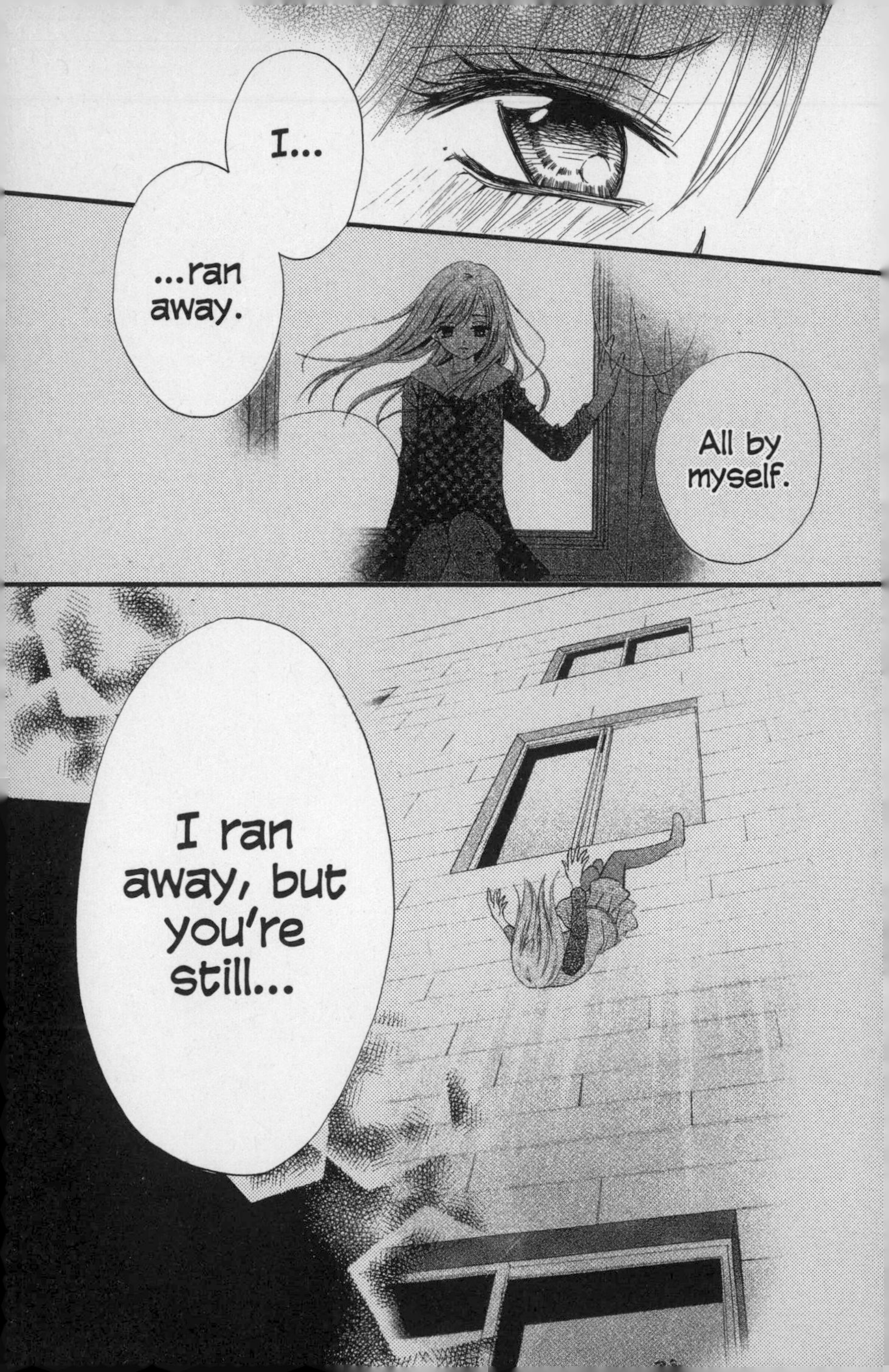
I...
...ran away.
All by myself.
I ran away, but you're still...

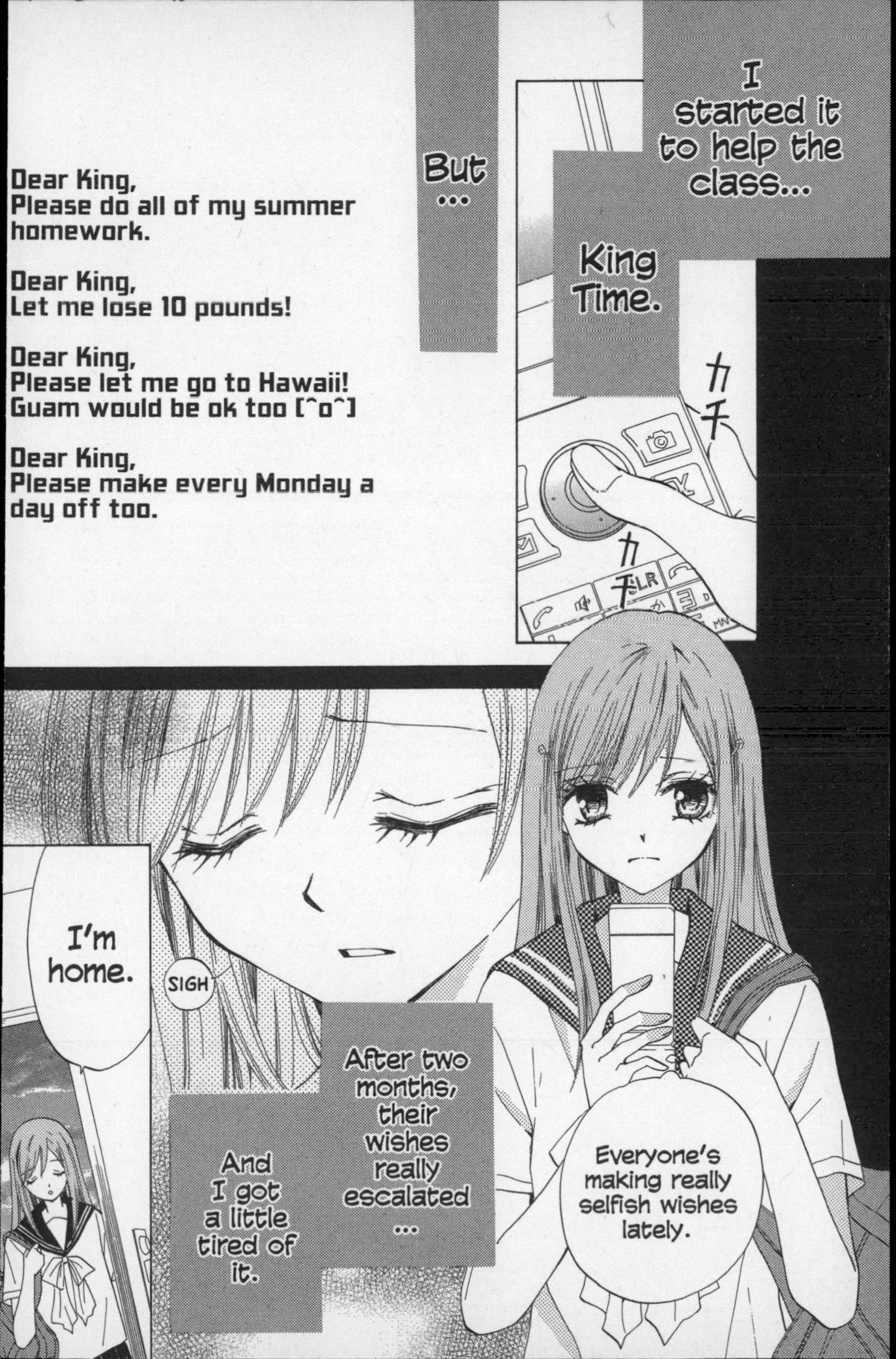
I started it to help the class...
King Time.
カチ
カチ
But...
Dear King,
Please do all of my summer homework.
Dear King,
Let me lose 10 pounds!
Dear King,
Please let me go to Hawaii! Guam would be ok too [^o^]
Dear King,
Please make every Monday a day off too.
Everyone's making really selfish wishes lately.
After two months, their wishes really escalated...
And I got a little tired of it.
SIGH
I'm home.

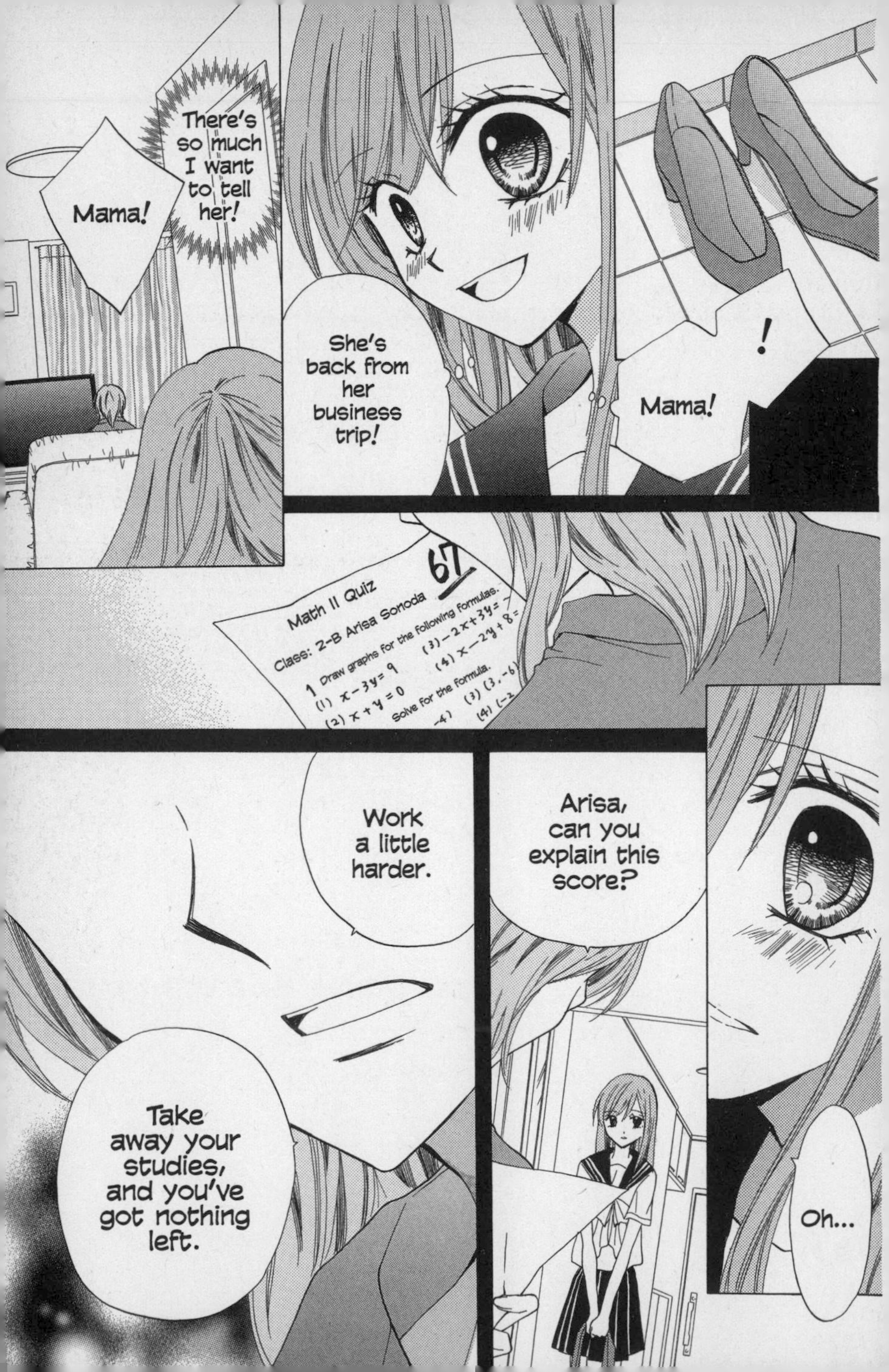
!
Mama!
She's back from her business trip!
There's so much I want to tell her!
Mama!
67
Math II Quiz
Class: 2-B Arisa Sonoda
1 Draw graphs for the following formulas.
(1) x-3y=9
(2) x+y=0
(3) -2x+3y=
(4) x-2y+8=
Solve for the formula.
Oh...
Arisa, can you explain this score?
Work a little harder.
Take away your studies, and you've got nothing left.

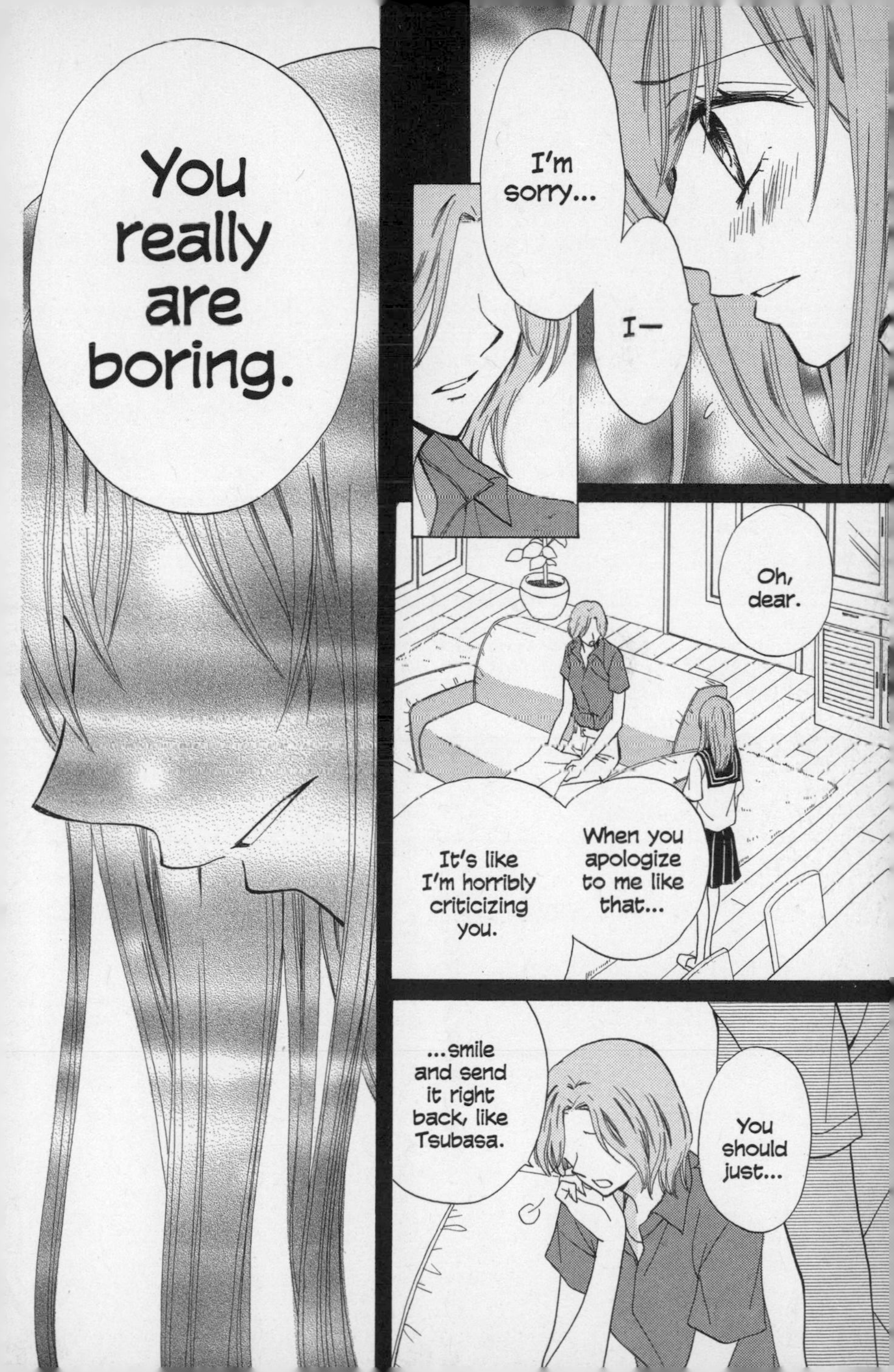

I'm sorry...
I—
Oh, dear.
When you apologize to me like that...
It's like I'm horribly criticizing you.
You should just...
...smile and send it right back, like Tsubasa.
You really are boring.

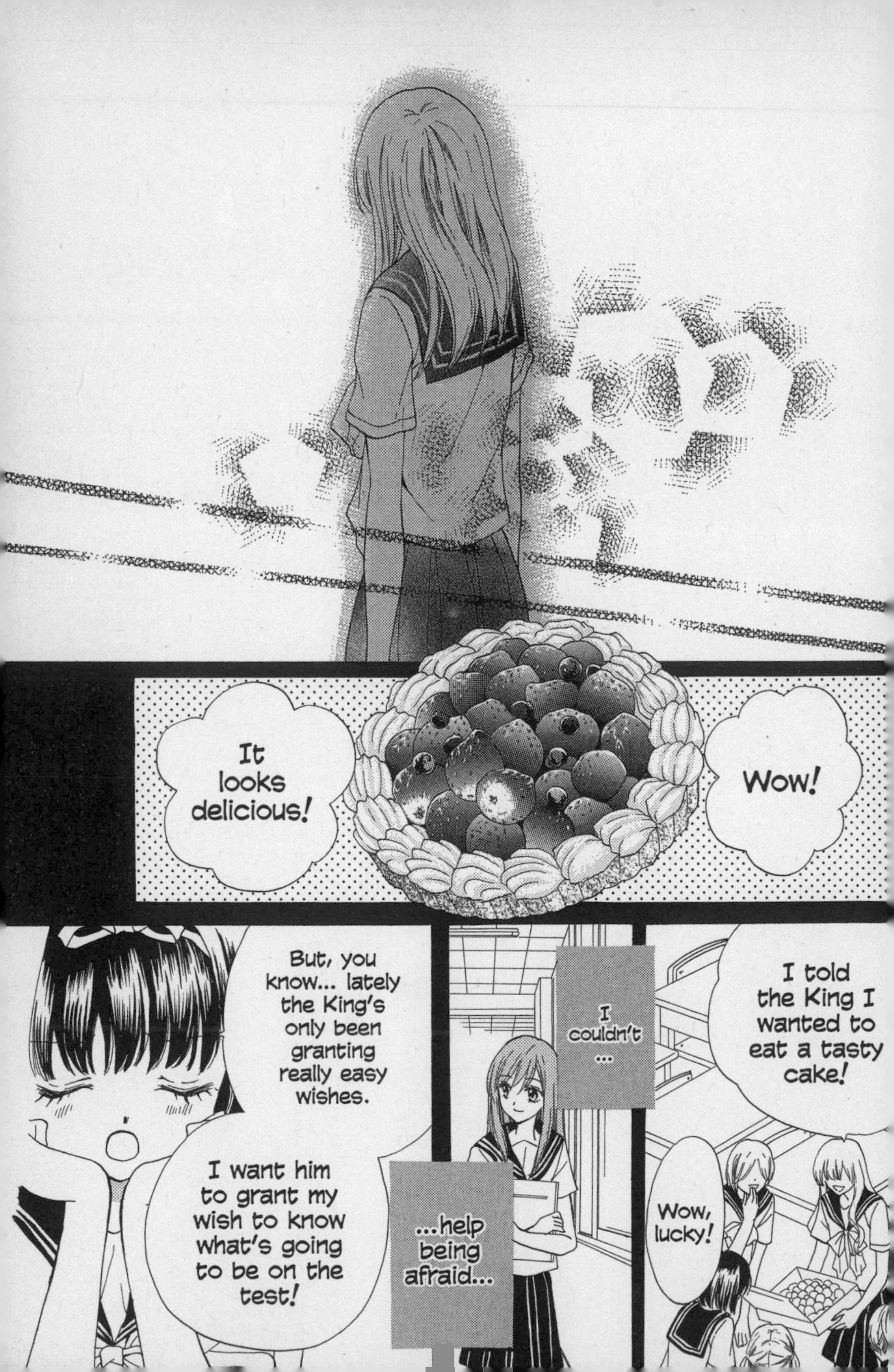
Wow!
It looks delicious!
I told the King I wanted to eat a tasty cake!
Wow, lucky!
I couldn't ...
...help being afraid...
But, you know... lately the King's only been granting really easy wishes.
I want him to grant my wish to know what's going to be on the test!

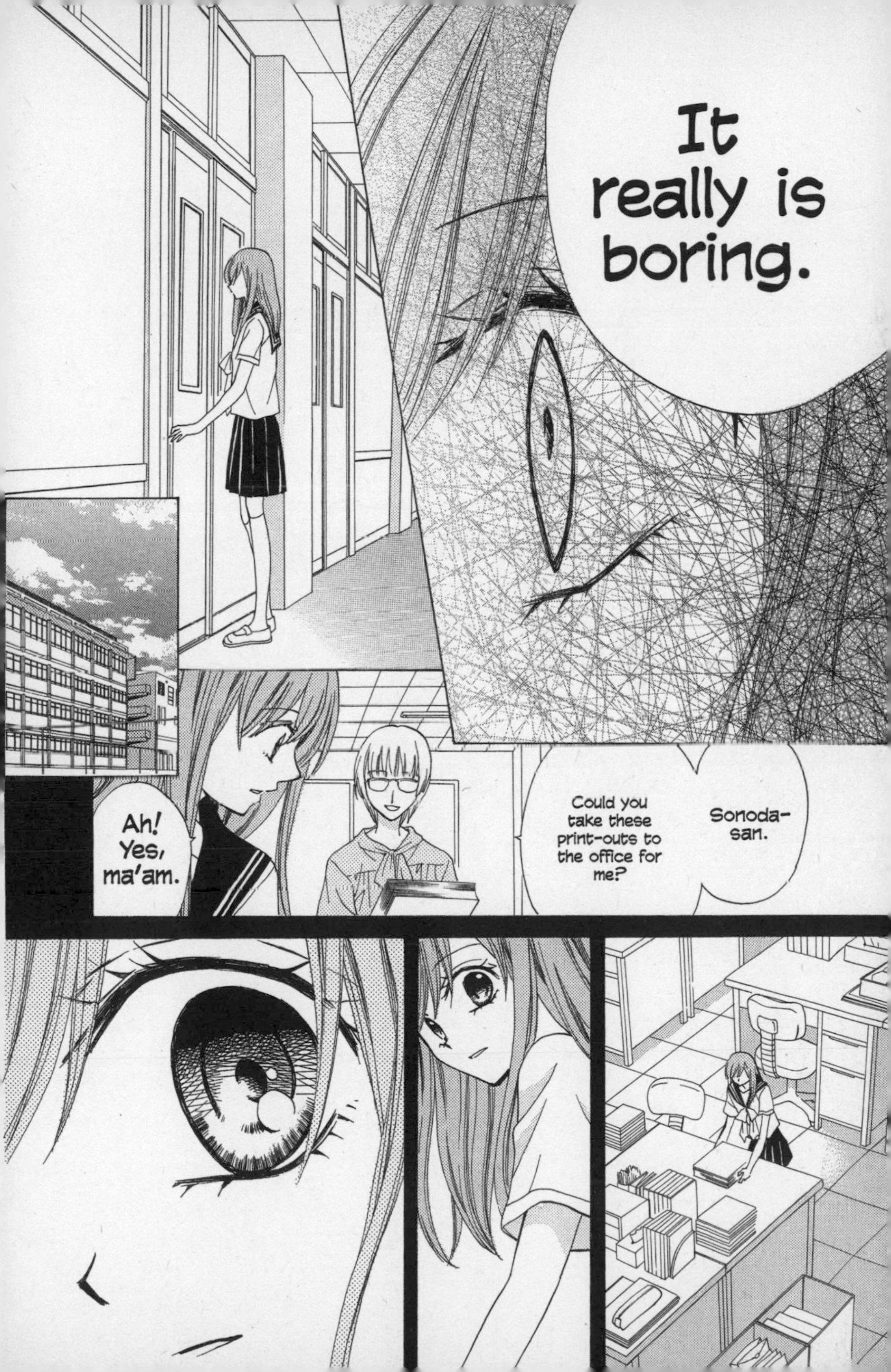
It really is boring.
Sonoda-san.
Could you take these print-outs to the office for me?
Ah! Yes, ma'am.

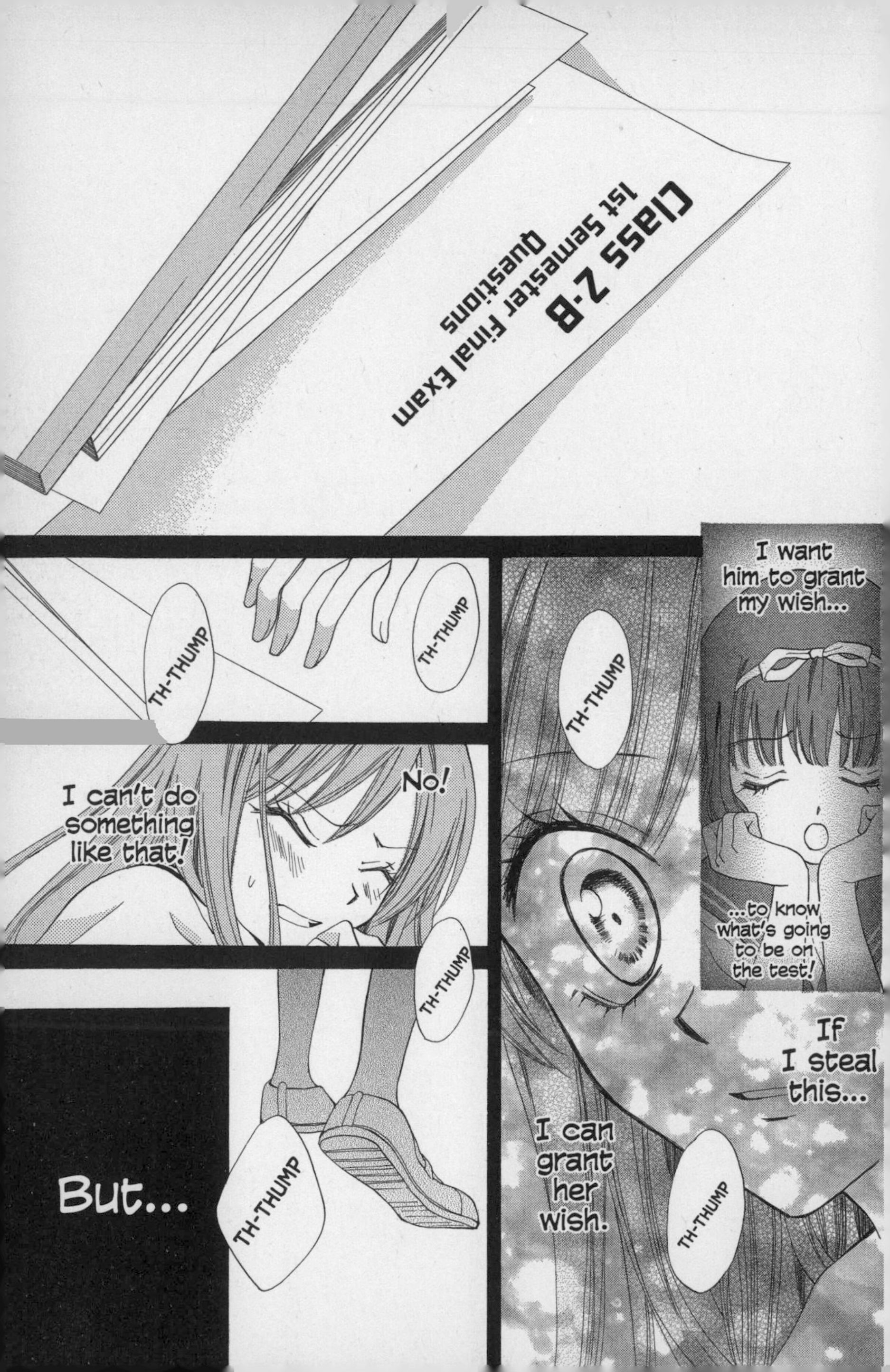
Class 2-B
1st Semester Final Exam
Questions
I want him to grant my wish...
...to know what's going to be on the test!
TH-THUMP
If I steal this...
I can grant her wish.
TH-THUMP
TH-THUMP
TH-THUMP
No!
I can't do something like that!
TH-THUMP
But...
TH-THUMP

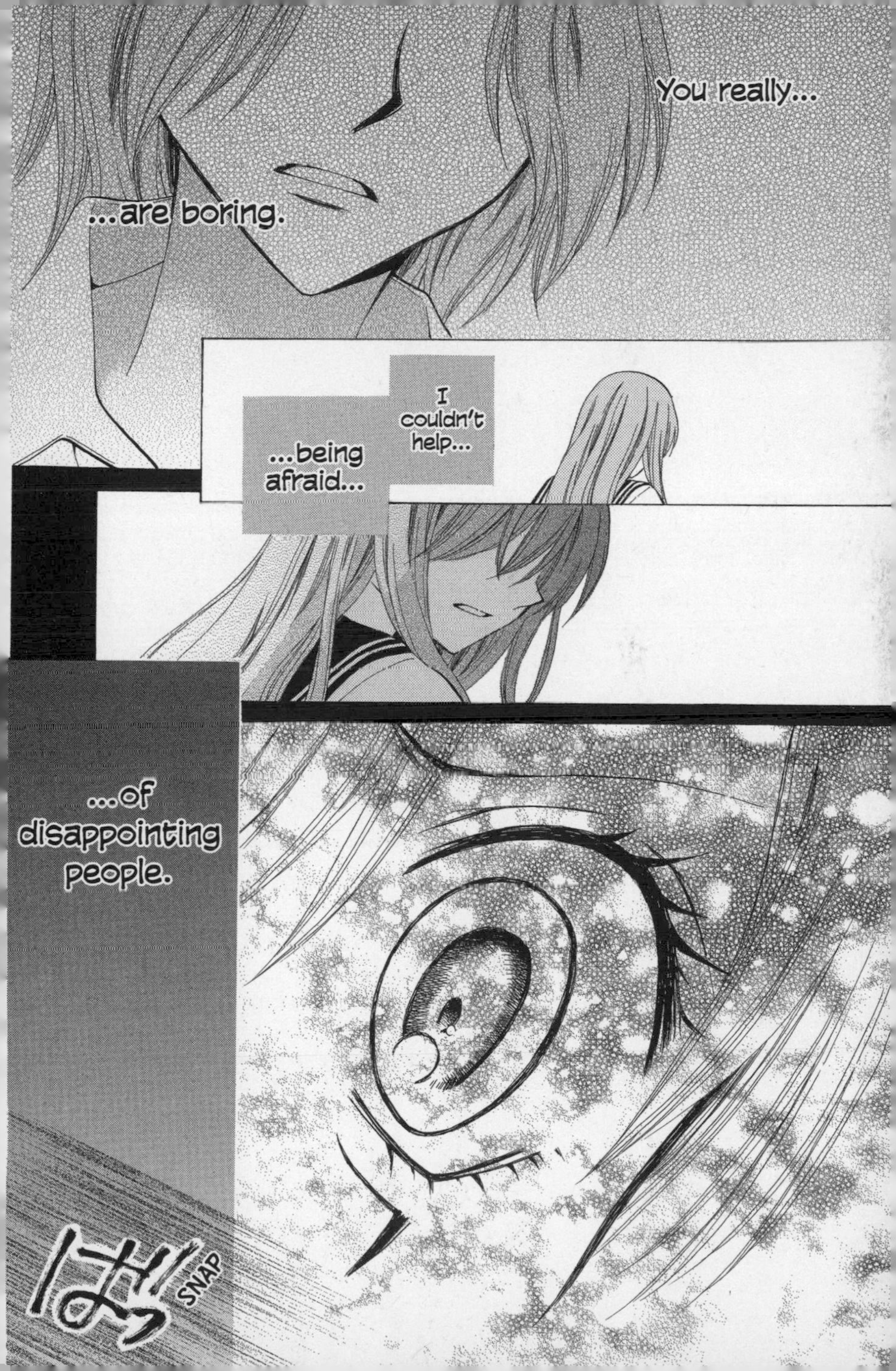
You really...
...are boring.
I couldn't help...
...being afraid...
...of disappointing people.
はっ
SNAP

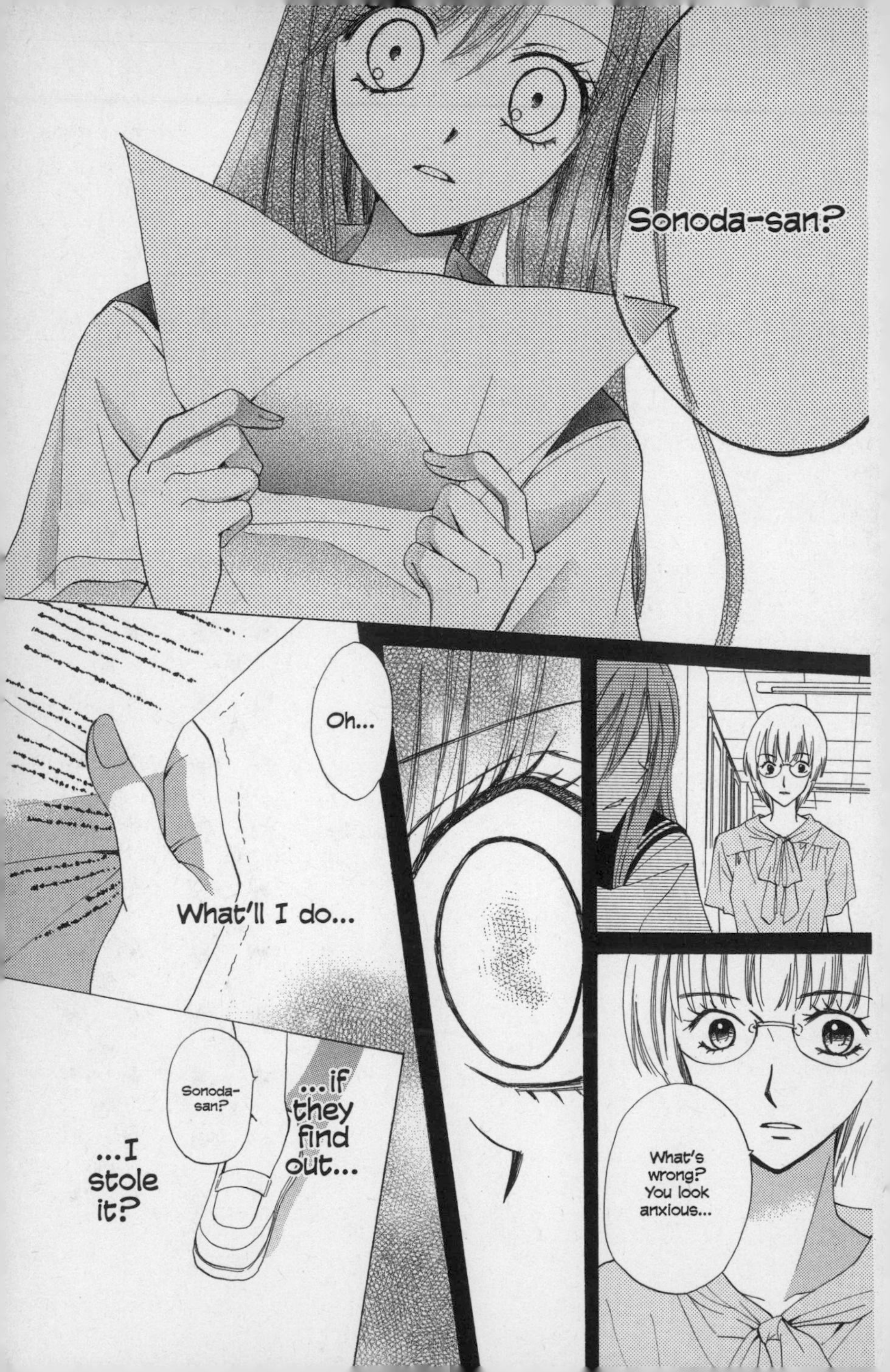
Sonoda-san?
What's wrong? You look anxious...
Oh...
What'll I do...
...if they find out...
Sonoda-san?
...I stole it?

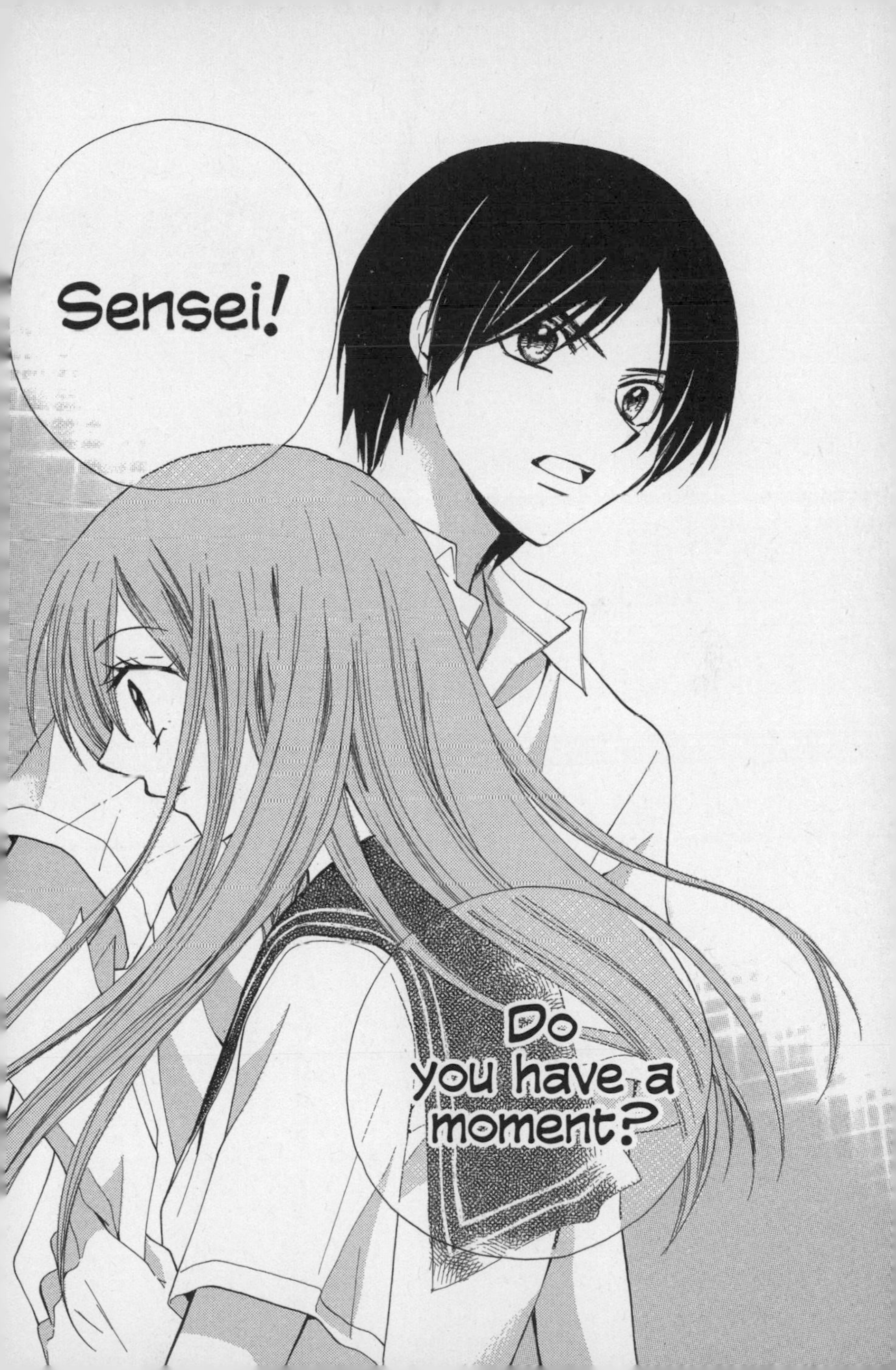
Sensei!
Do you have a moment?

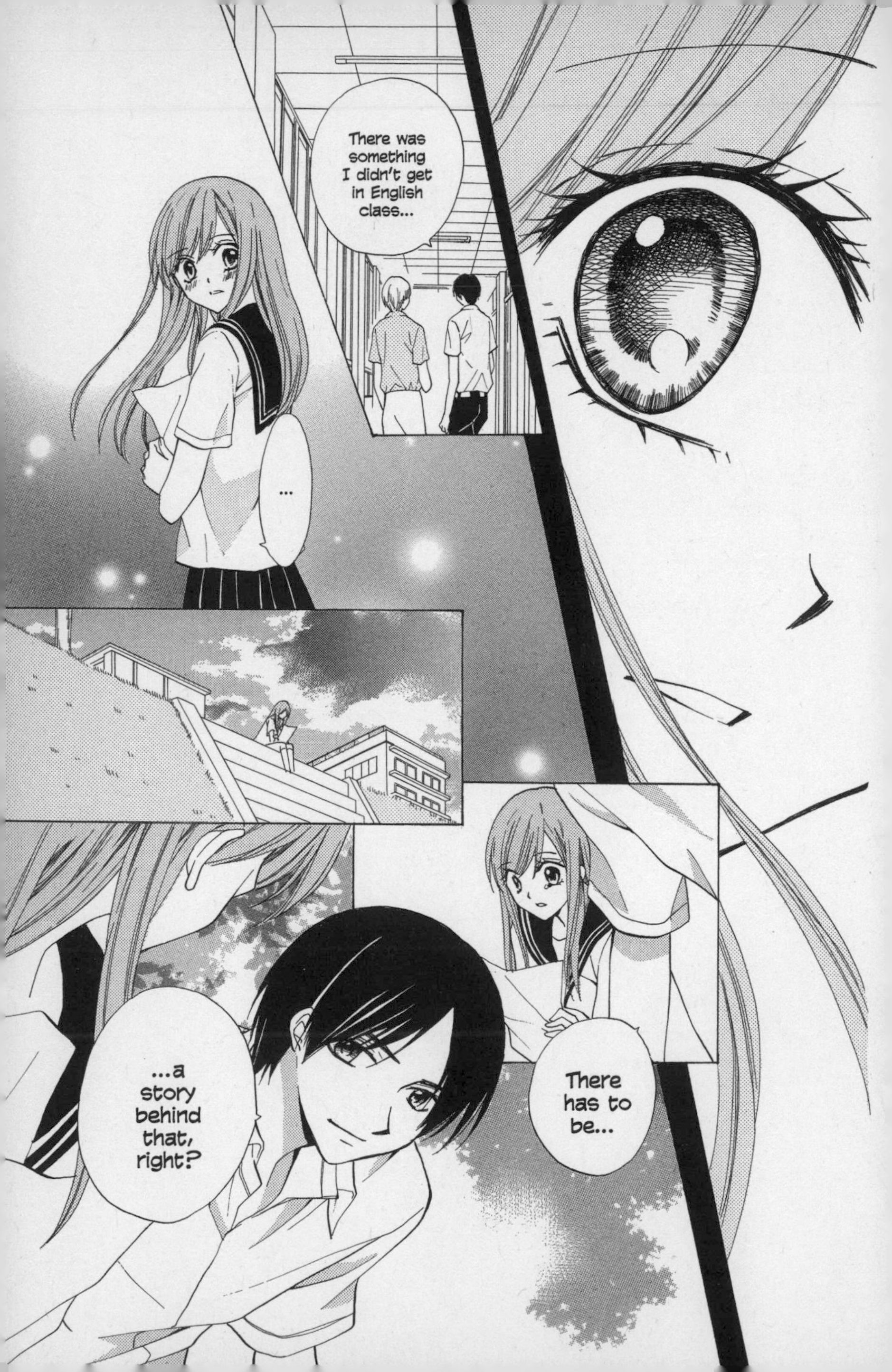
There was something I didn't get in English class...
...
There has to be...
...a story behind that, right?

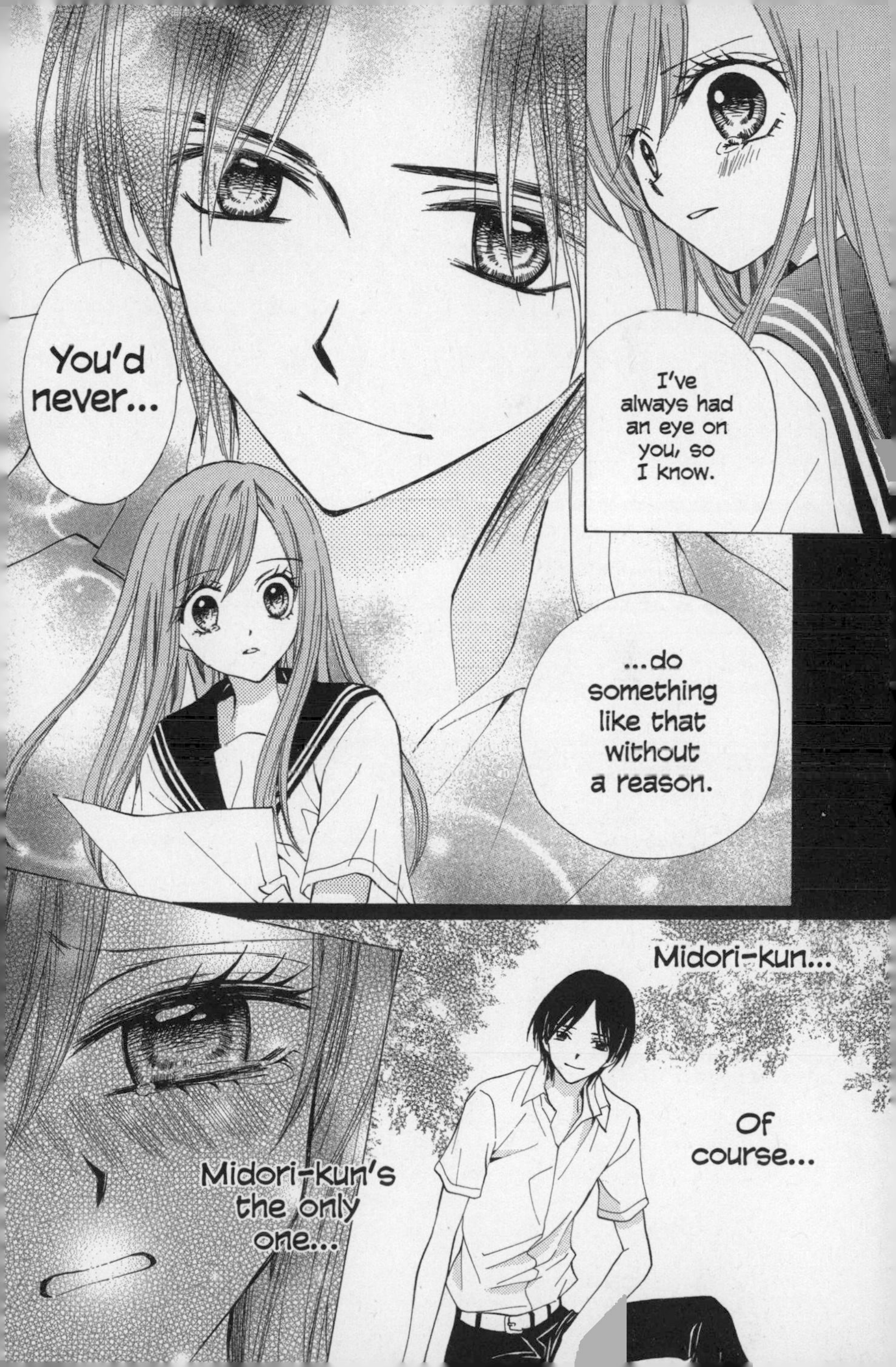
I've always had an eye on you, so I know.
You'd never...
...do something like that without a reason.
Midori-kun...
Of course...
Midori-kun's the only one...

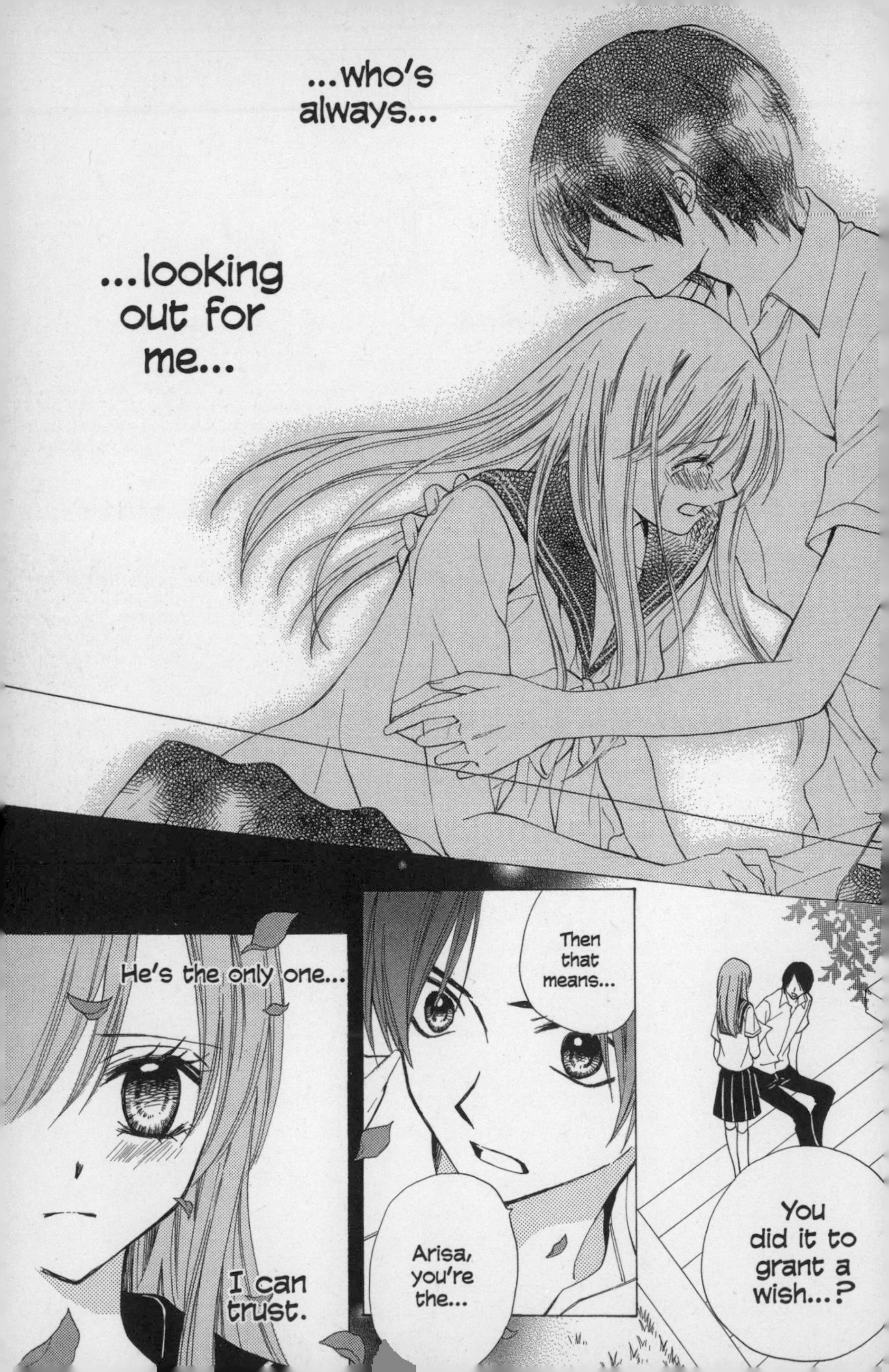
...who's always...
...looking out for me...
You did it to grant a wish...?
Then that means...
Arisa, you're the...
He's the only one...
I can trust.

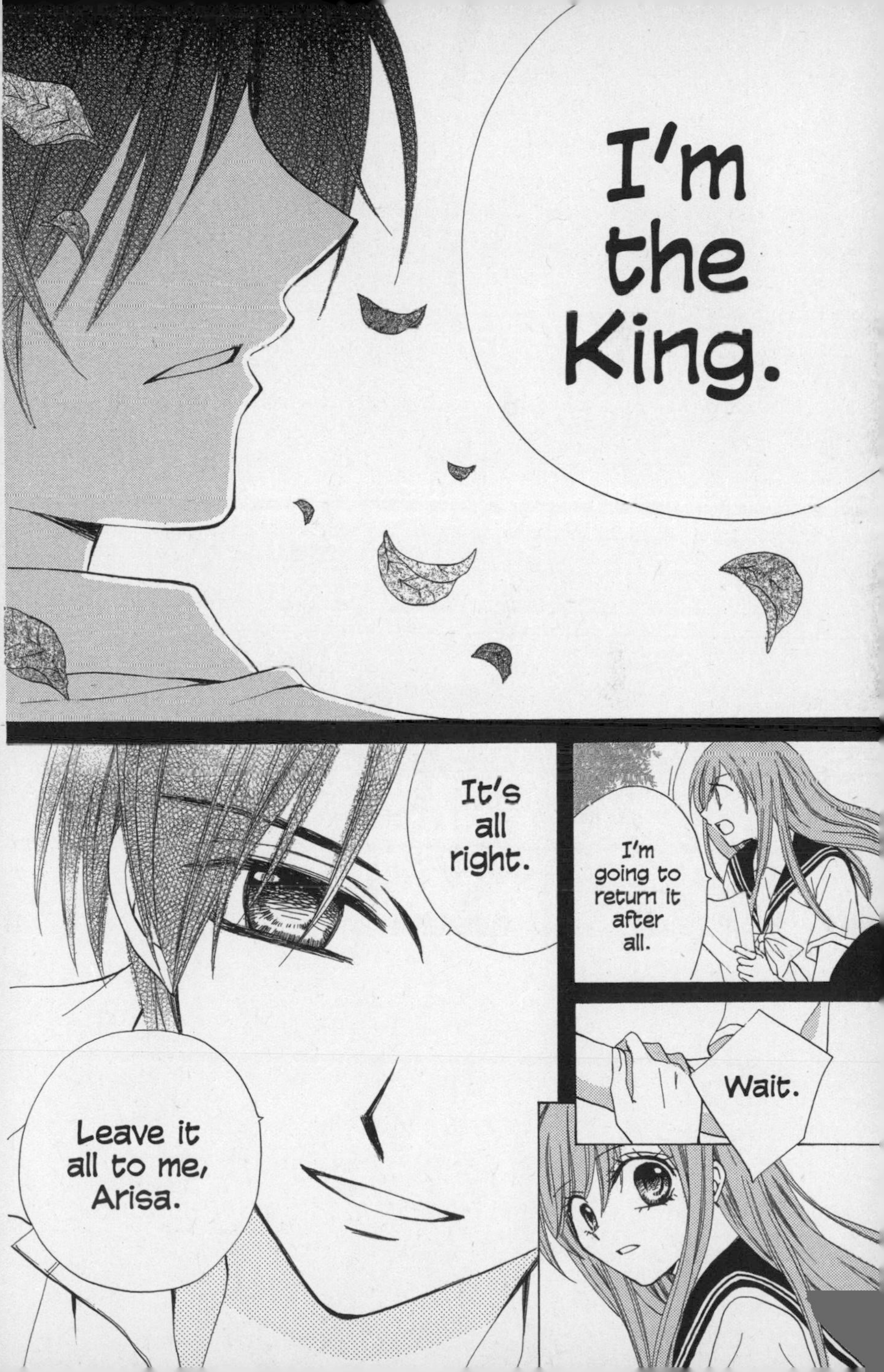
I'm the King.
I'm going to return it after all.
Wait.
It's all right.
Leave it all to me, Arisa.

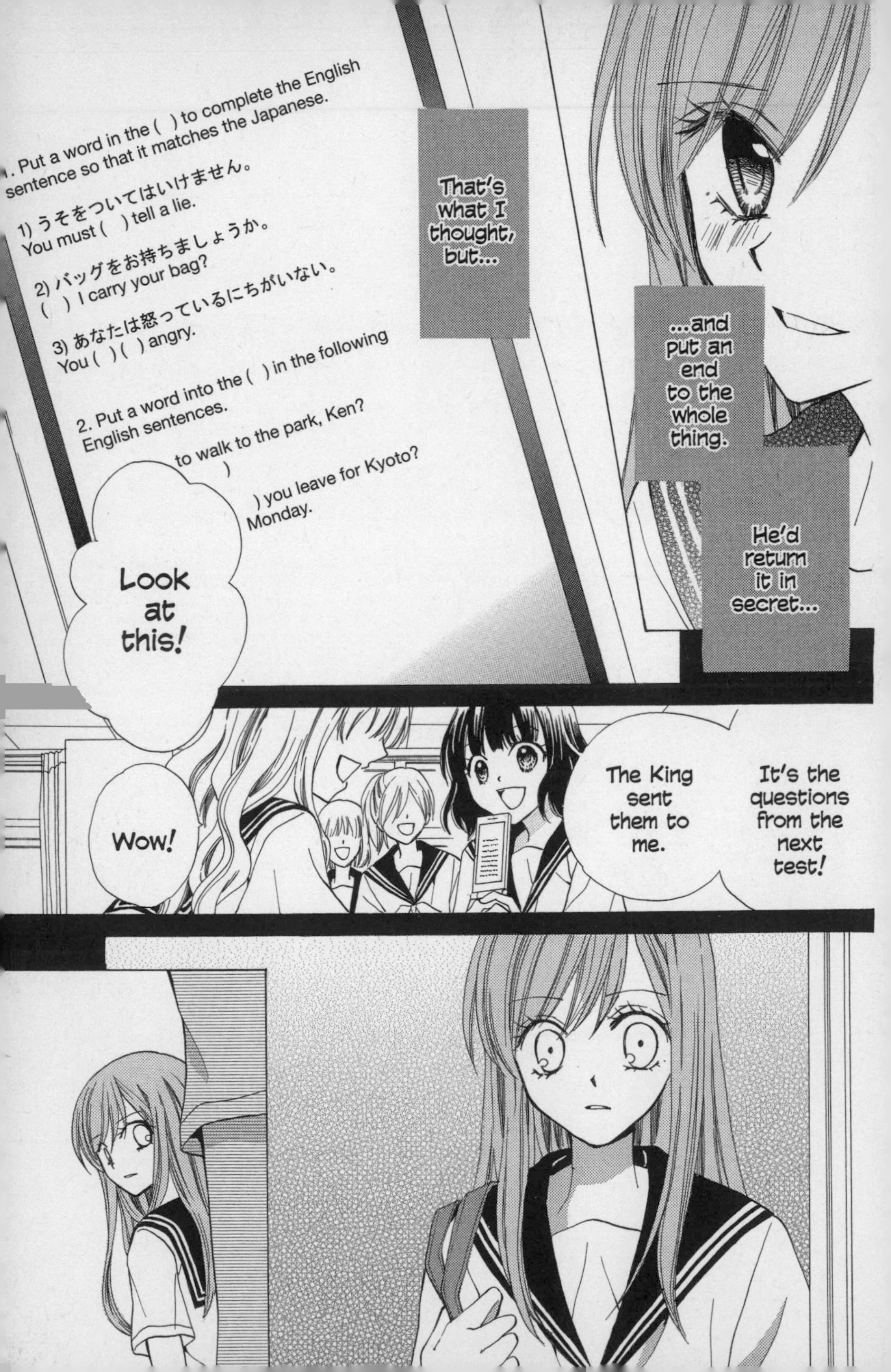
He'd return it in secret...
...and put an end to the whole thing.
That's what I thought, but...
. Put a word in the ( ) to complete the English sentence so that it matches the Japanese.
1) うそをついてはいけません。
You must ( ) tell a lie.
2) バッグをお持ちましょうか。
( ) I carry your bag?
3) あなたは怒っているにちがいない。
You ( ) ( ) angry.
2. Put a word into the ( ) in the following English sentences.
to walk to the park, Ken?
)
) you leave for Kyoto?
Monday.
Look at this!
It's the questions from the next test!
The King sent them to me.
Wow!

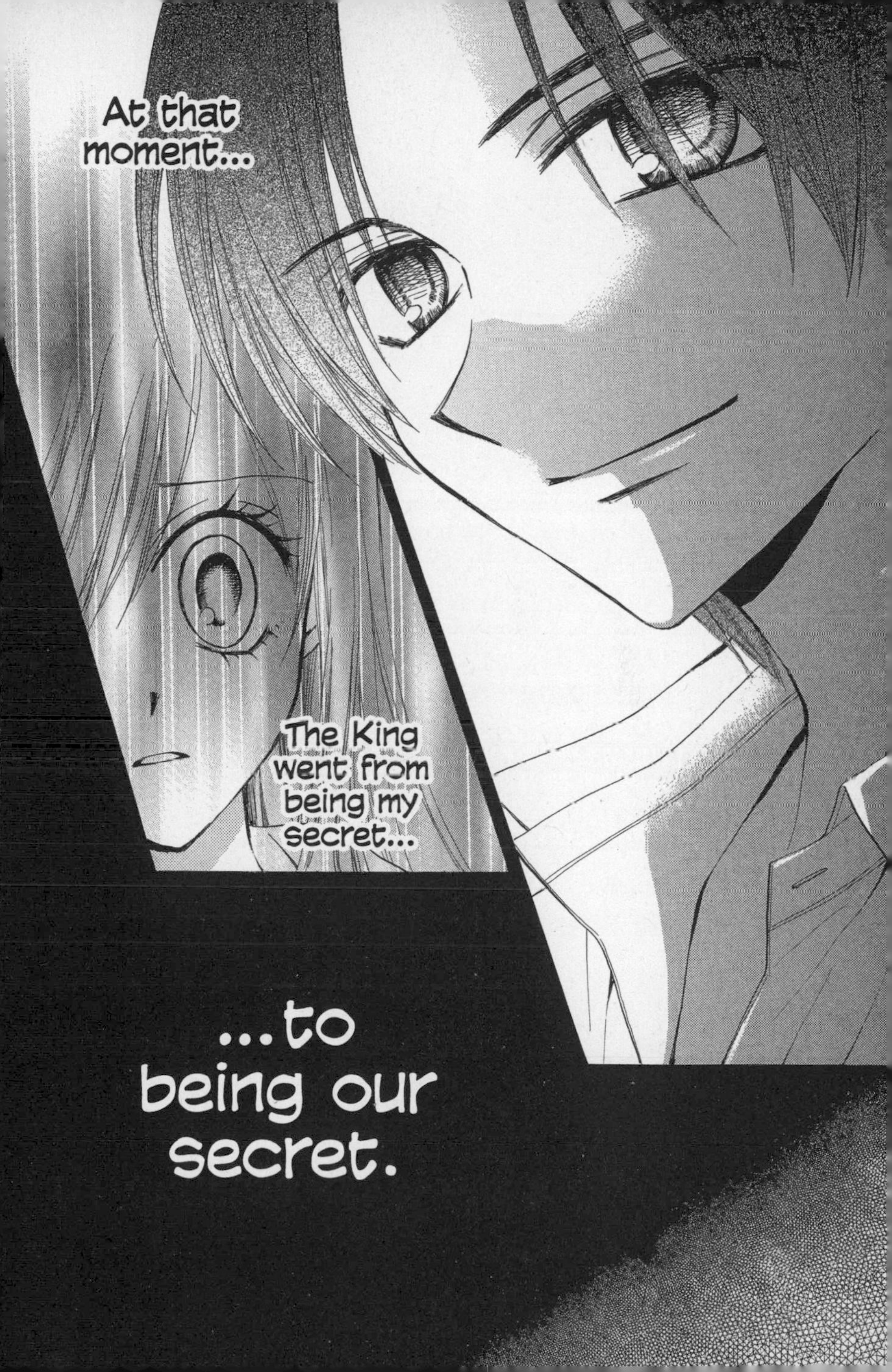
At that moment...
The King went from being my secret...
...to being our secret.

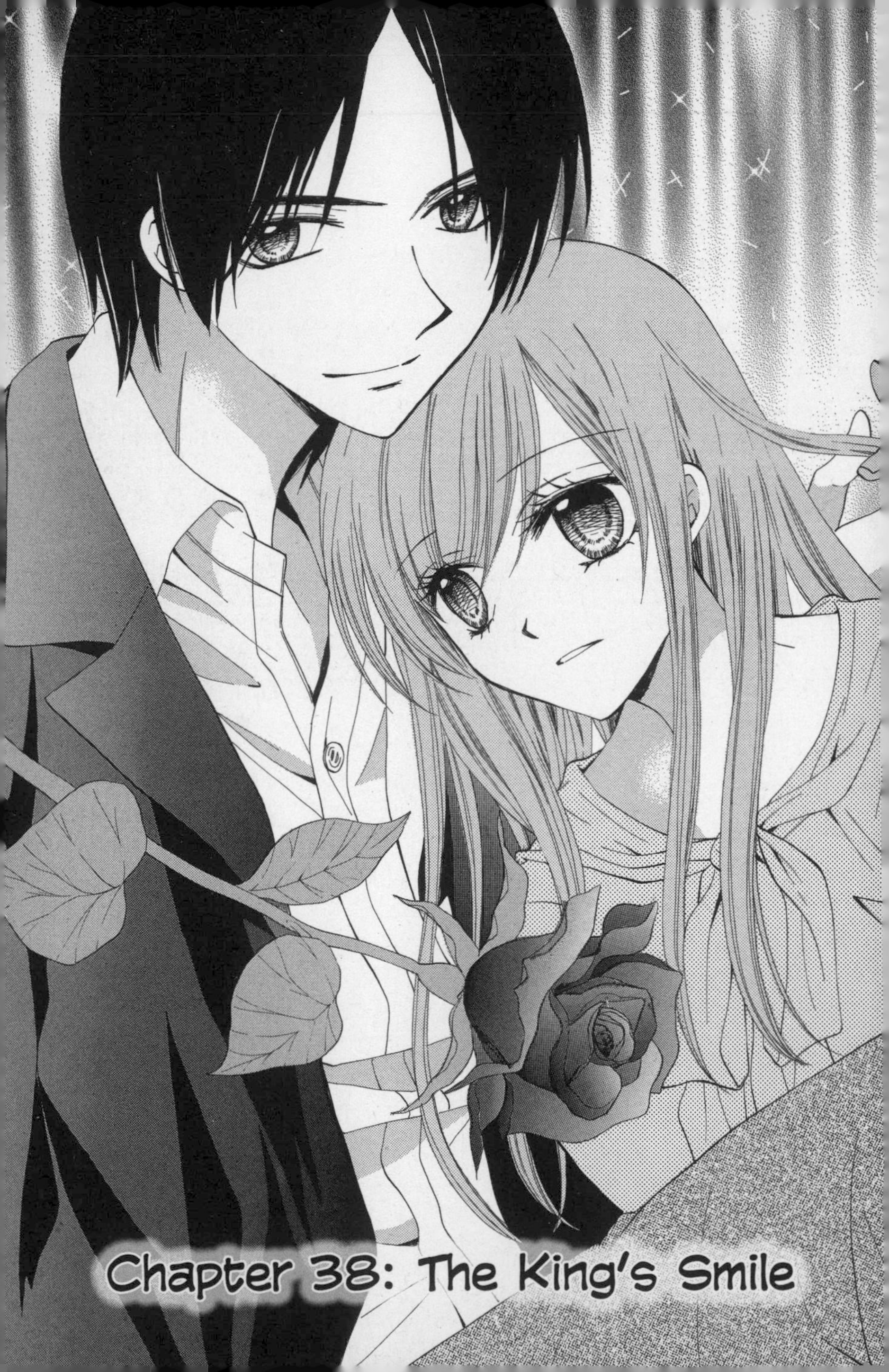
Chapter 38: The King's Smile

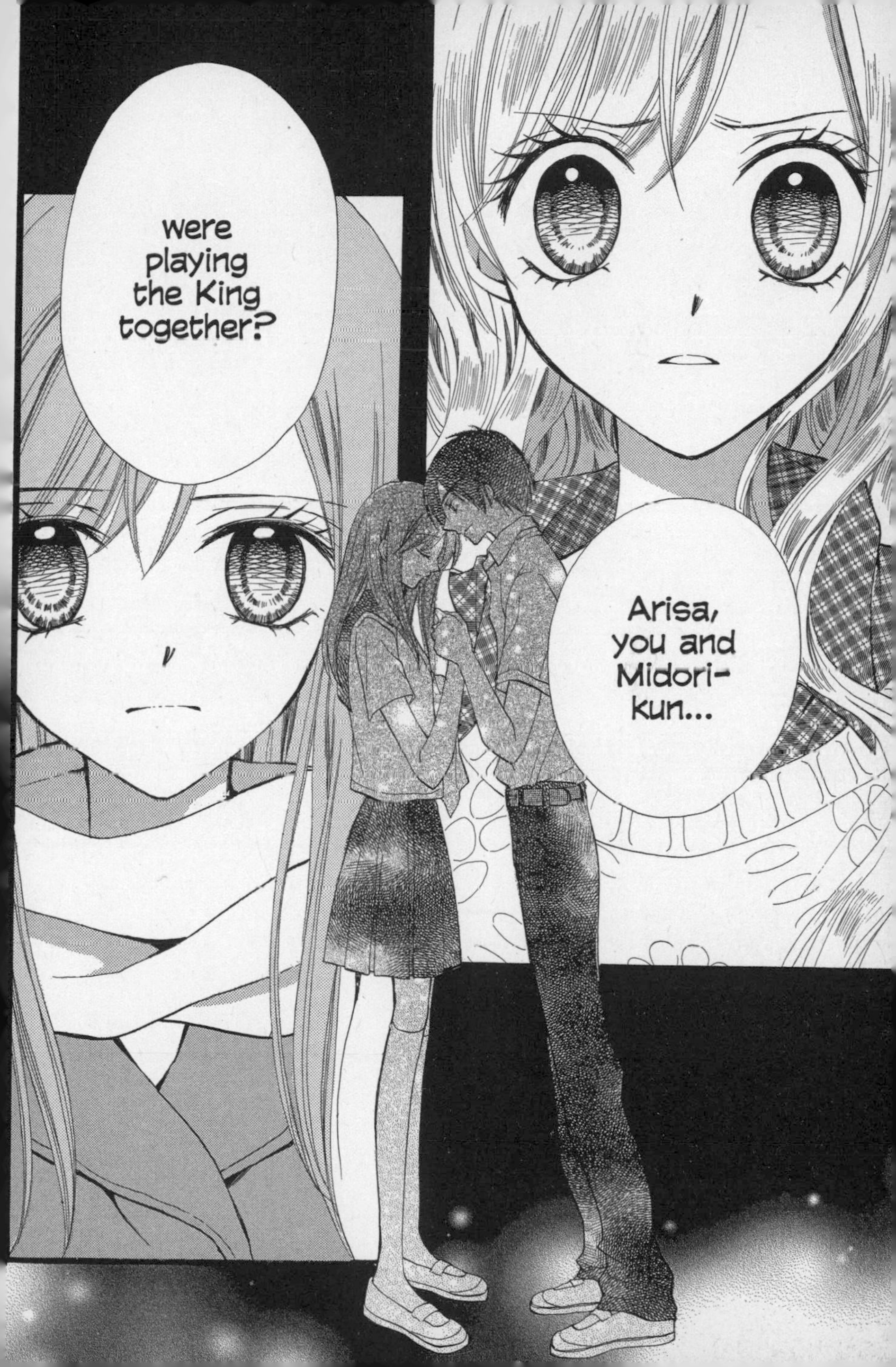
Arisa, you and Midori-kun...
were playing the King together?

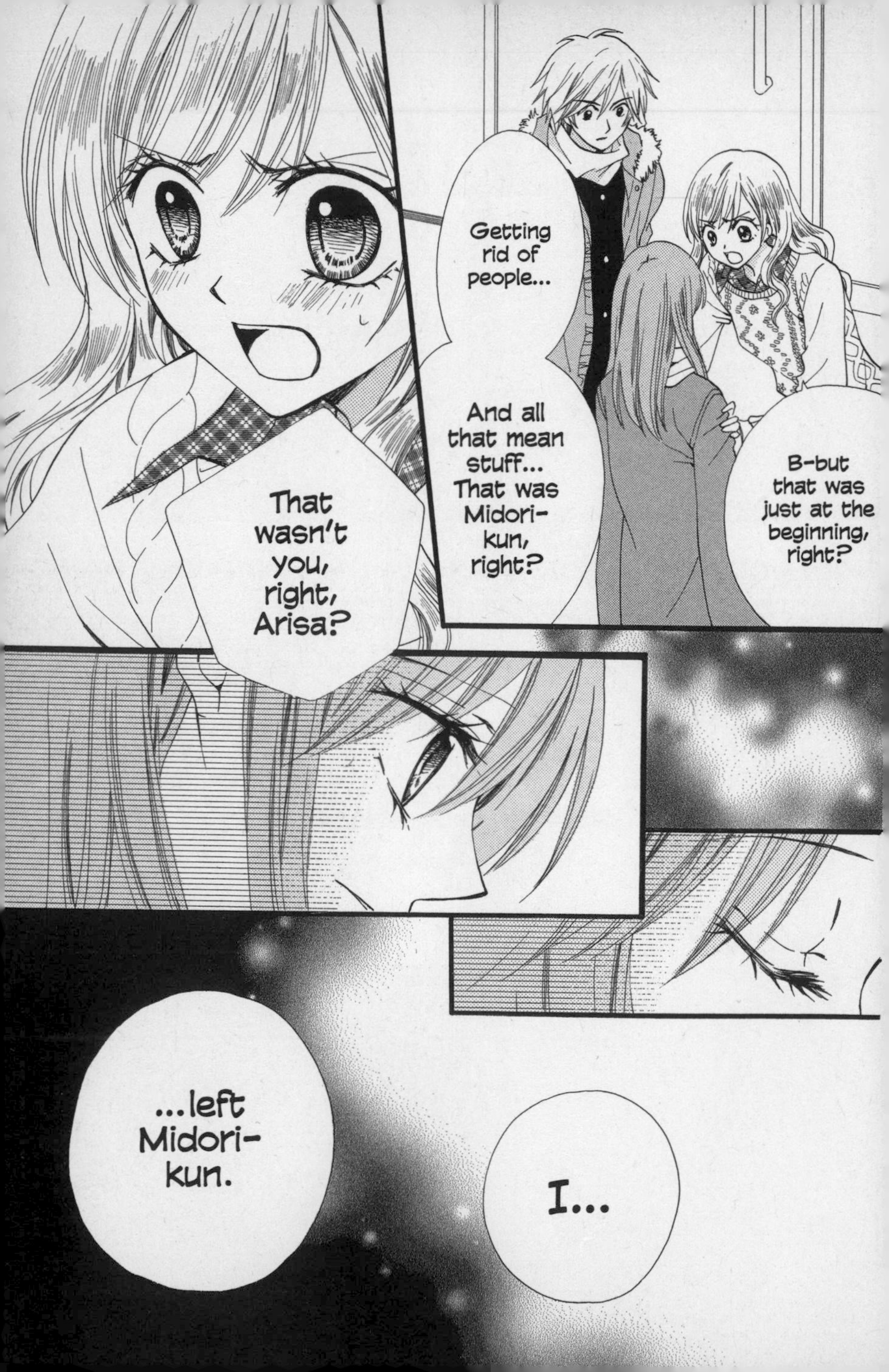

Getting rid of people...
And all that mean stuff... That was Midori-kun, right?
B-but that was just at the beginning, right?
That wasn't you, right, Arisa?
I...
...left Midori-kun.

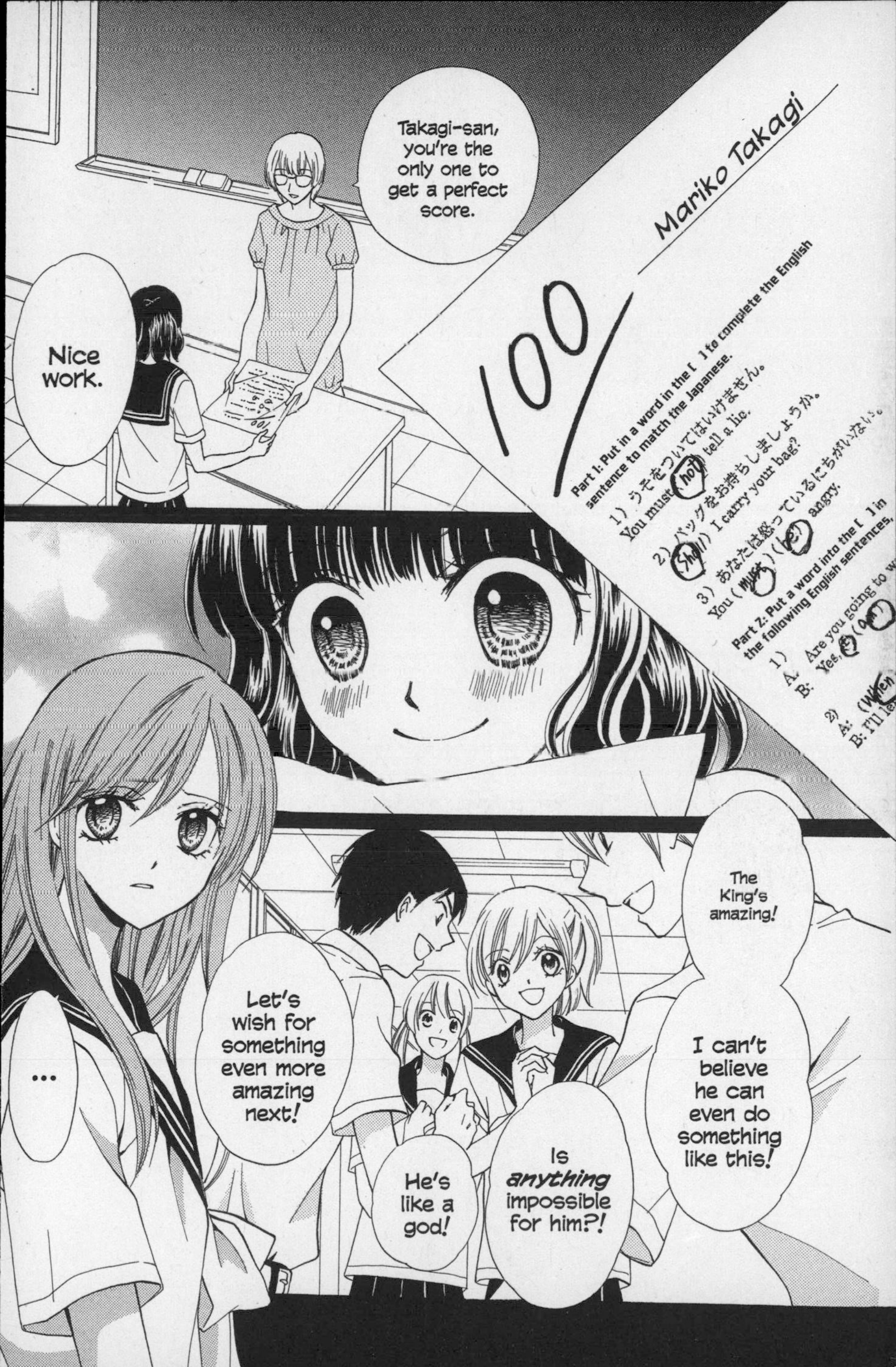
Takagi-san, you're the only one to get a perfect score.
Nice work.
Mariko Takagi
100
Part 1: Put in a word in the [ ] to complete the English sentence to match the Japanese.
1) うそをついてはいけません。 You must (not) tell a lie.
2) バッグをお持ちしましょうか。 (Shall) I carry your bag?
3) あなたは怒っているにちがいない。 You (must) (be) angry.
Part 2: Put a word into the [ ] in the following English sentences.
The King's amazing!
I can't believe he can even do something like this!
Is *anything* impossible for him?!
He's like a god!
Let's wish for something even more amazing next!
...

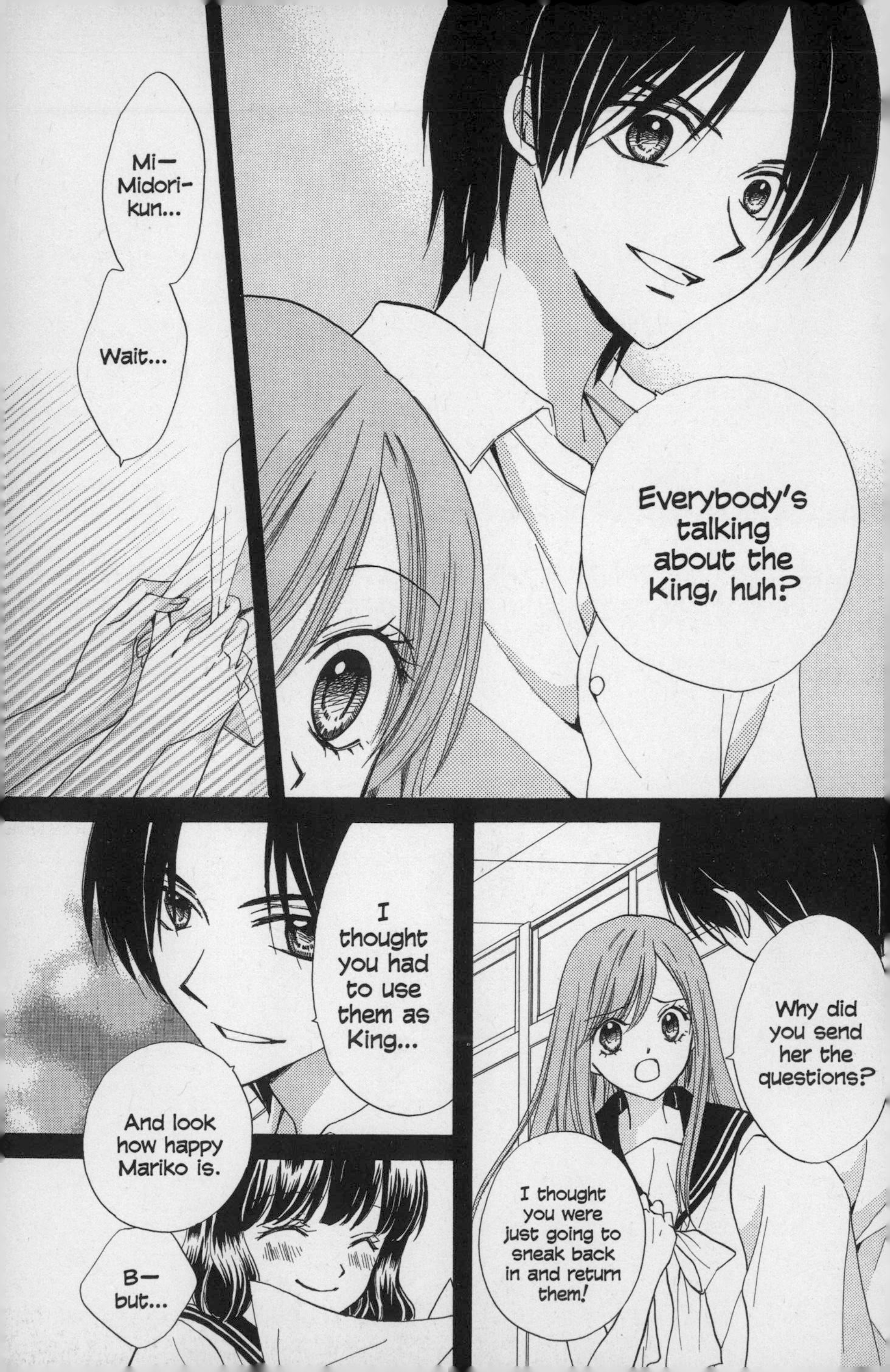
Everybody's talking about the King, huh?
Mi—Midori-kun...
Wait...
Why did you send her the questions?
I thought you were just going to sneak back in and return them!
I thought you had to use them as King...
And look how happy Mariko is.
B—but...

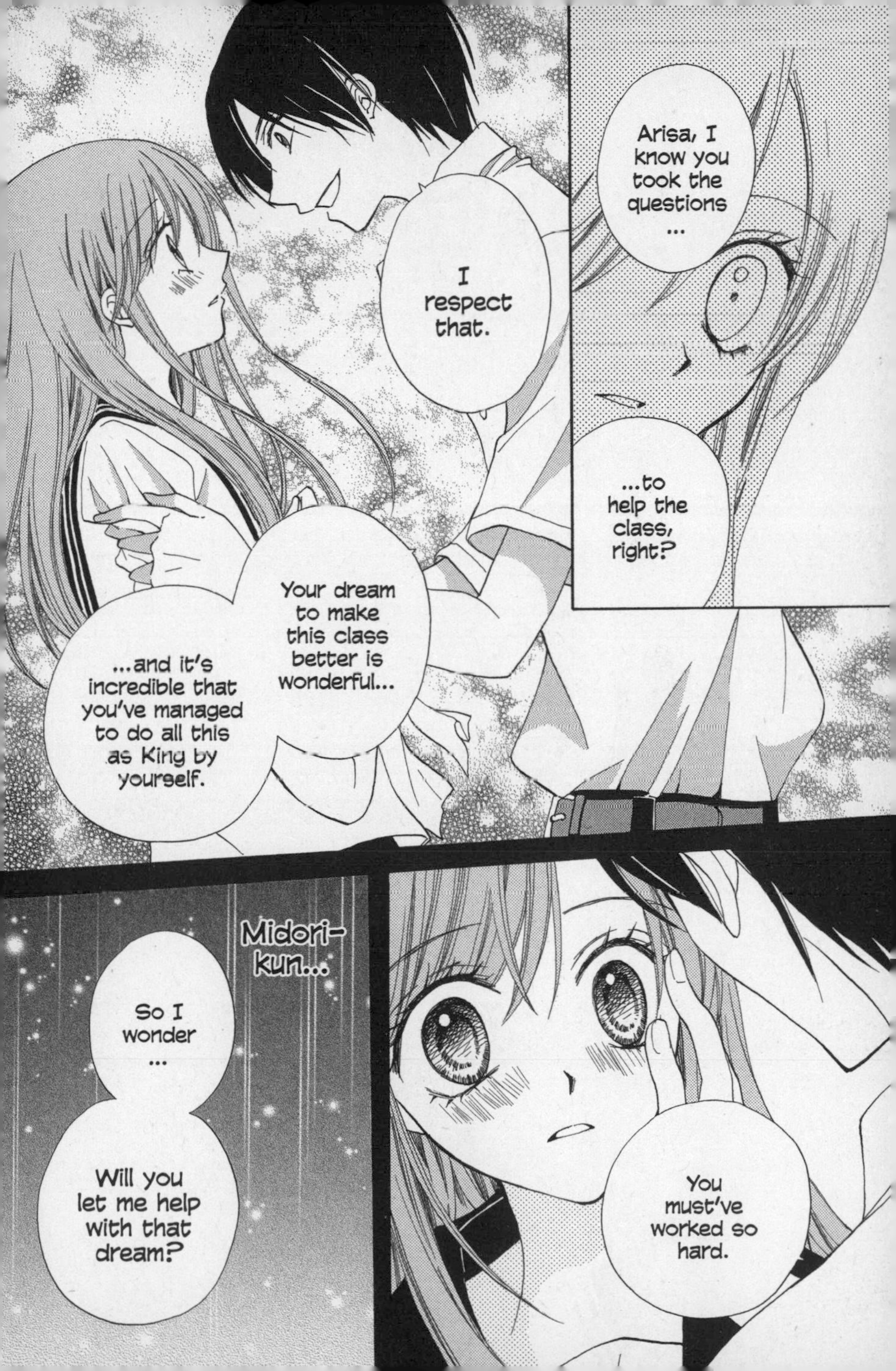
Arisa, I know you took the questions ...
...to help the class, right?
I respect that.
Your dream to make this class better is wonderful...
...and it's incredible that you've managed to do all this as King by yourself.
You must've worked so hard.
Midori-kun...
So I wonder ...
Will you let me help with that dream?

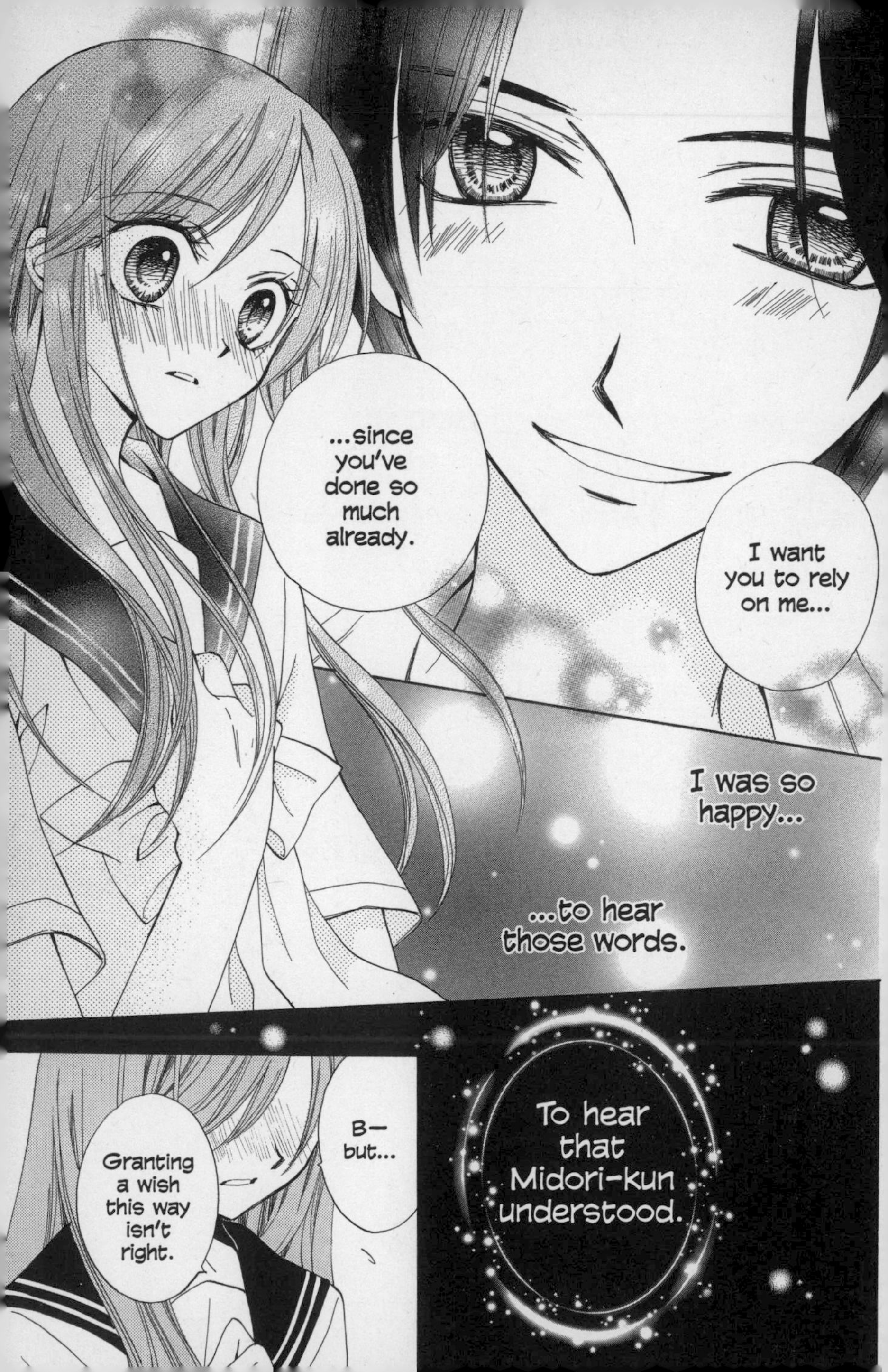
I want you to rely on me...
...since you've done so much already.
I was so happy...
...to hear those words.
To hear that Midori-kun understood.
B— but...
Granting a wish this way isn't right.

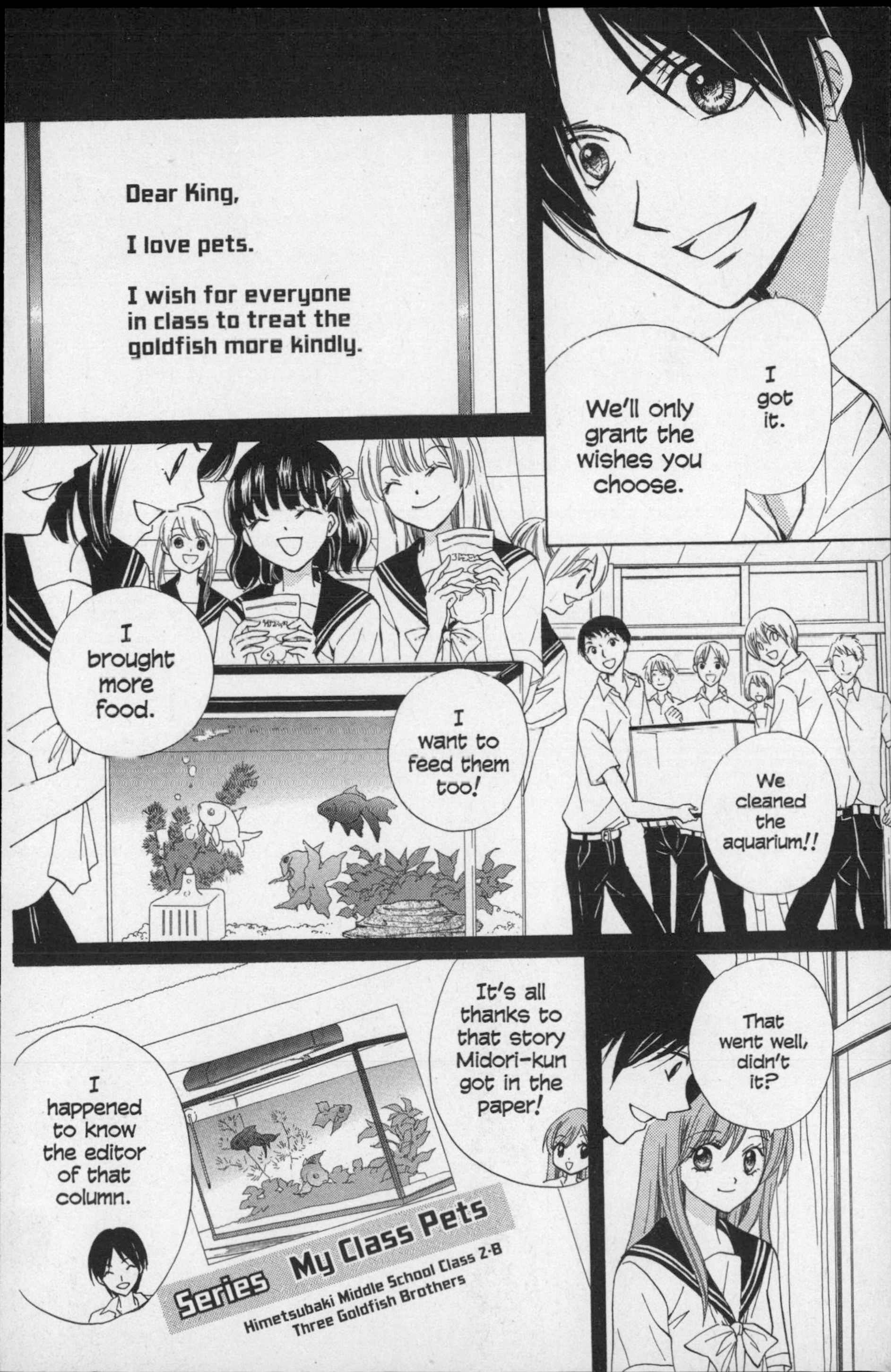
I got it.
We'll only grant the wishes you choose.
Dear King,
I love pets.
I wish for everyone in class to treat the goldfish more kindly.
We cleaned the aquarium!!
I want to feed them too!
I brought more food.
That went well, didn't it?
It's all thanks to that story Midori-kun got in the paper!
I happened to know the editor of that column.
Series My Class Pets
Himetsubaki Middle School Class 2-B
Three Goldfish Brothers

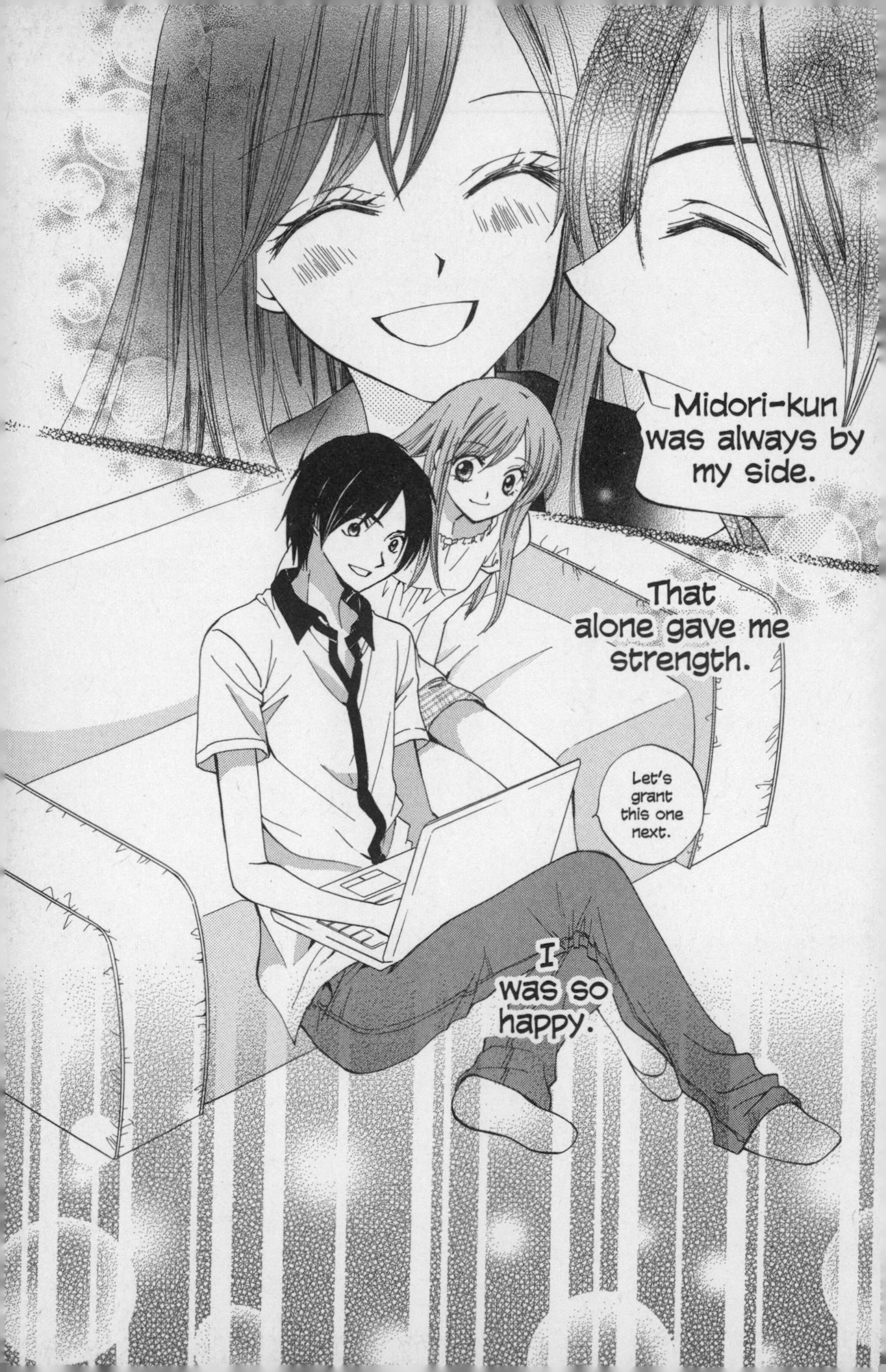
Midori-kun was always by my side.
That alone gave me strength.
Let's grant this one next.
I was so happy.

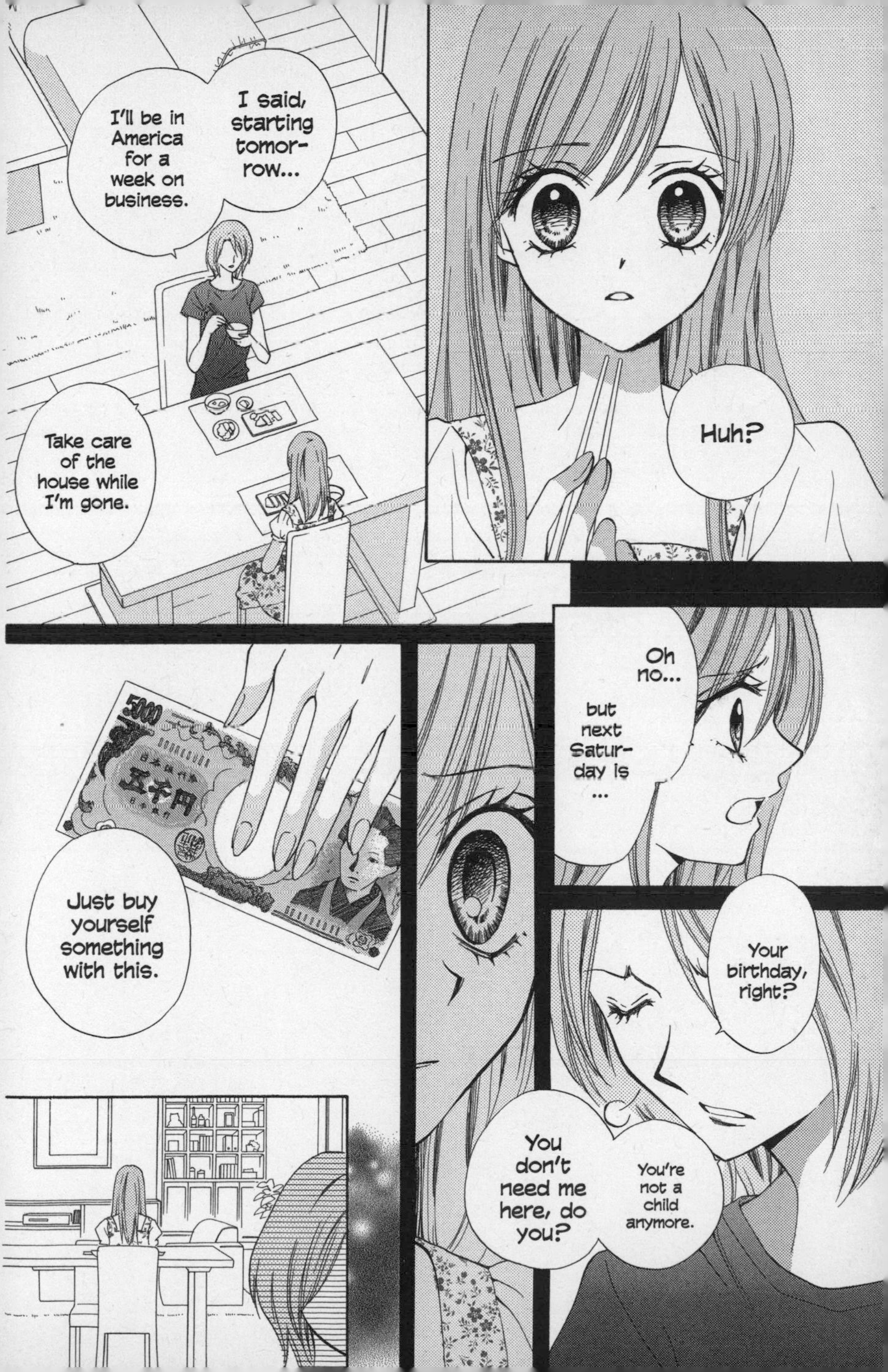
Huh?
I said, starting tomorrow...
I'll be in America for a week on business.
Take care of the house while I'm gone.
Oh no...
but next Saturday is ...
Your birthday, right?
You're not a child anymore.
You don't need me here, do you?
Just buy yourself something with this.

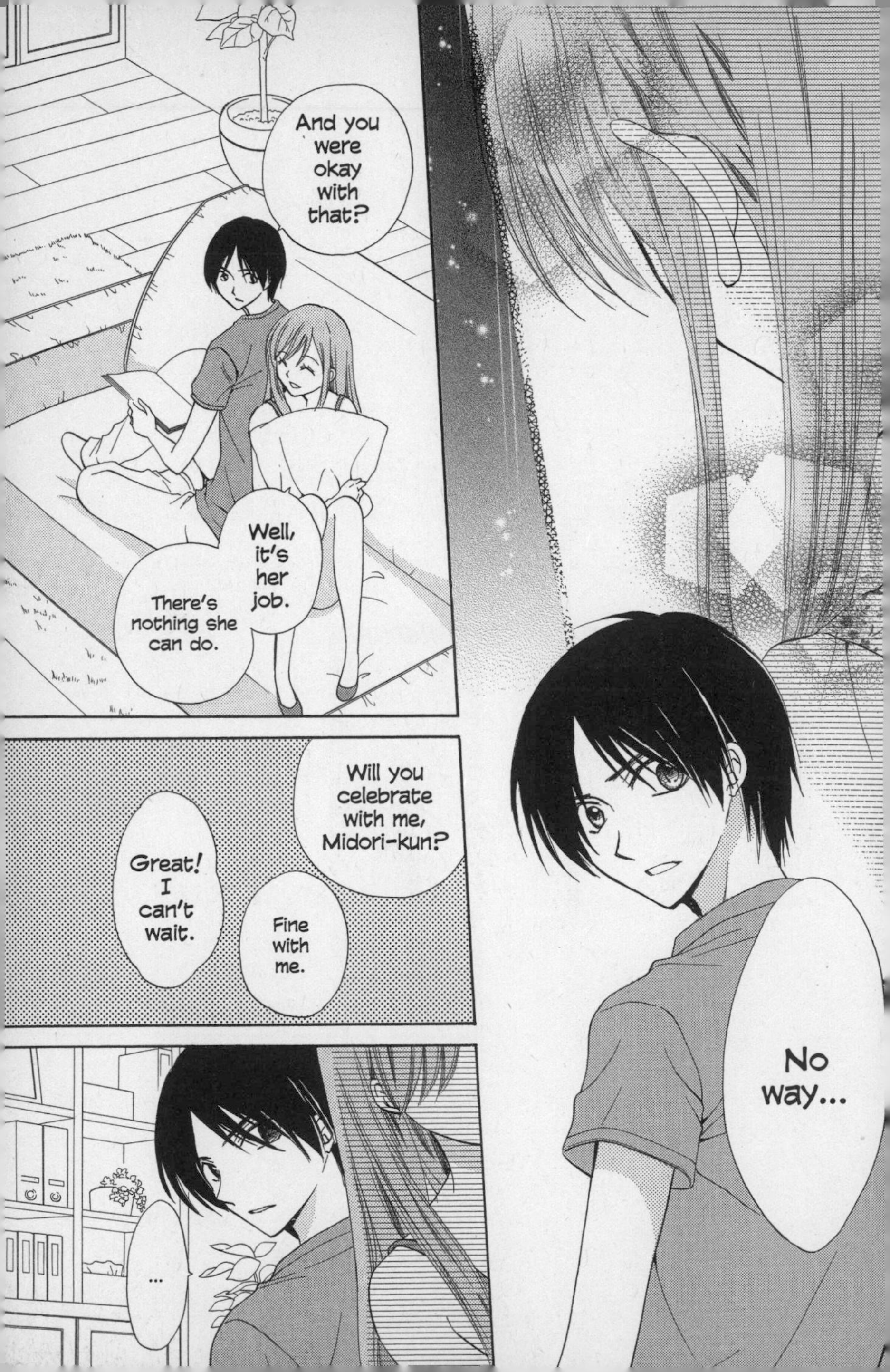
No way...
And you were okay with that?
Well, it's her job.
There's nothing she can do.
Will you celebrate with me, Midori-kun?
Fine with me.
Great! I can't wait.
...

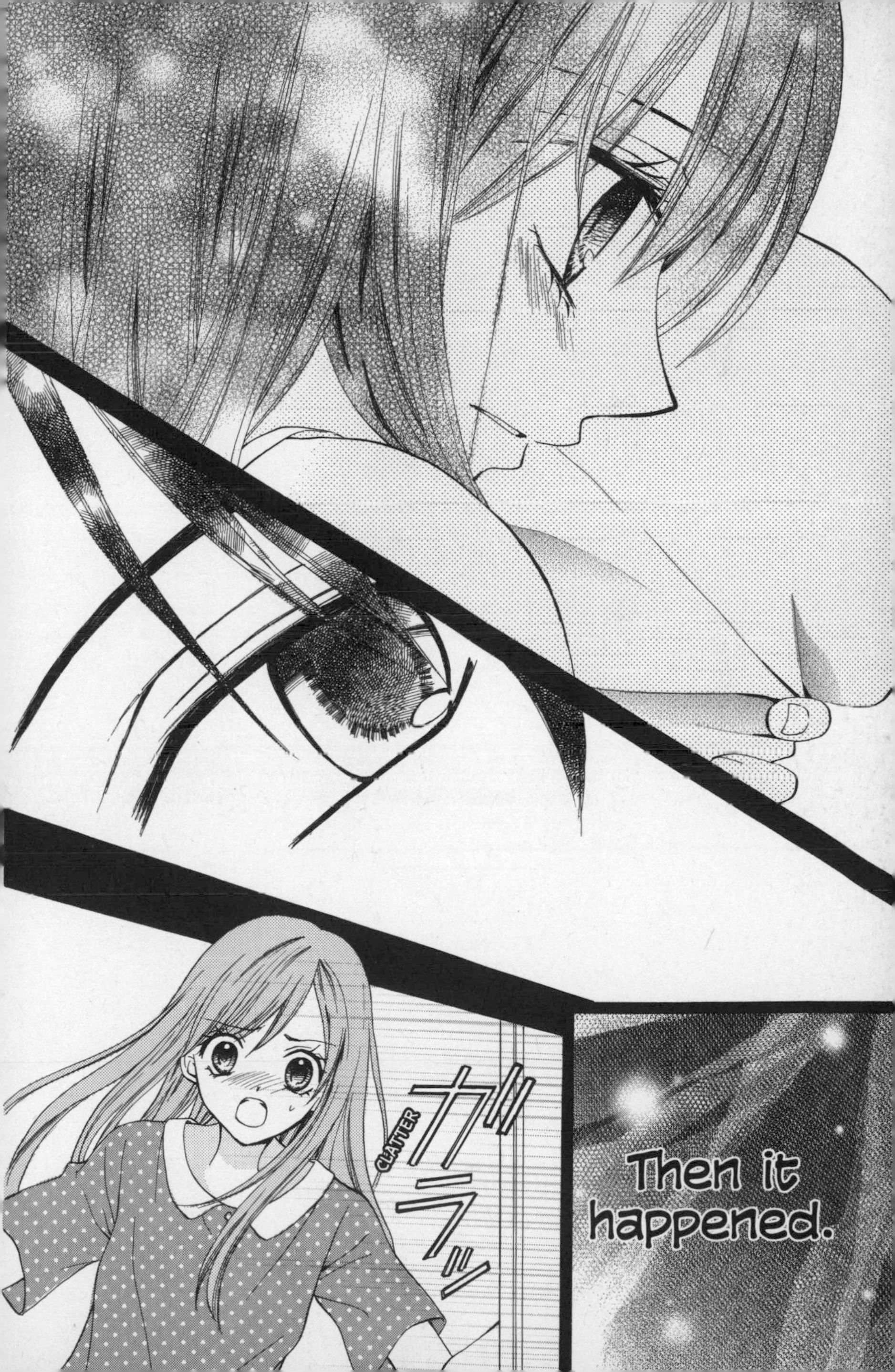
Then it happened.
CLATTER
ガラッ

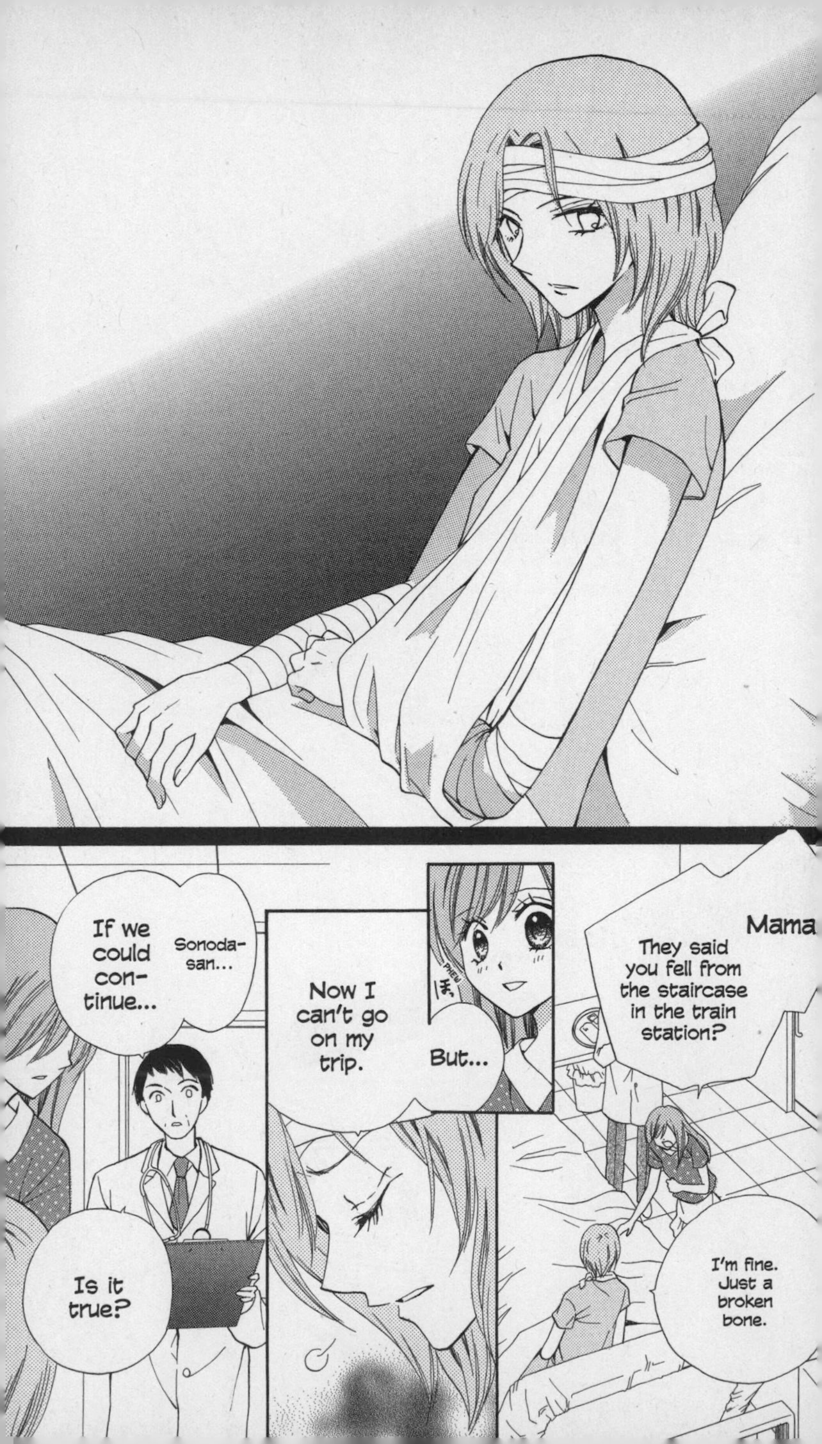
Mama
They said you fell from the staircase in the train station?
I'm fine. Just a broken bone.
ほっ
PHEW
But...
Now I can't go on my trip.
Sonoda-san...
If we could continue...
Is it true?

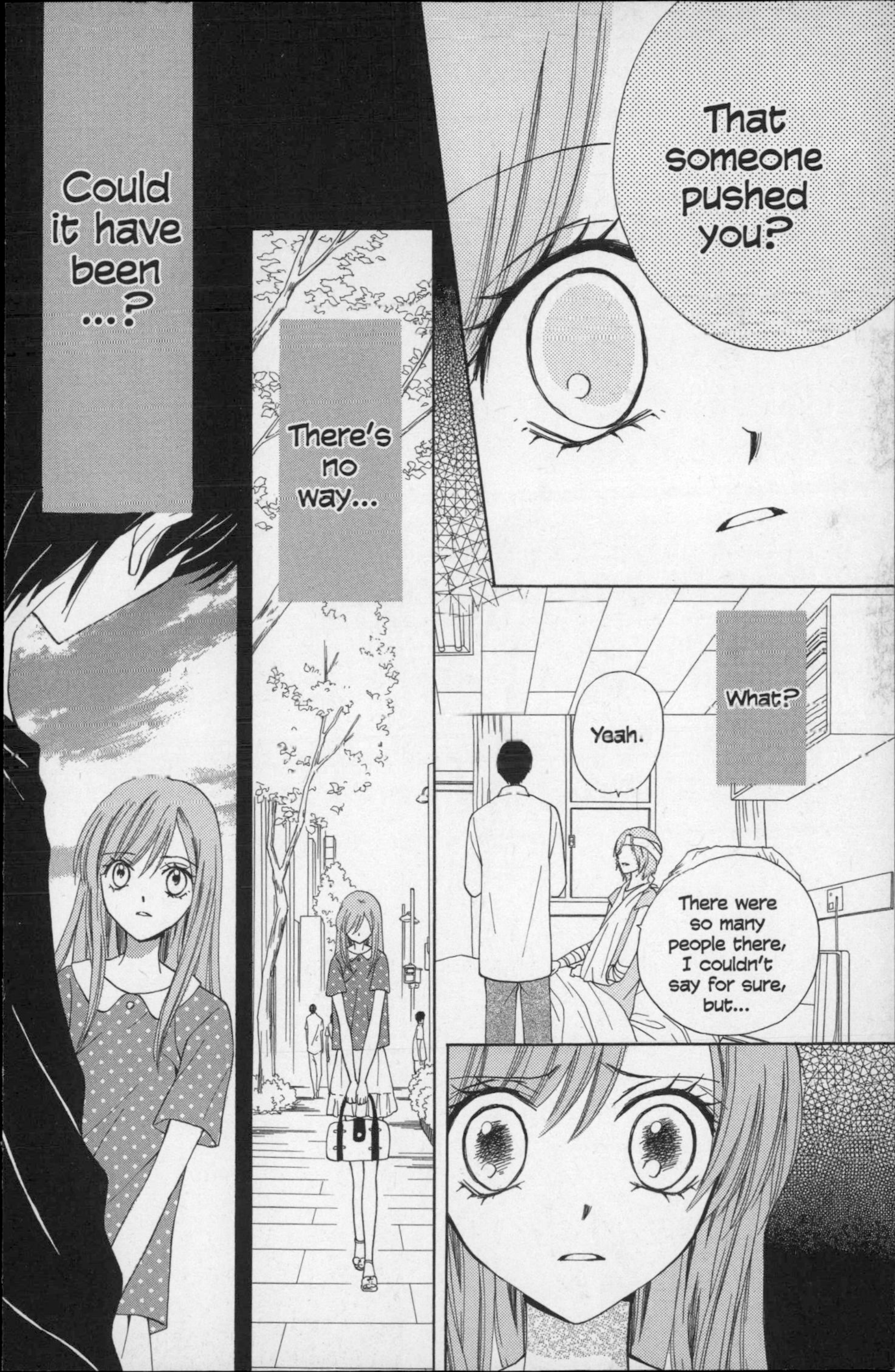
That someone pushed you?
What?
Yeah.
There were so many people there, I couldn't say for sure, but...
There's no way...
Could it have been ...?

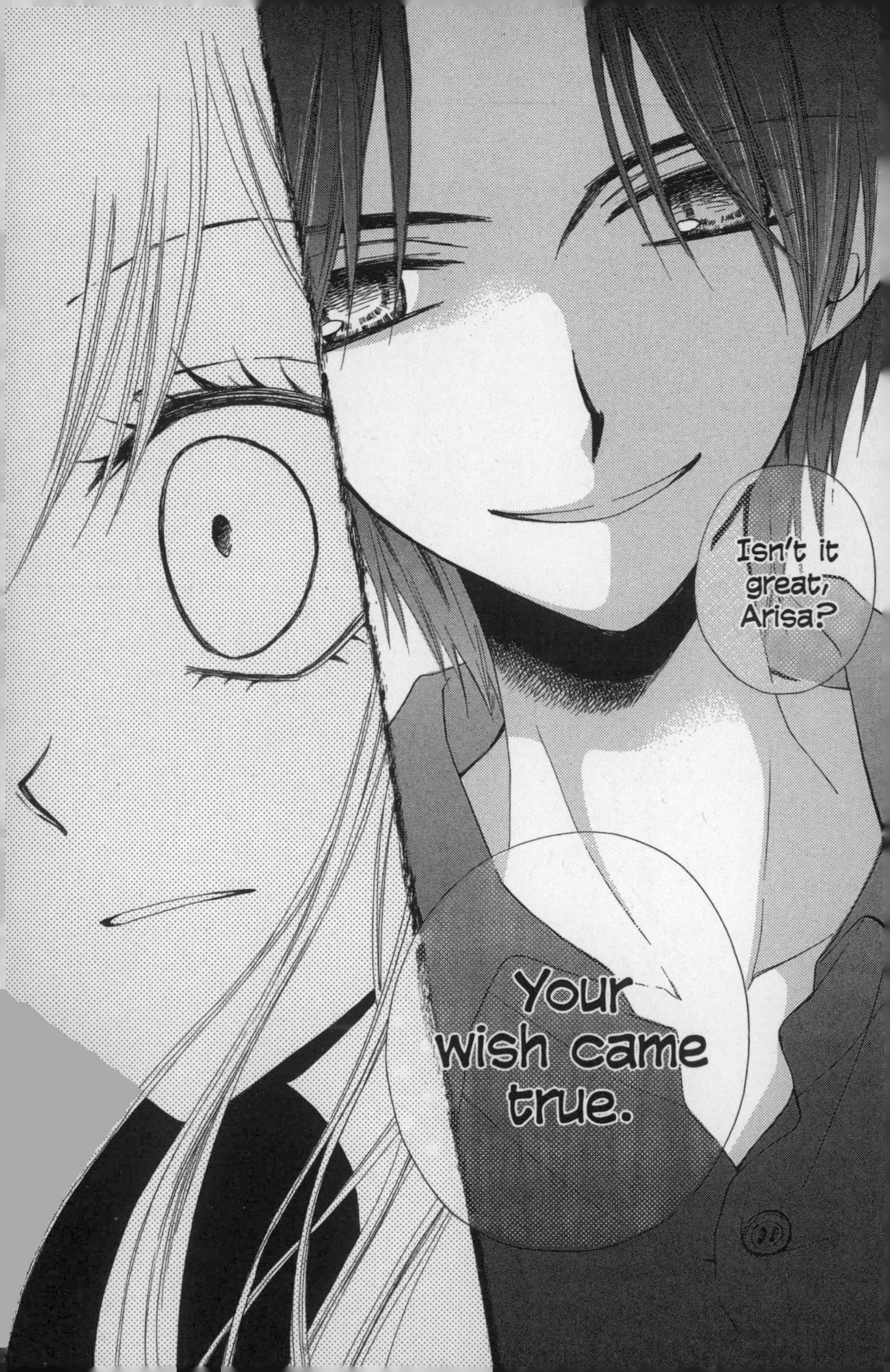
Isn't it great, Arisa?
Your wish came true.

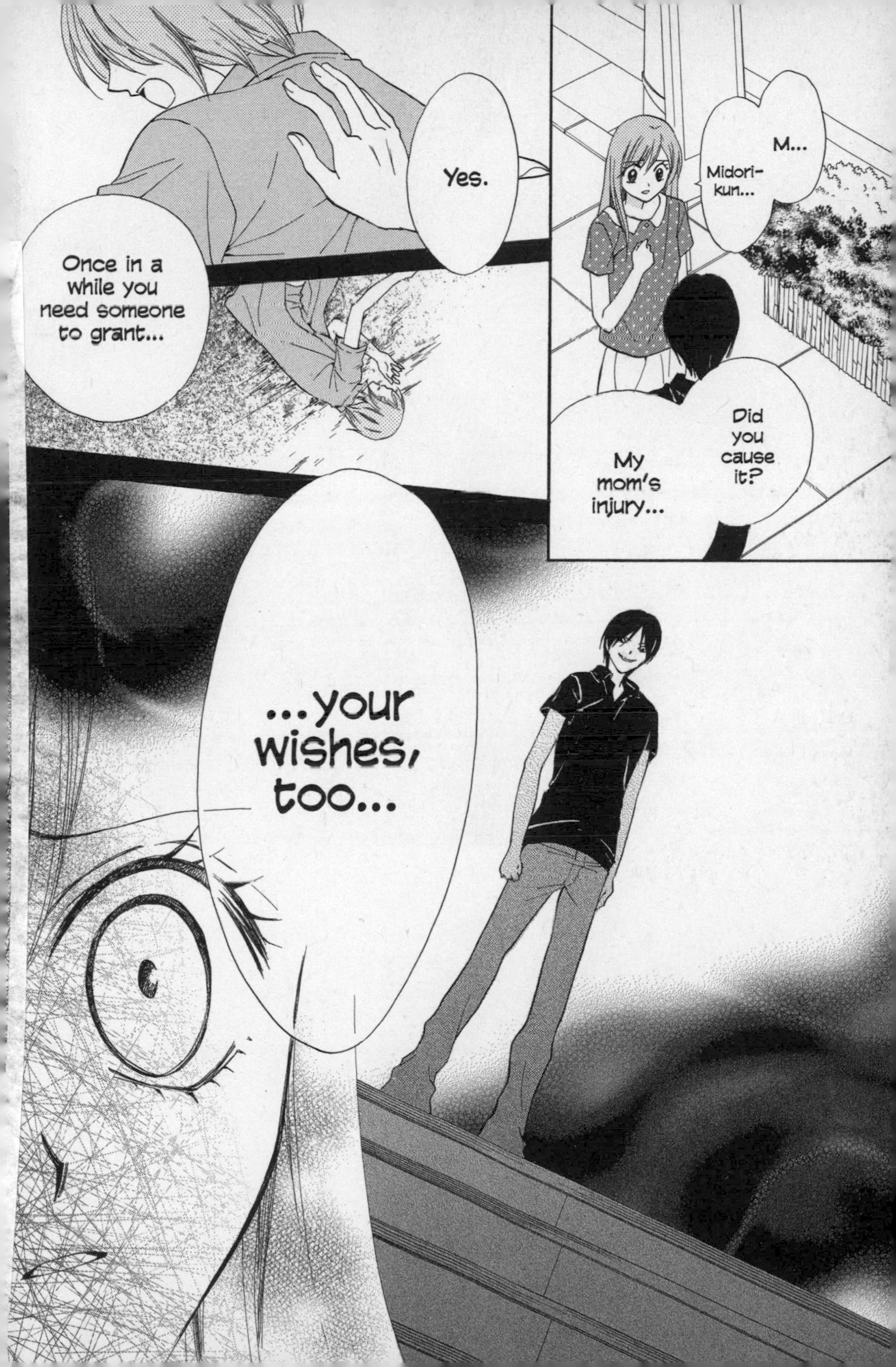
M... Midori-kun...
Did you cause it?
My mom's injury...
Yes.
Once in a while you need someone to grant...
...your wishes, too...

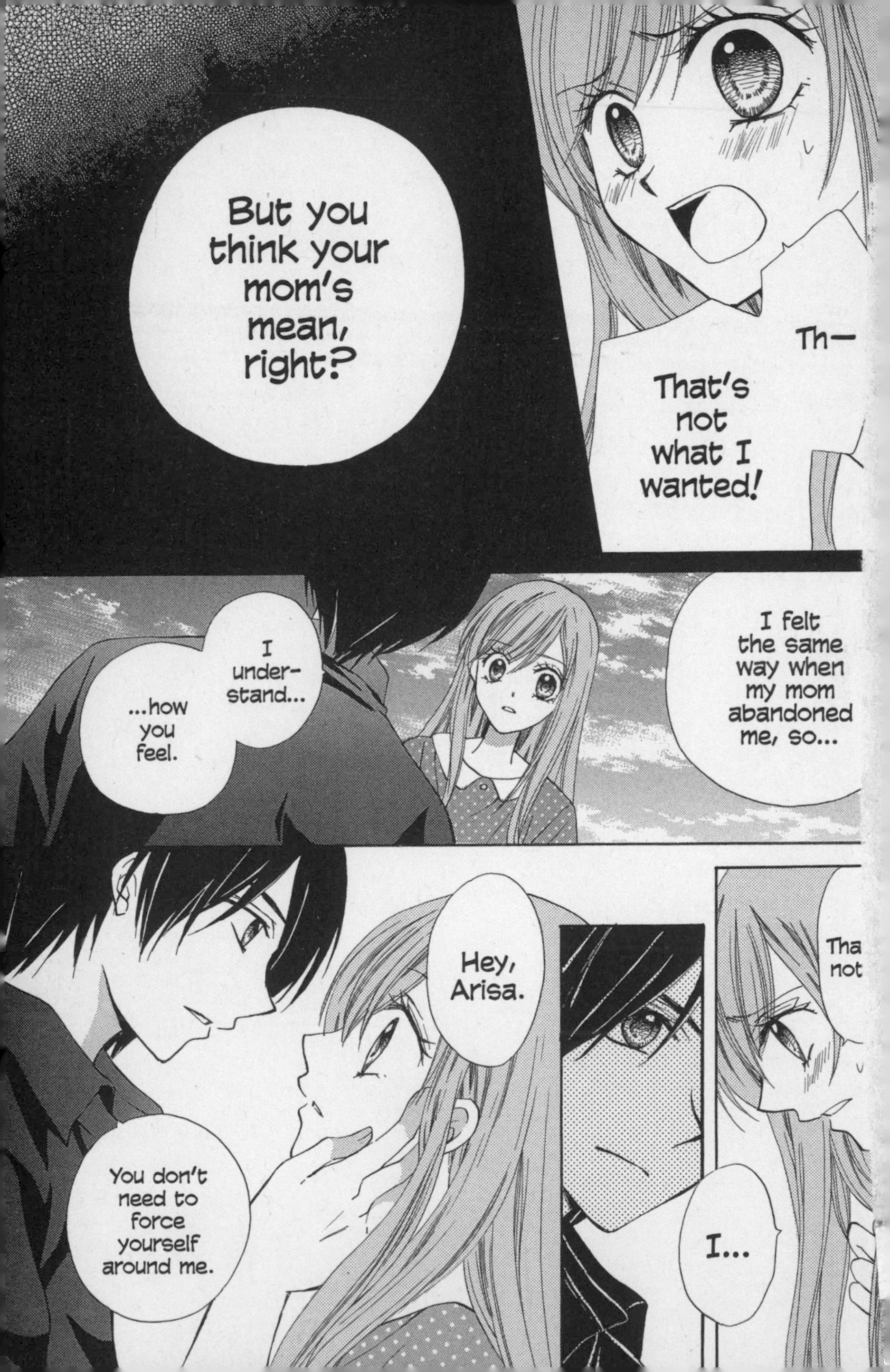

Th—
That's not what I wanted!
But you think your mom's mean, right?
I felt the same way when my mom abandoned me, so...
I understand...
...how you feel.
Tha not
I...
Hey, Arisa.
You don't need to force yourself around me.

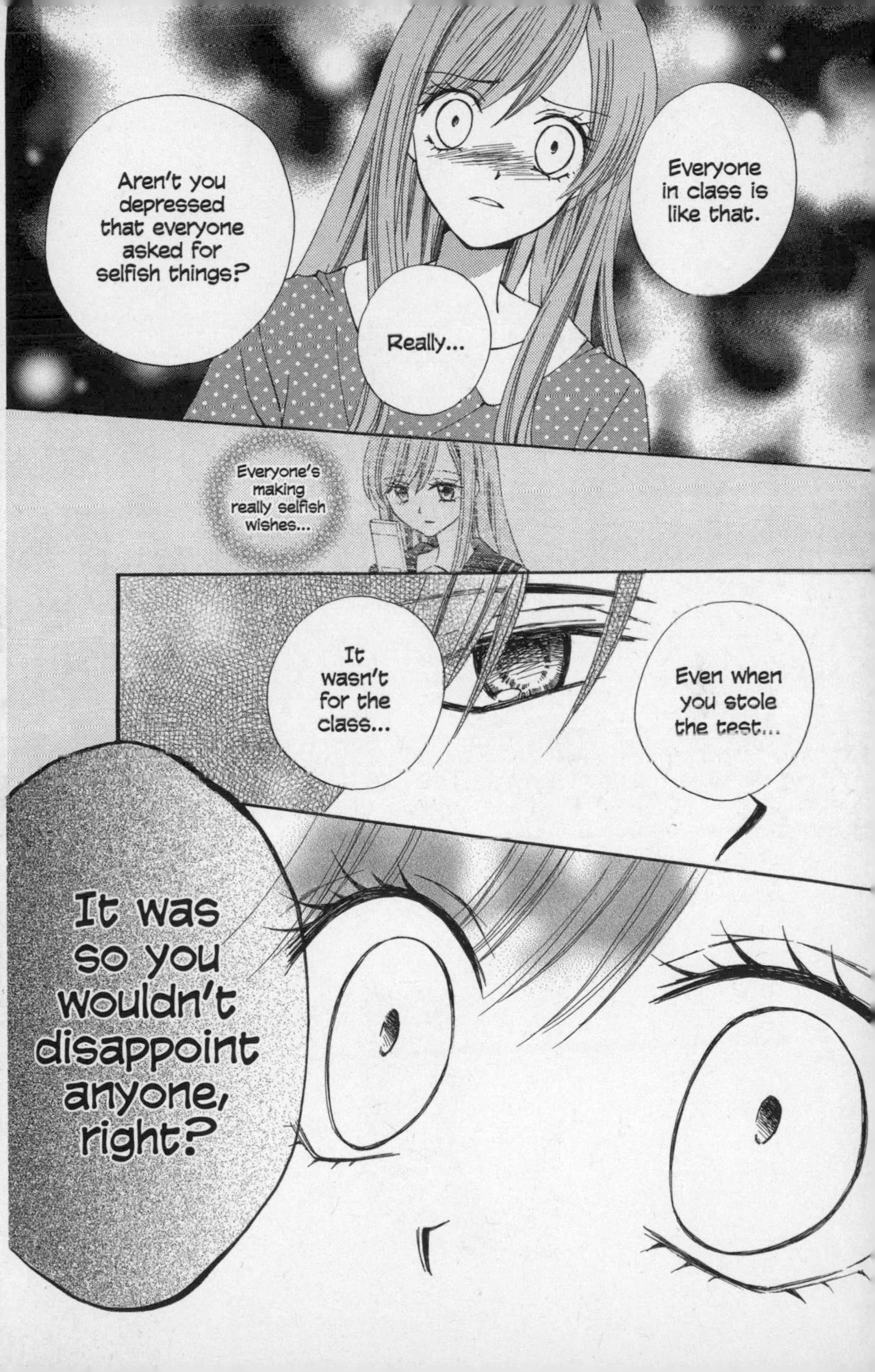
Everyone in class is like that.
Aren't you depressed that everyone asked for selfish things?
Really...
Everyone's making really selfish wishes...
Even when you stole the test...
It wasn't for the class...
It was so you wouldn't disappoint anyone, right?

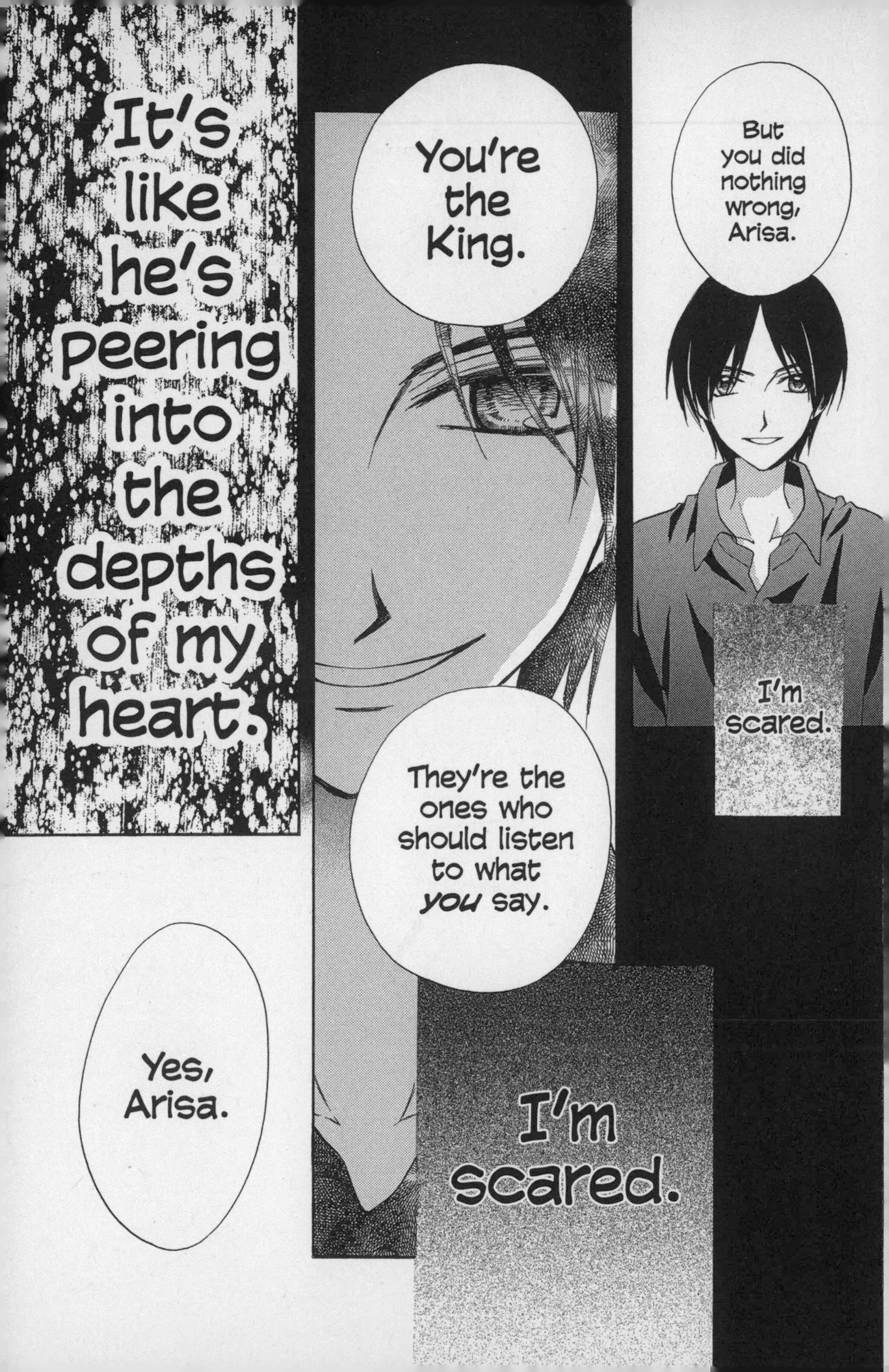
But you did nothing wrong, Arisa.
I'm scared.
You're the King.
They're the ones who should listen to what *you* say.
It's like he's peering into the depths of my heart.
I'm scared.
Yes, Arisa.

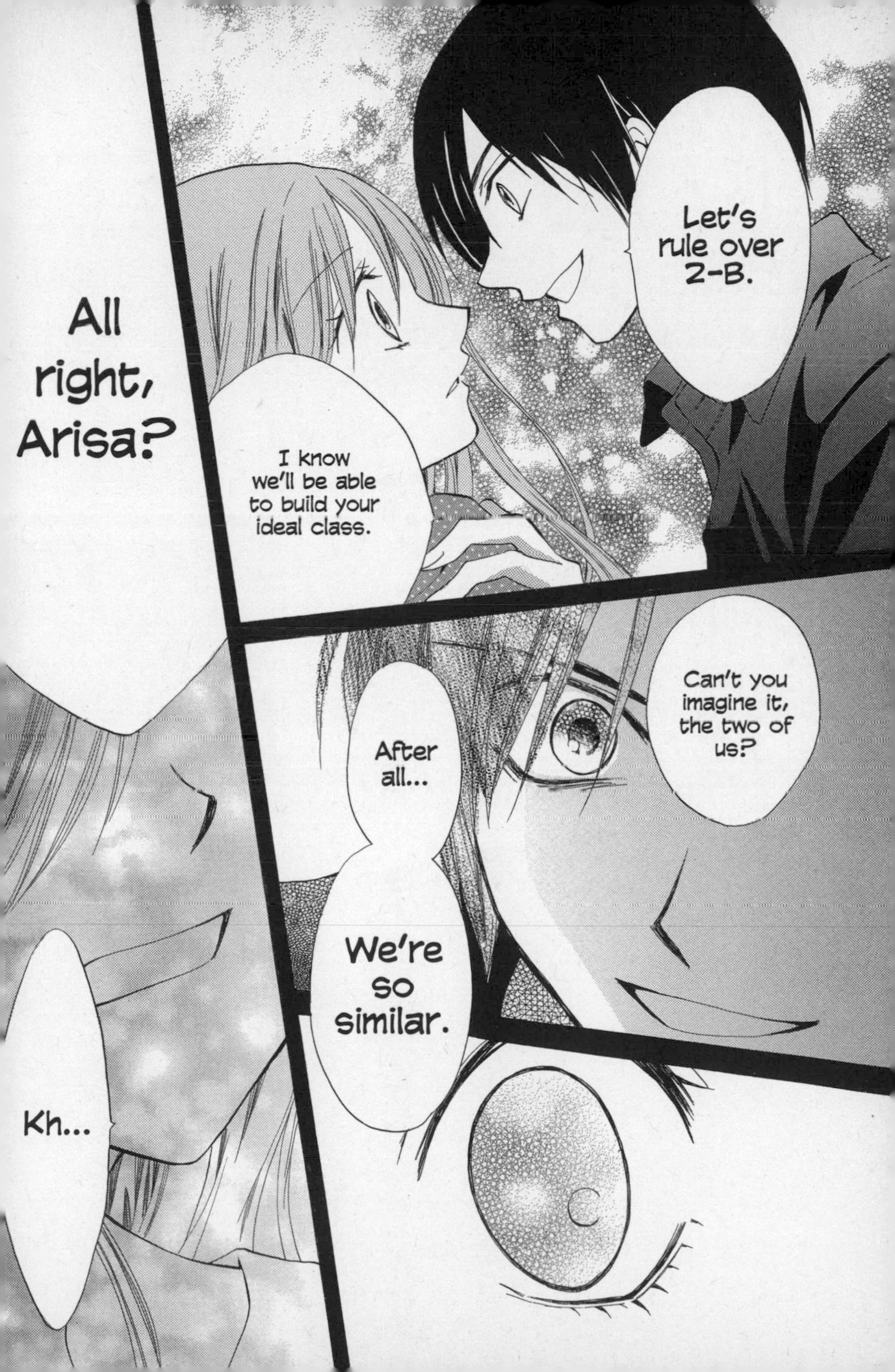
Let's rule over 2-B.
I know we'll be able to build your ideal class.
Can't you imagine it, the two of us?
After all...
We're so similar.
All right, Arisa?
Kh...

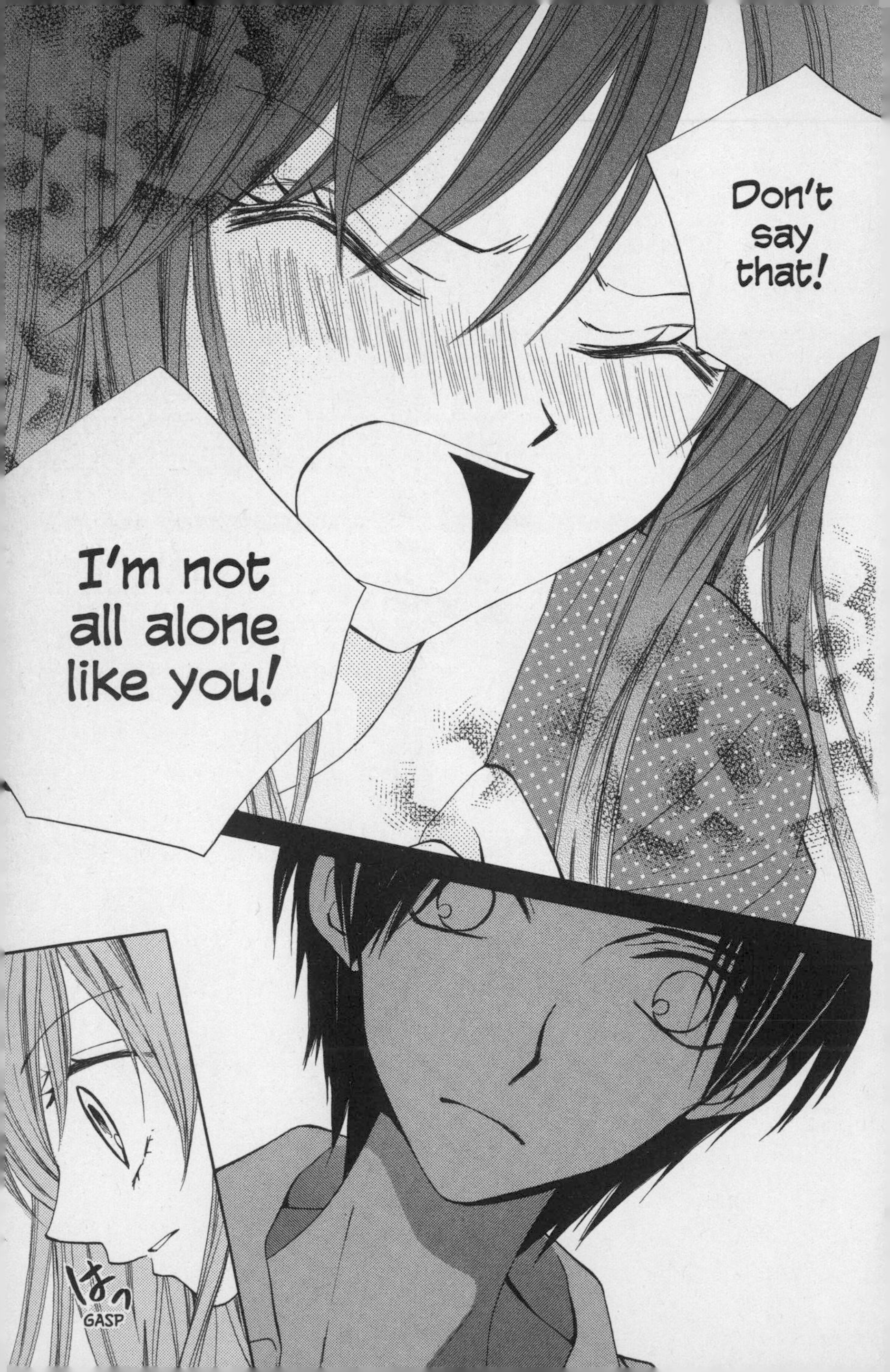
Don't say that!
I'm not all alone like you!
はっ
GASP

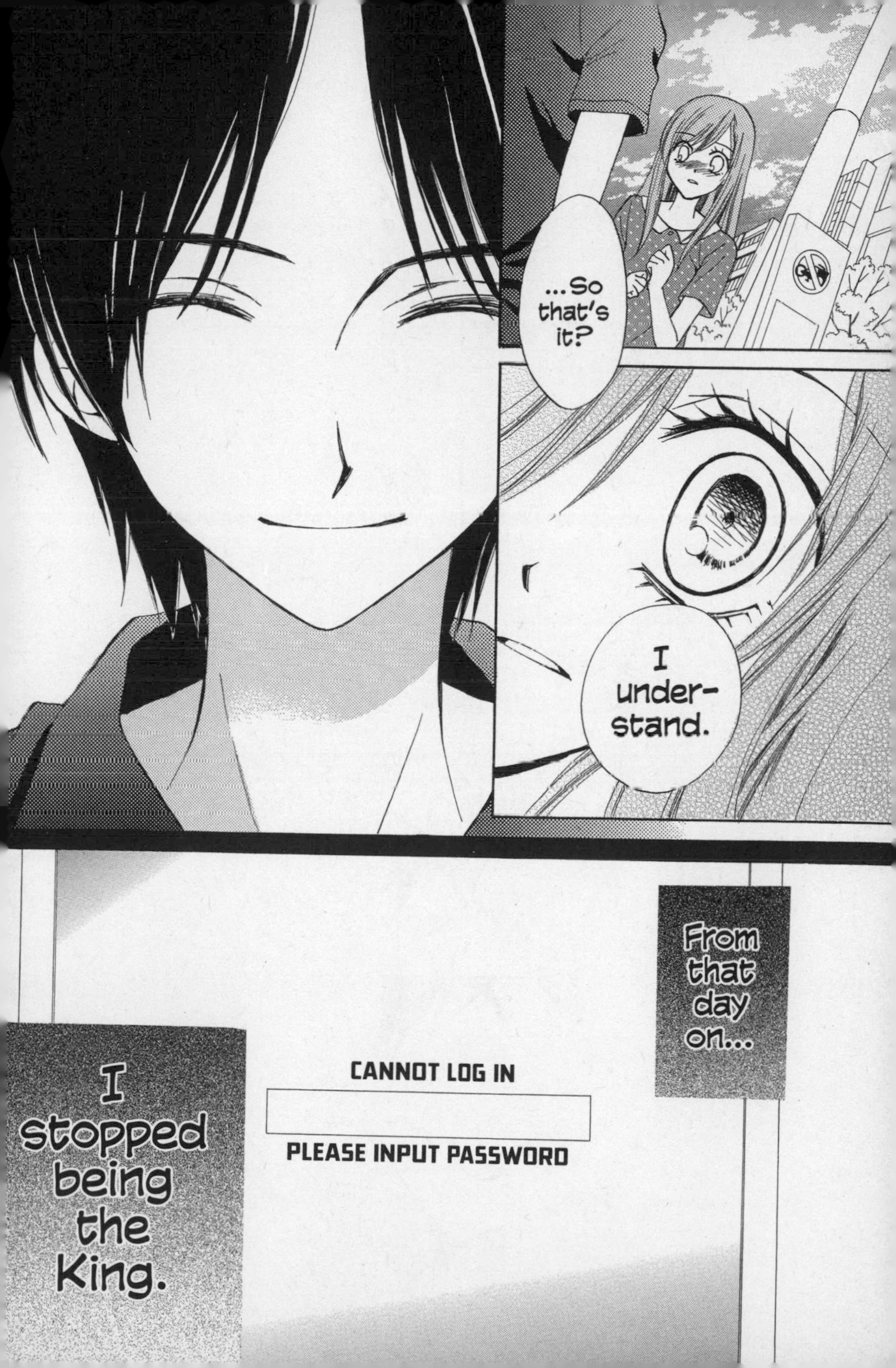
...So that's it?
I under-stand.
From that day on...
CANNOT LOG IN
PLEASE INPUT PASSWORD
I stopped being the King.

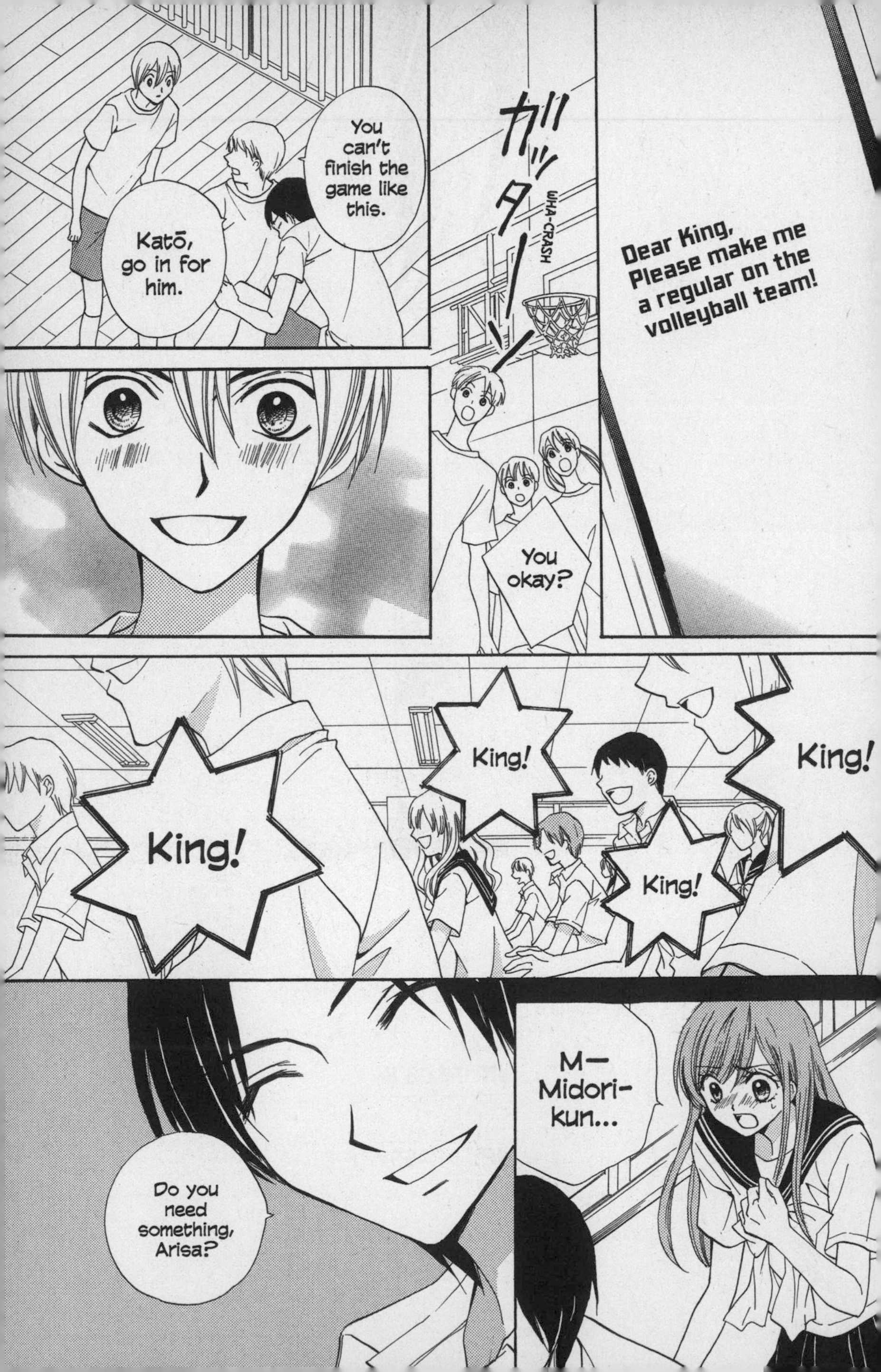
Dear King, Please make me a regular on the volleyball team!
WHA-CRASH
You okay?
You can't finish the game like this.
Katō, go in for him.
King!
King!
King!
King!
M—Midori-kun...
Do you need something, Arisa?

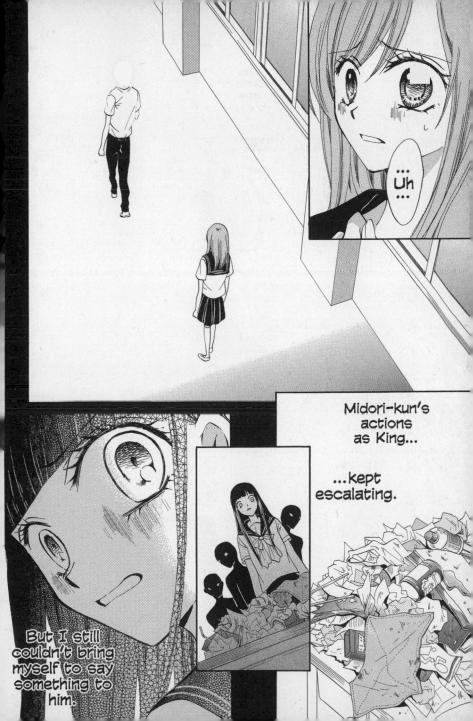

...
Üh
...

Midori-kun's
actions
as King...

...kept
escalating.

But I still
couldn't bring
myself to say
something to
him.

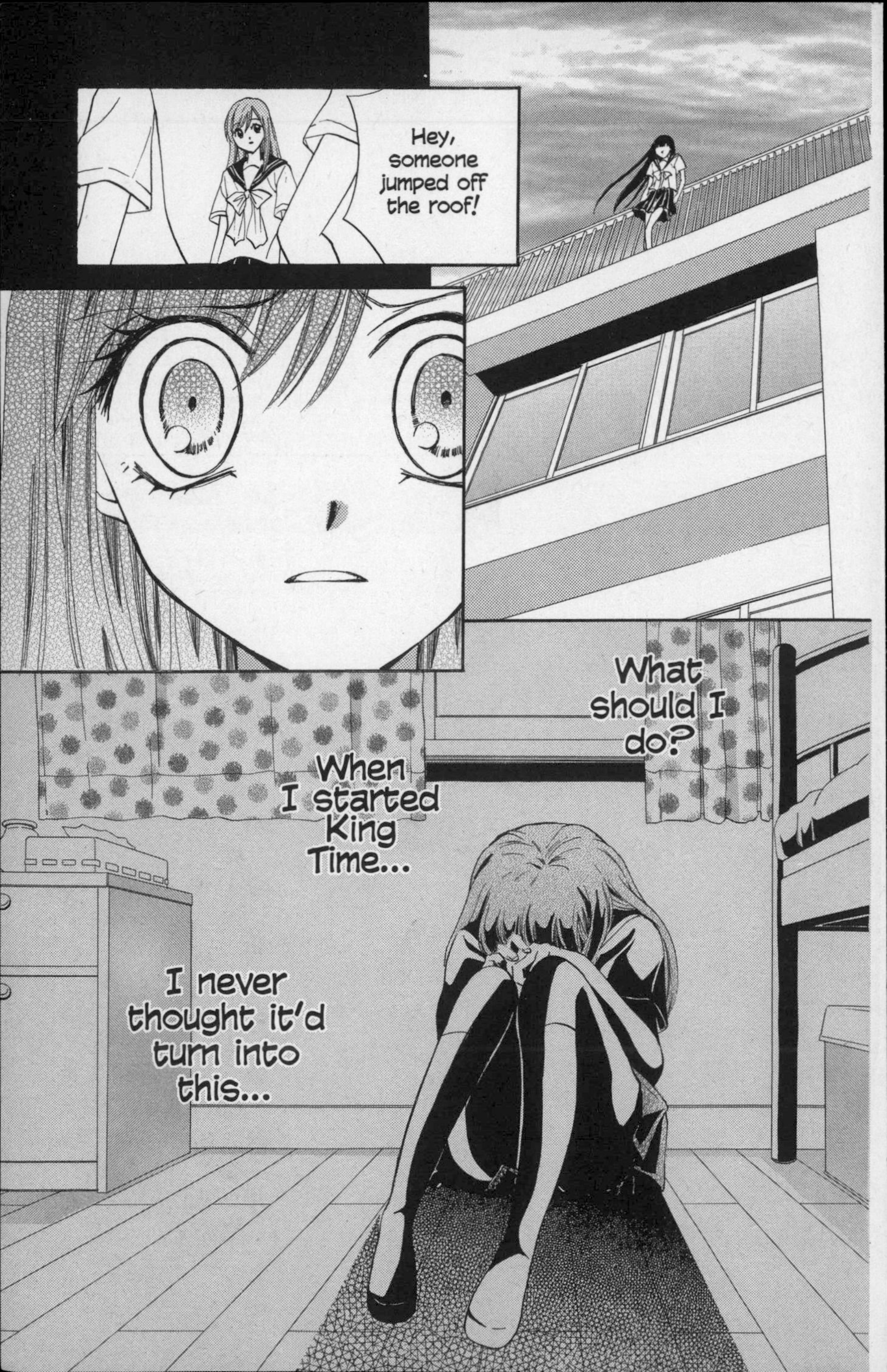
Hey, someone jumped off the roof!
What should I do?
When I started King Time...
I never thought it'd turn into this...

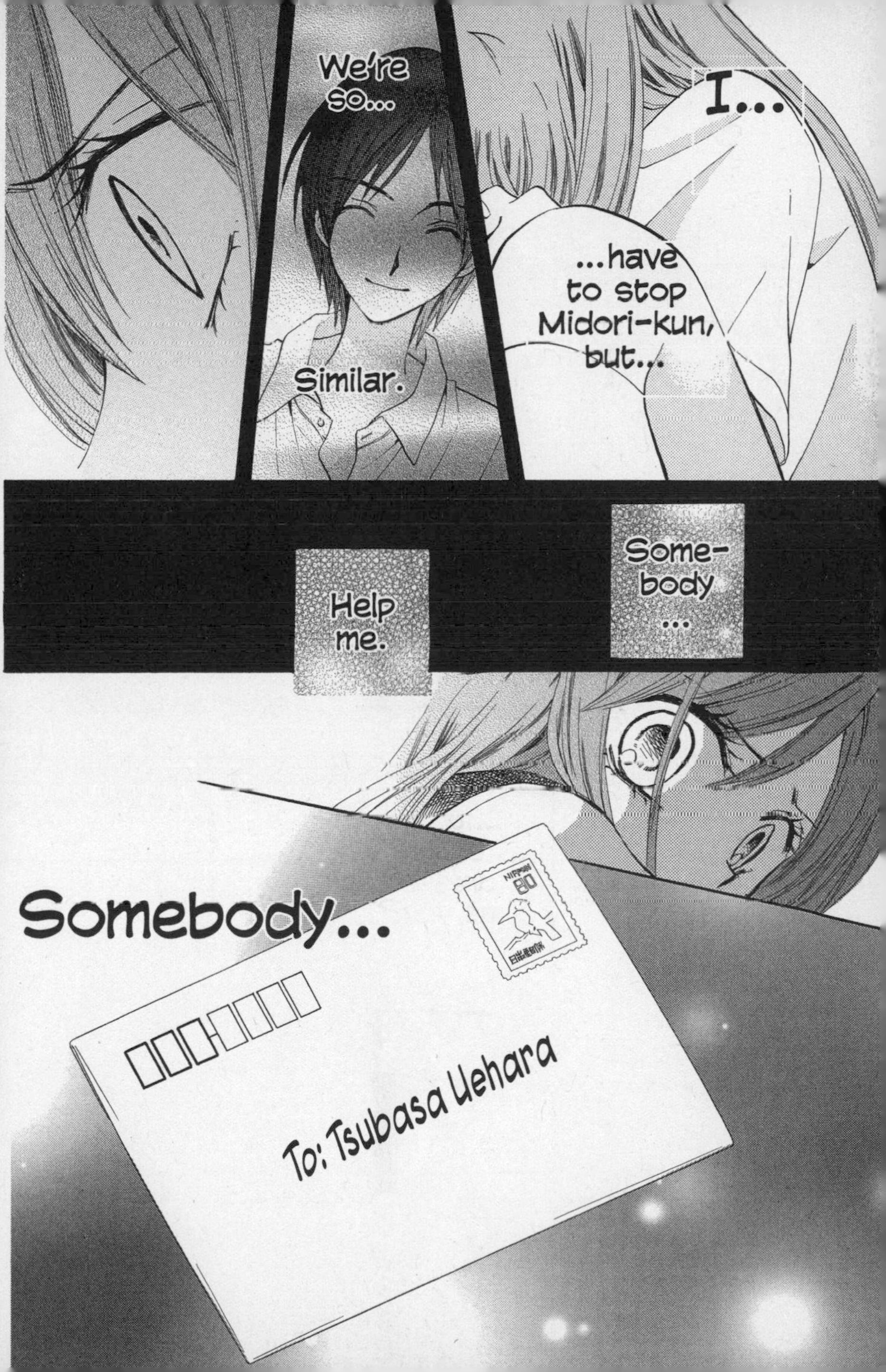
I...
...have to stop Midori-kun, but...
We're so...
Similar.
Some-body...
Help me.
Somebody...
NIPPON 80
To: Tsubasa Uehara

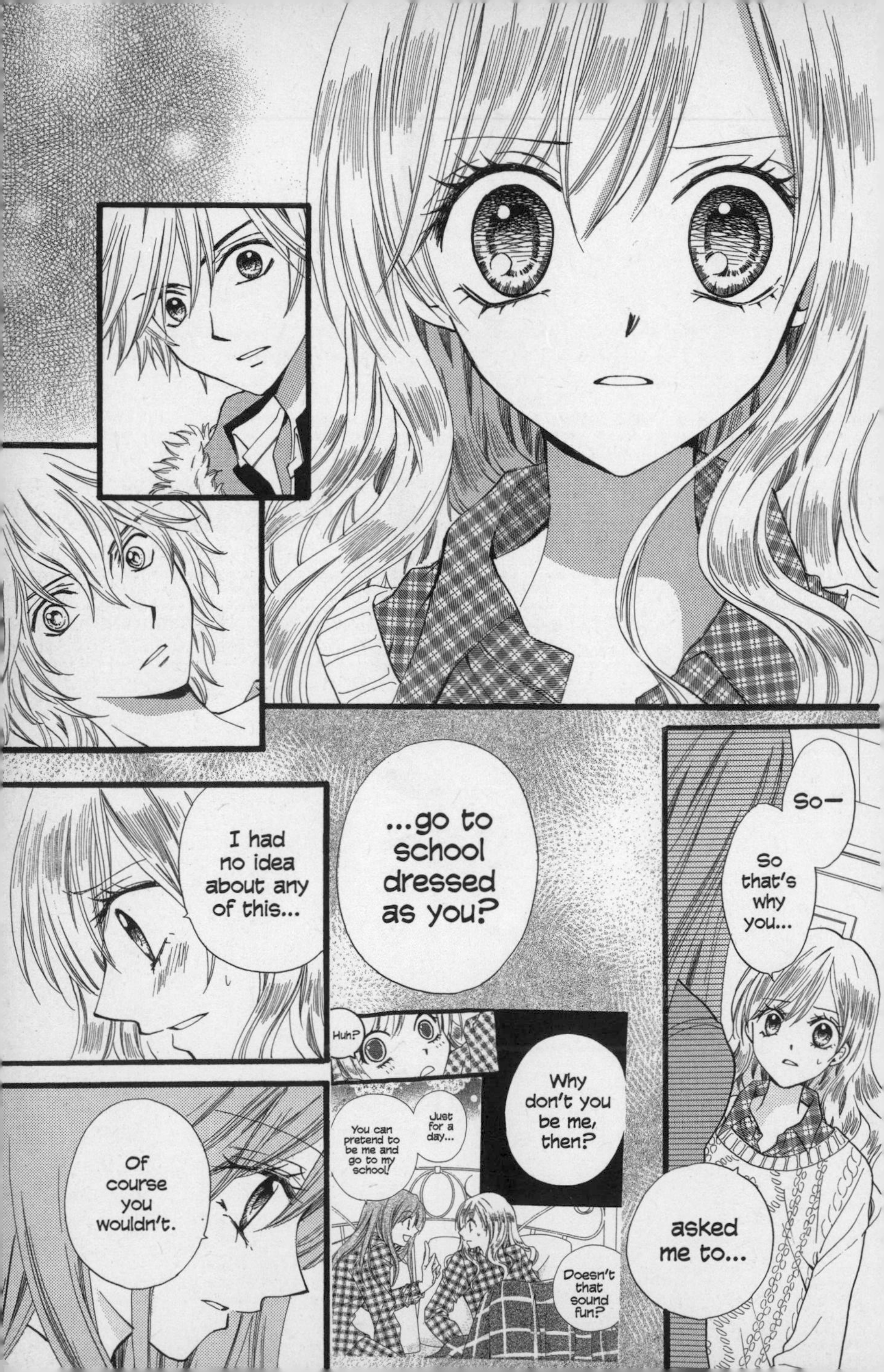
So—
So that's why you...
asked me to...
...go to school dressed as you?
Why don't you be me, then?
Huh?
Just for a day...
You can pretend to be me and go to my school!
Doesn't that sound fun?
I had no idea about any of this...
Of course you wouldn't.

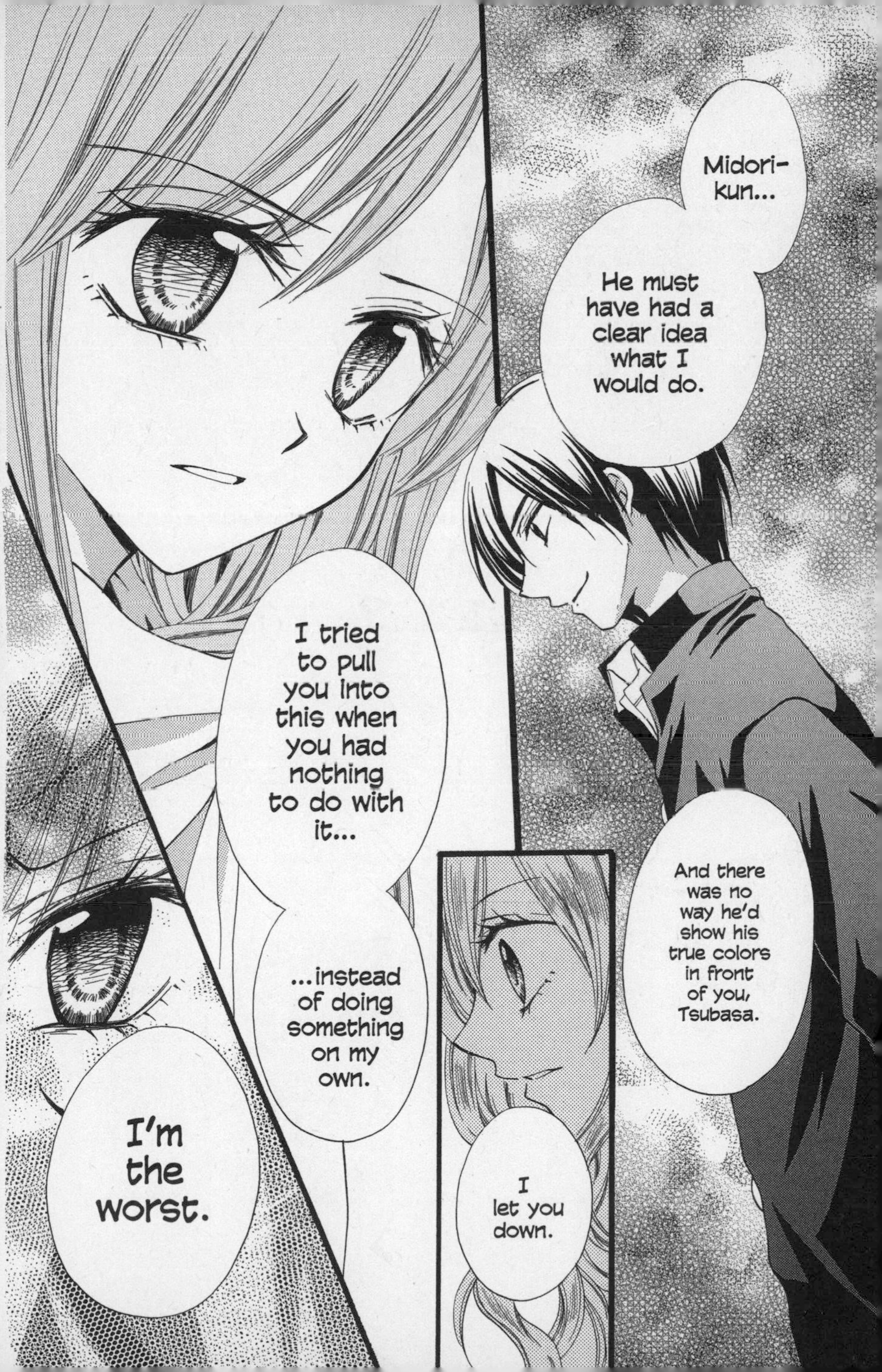
Midori-kun...
He must have had a clear idea what I would do.
And there was no way he'd show his true colors in front of you, Tsubasa.
I tried to pull you into this when you had nothing to do with it...
...instead of doing something on my own.
I let you down.
I'm the worst.

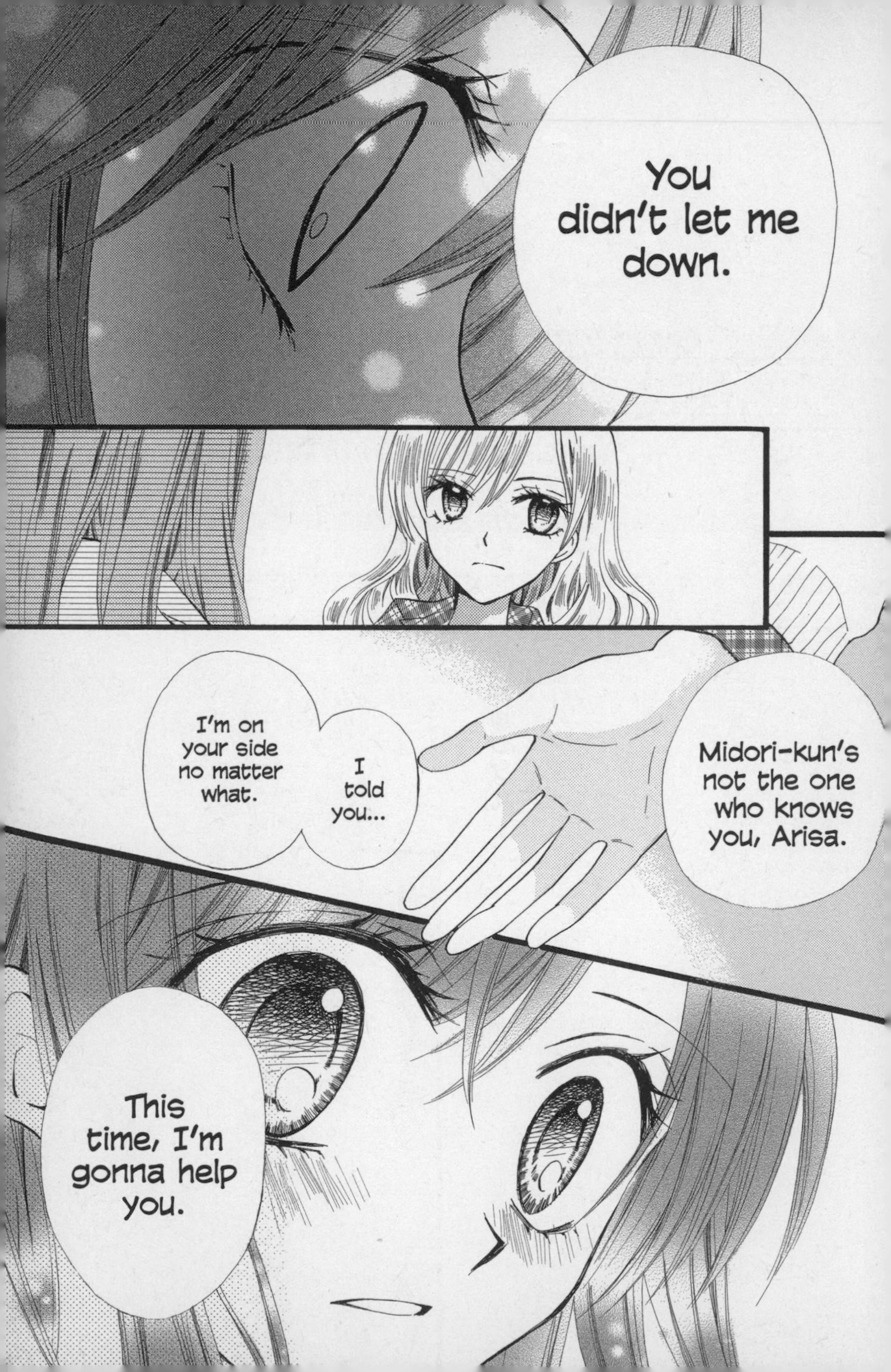
You didn't let me down.
Midori-kun's not the one who knows you, Arisa.
I told you...
I'm on your side no matter what.
This time, I'm gonna help you.

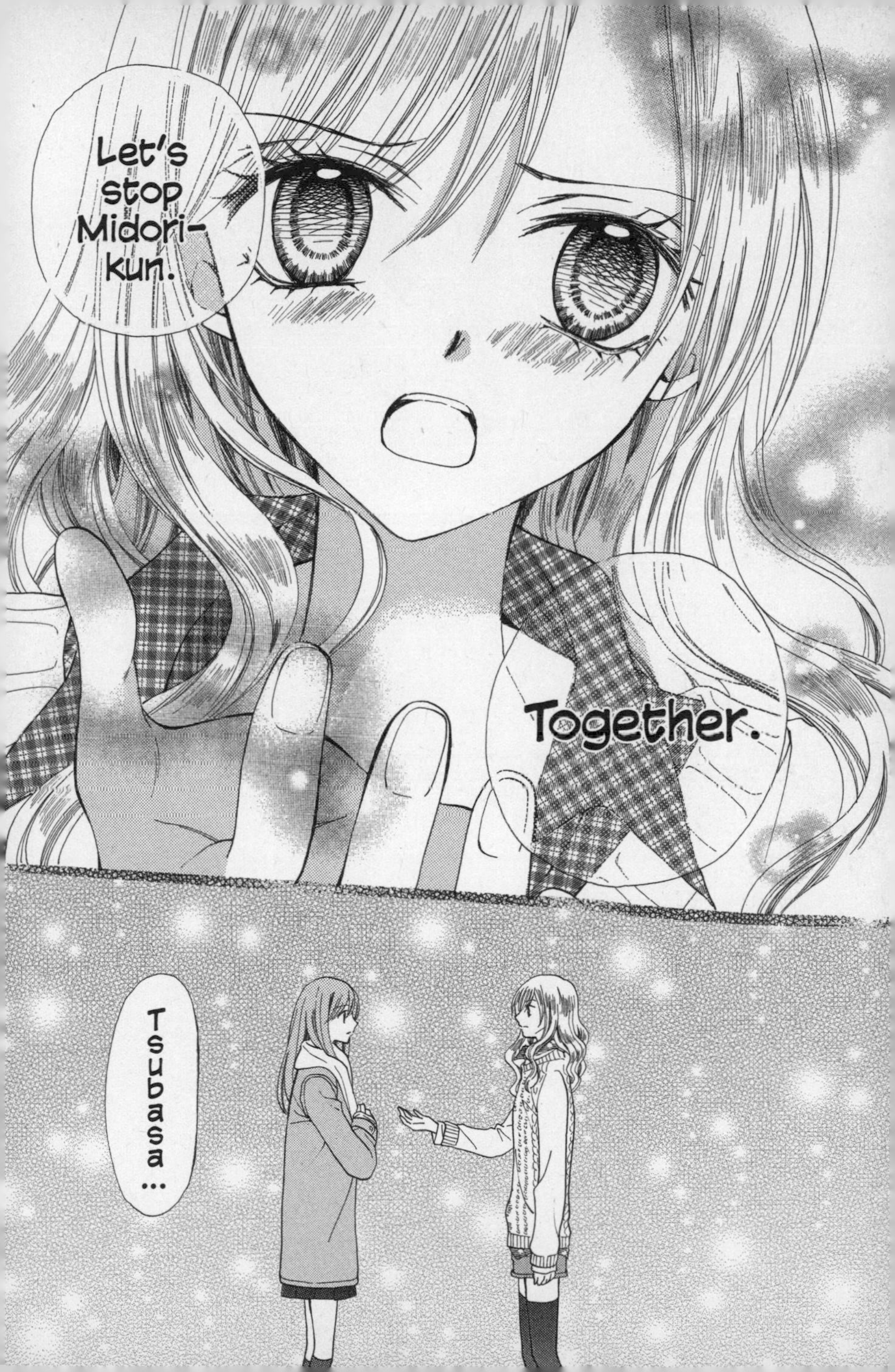
Let's stop Midori-kun.
Together.
Tsubasa...

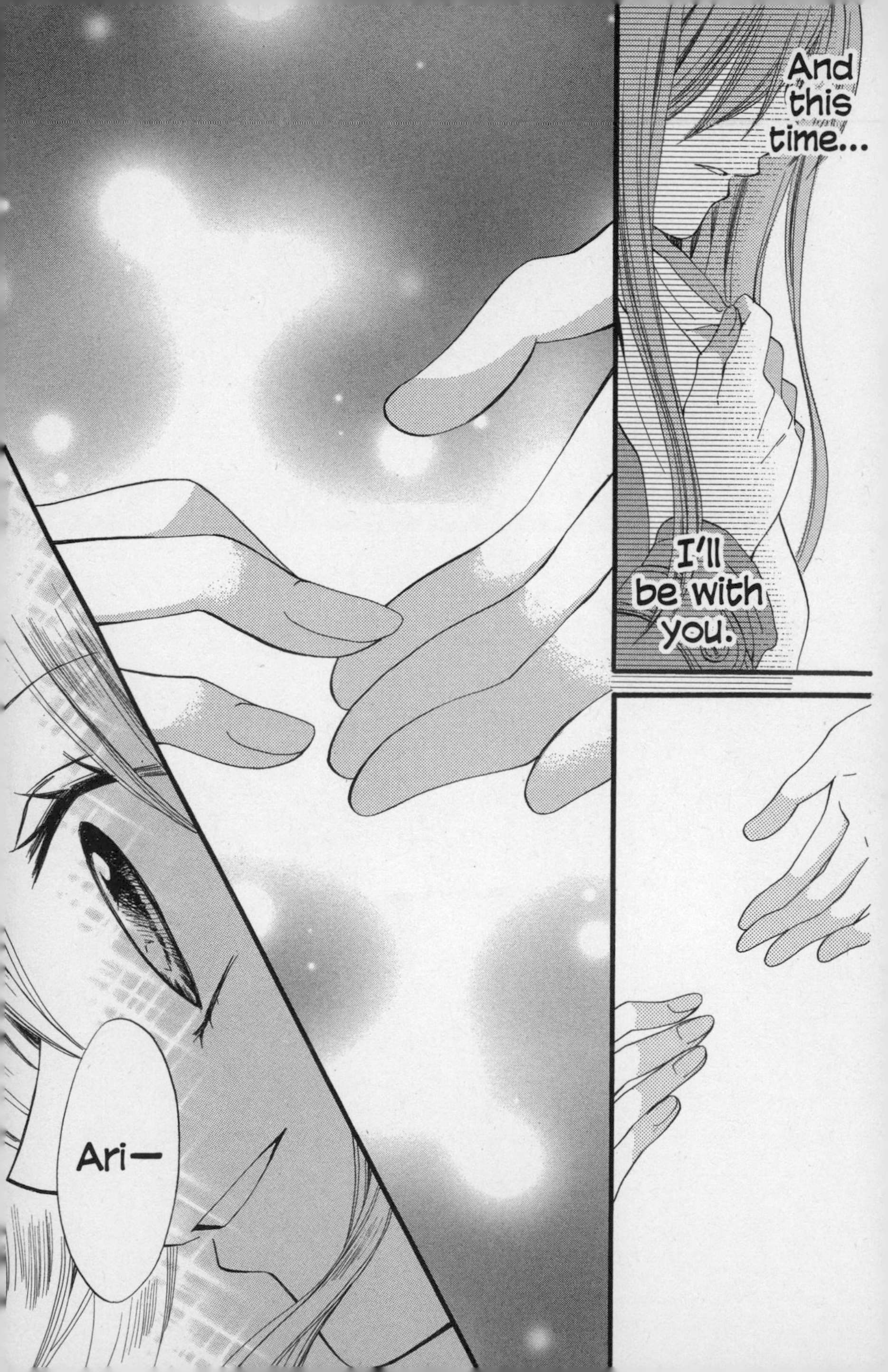
And this time...
I'll be with you.
Ari—

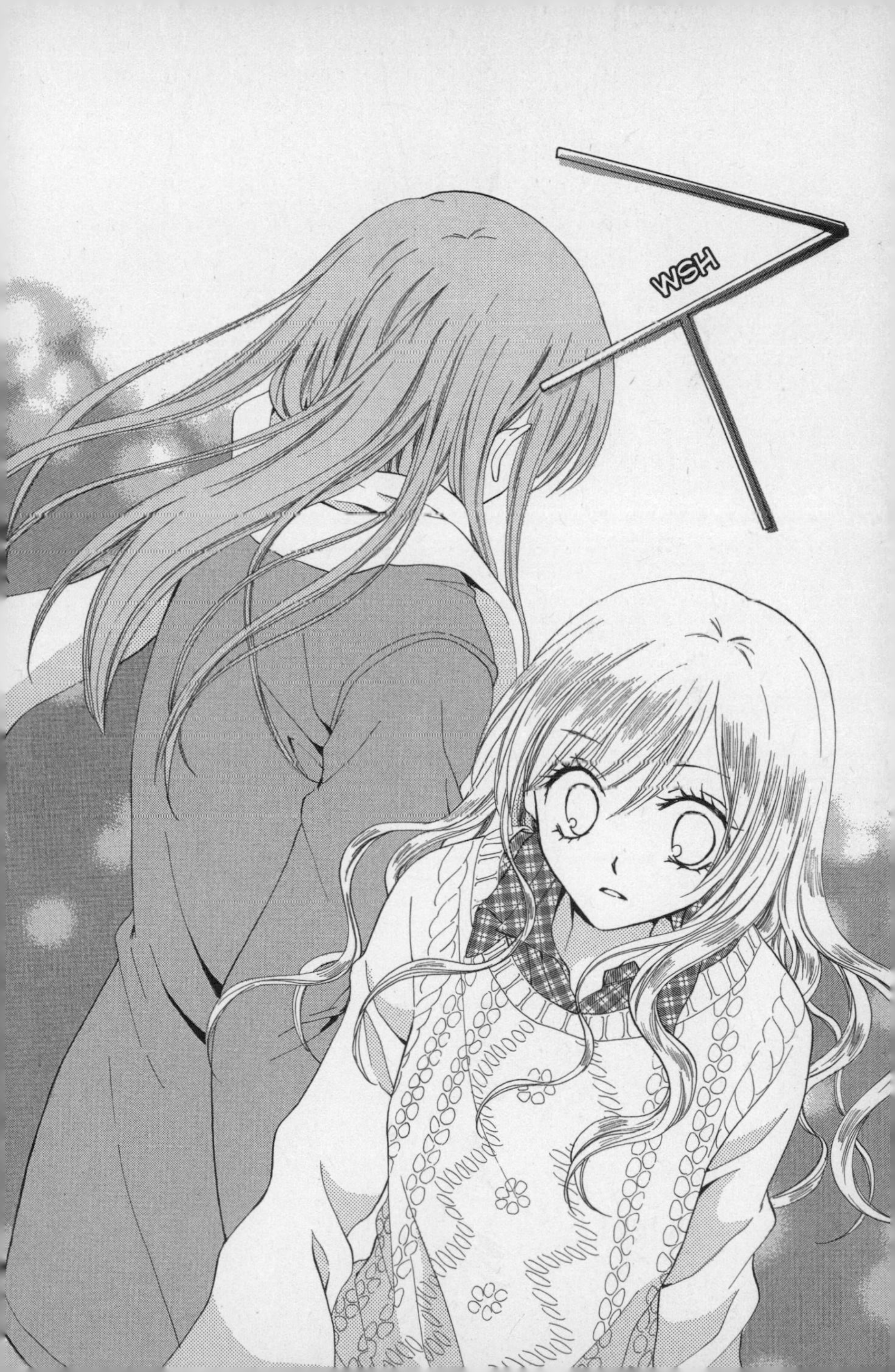
WSH

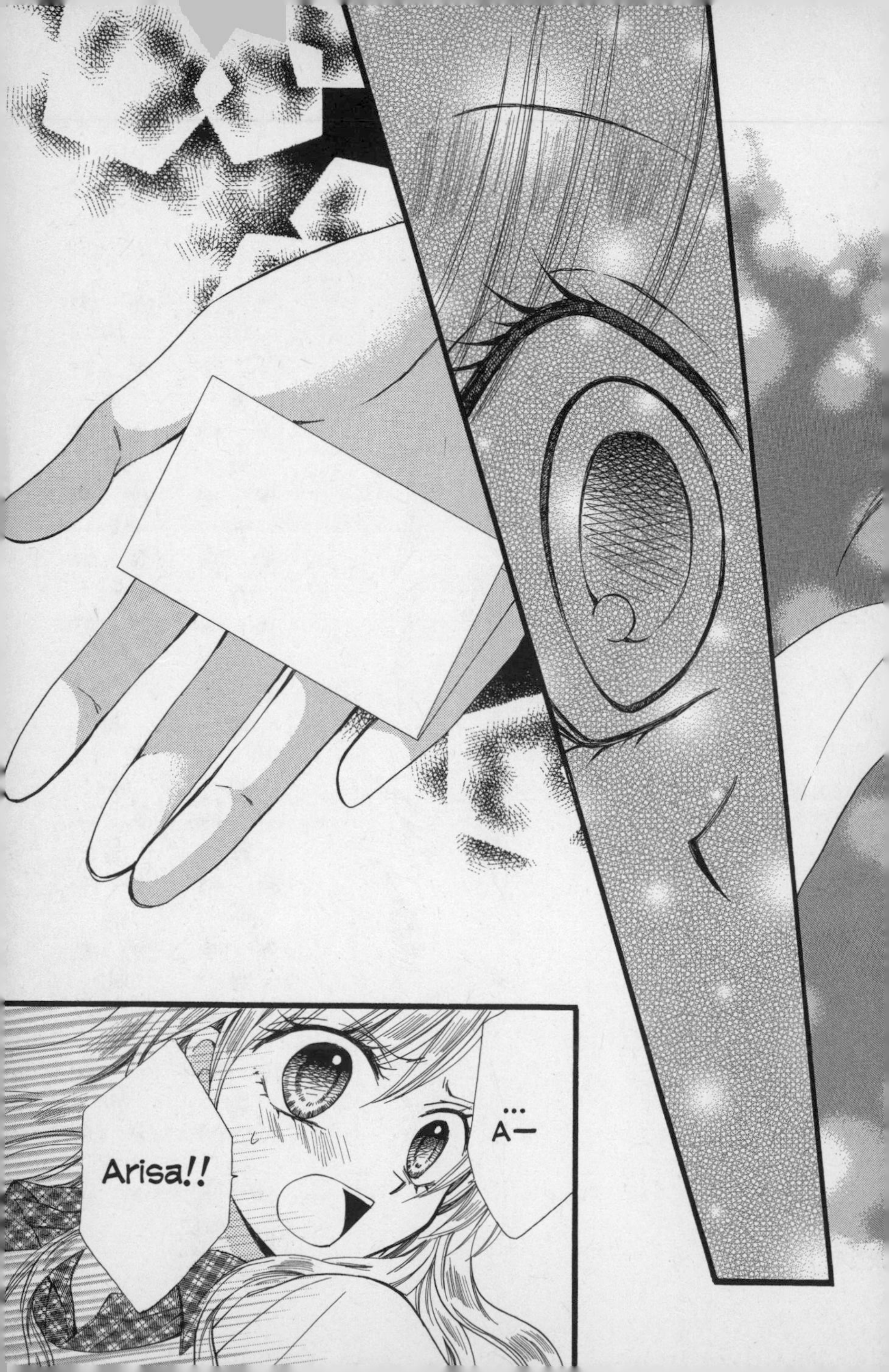
...
A—
Arisa!!

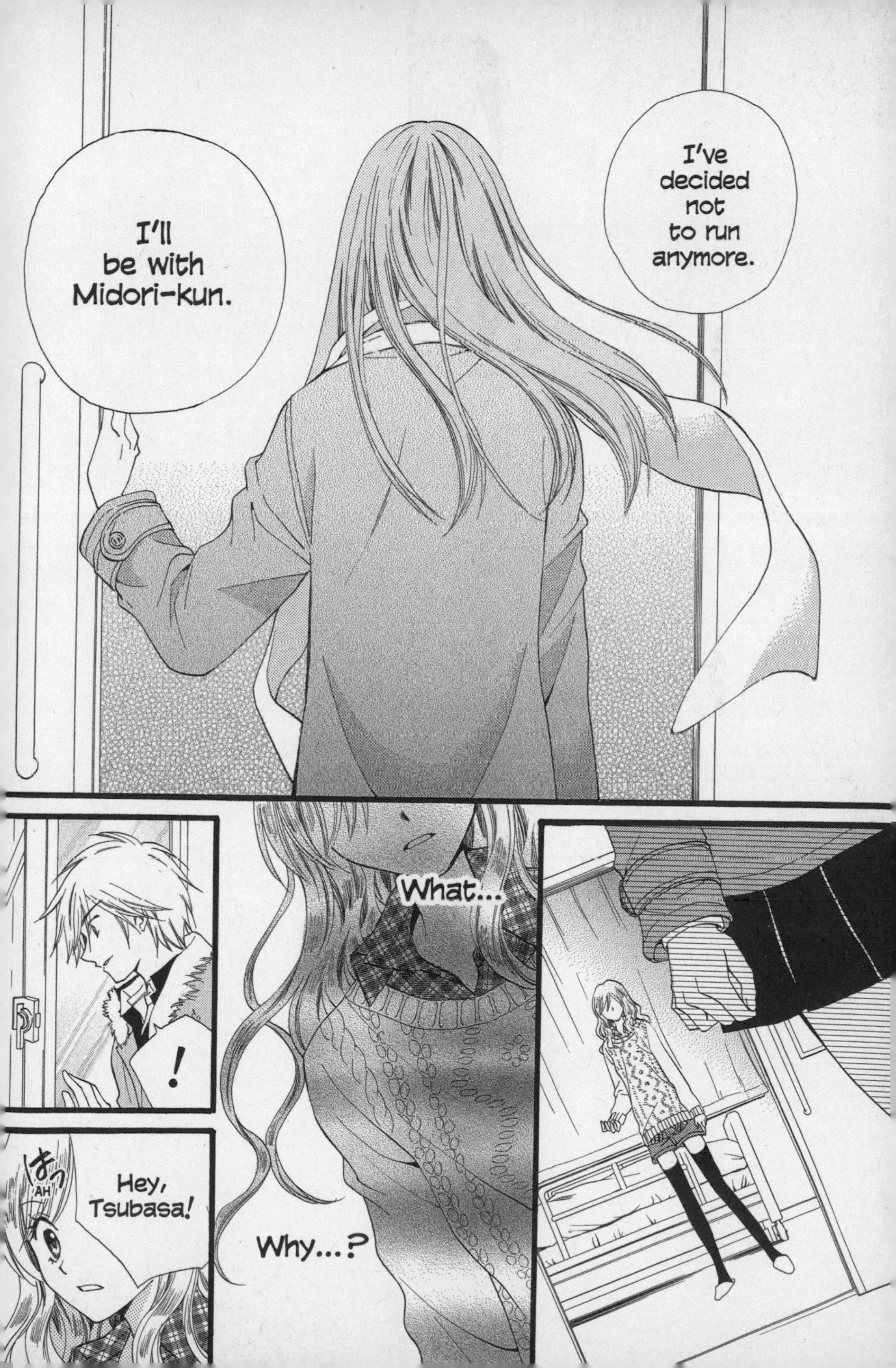
I've decided not to run anymore.
I'll be with Midori-kun.
What...
Why...?
!
AH
Hey, Tsubasa!

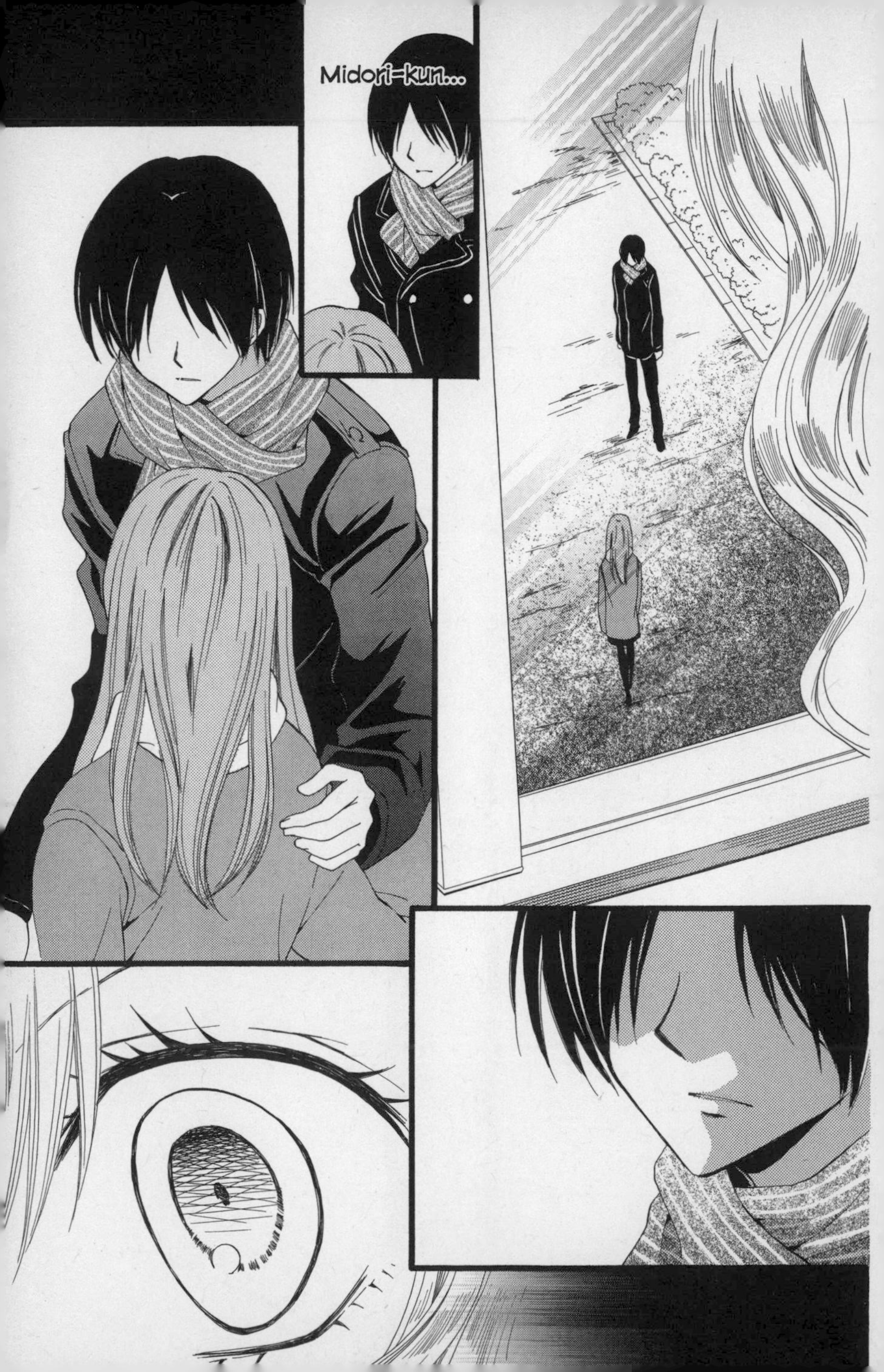
Midori-kun...

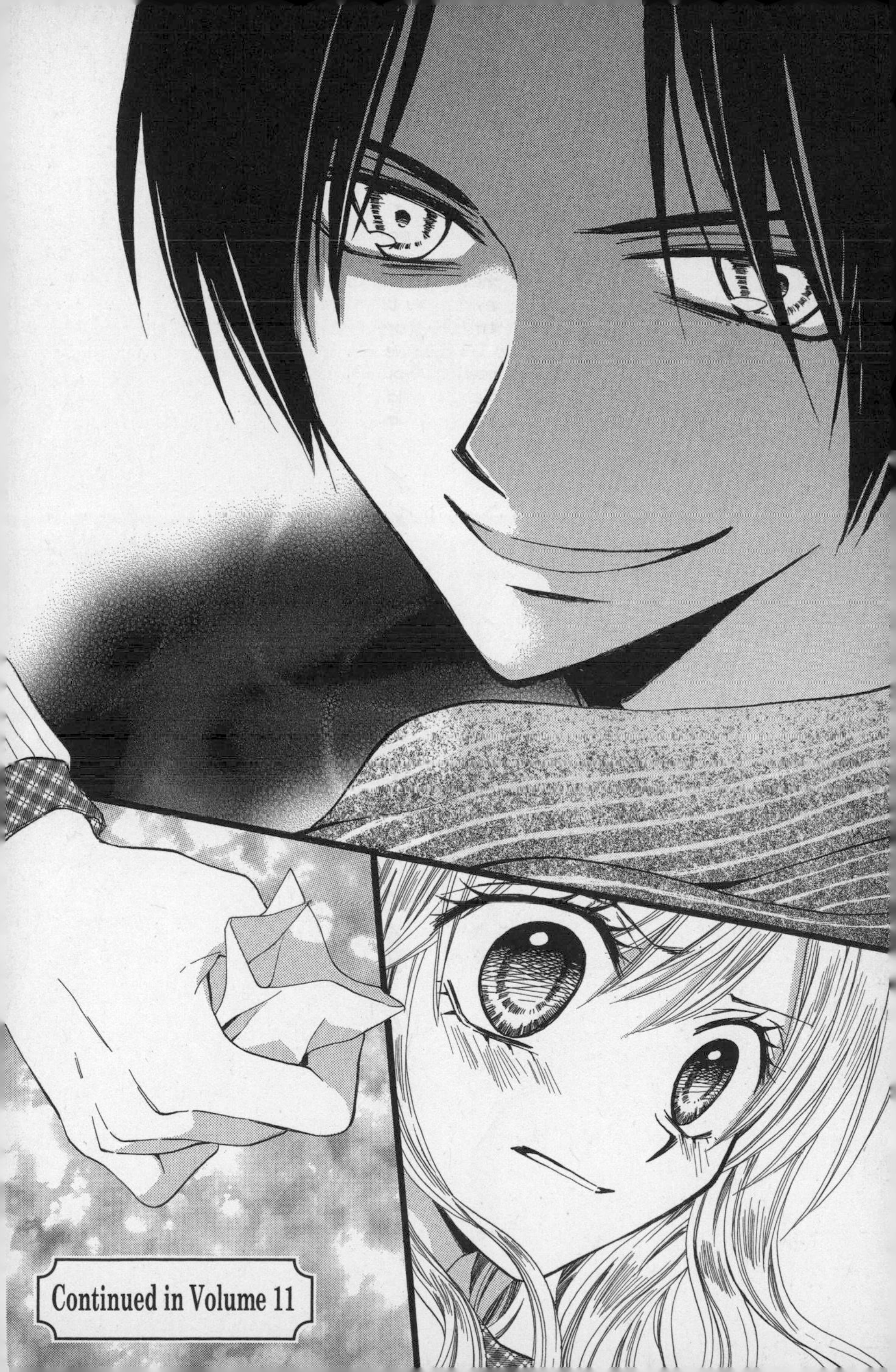
Continued in Volume 11

Vol. 10's done!! To celebrate, I drew the sisters smiling together, which I don't normally do. Speaking of which, when I met the new editor in charge of "Arisa," we sometimes referred to Tsubasa as Arisa...They just have the same number of letters* and the final vowel sound is the same, but I guess they're easy to mix up. At first I tried to give them even more similar names, but if I'd done that I'm sure we would've gotten so confused that meetings would've become totally incomprehensible! I'm glad I didn't. That's it! See you in Volume 11 too!

*In Japanese.

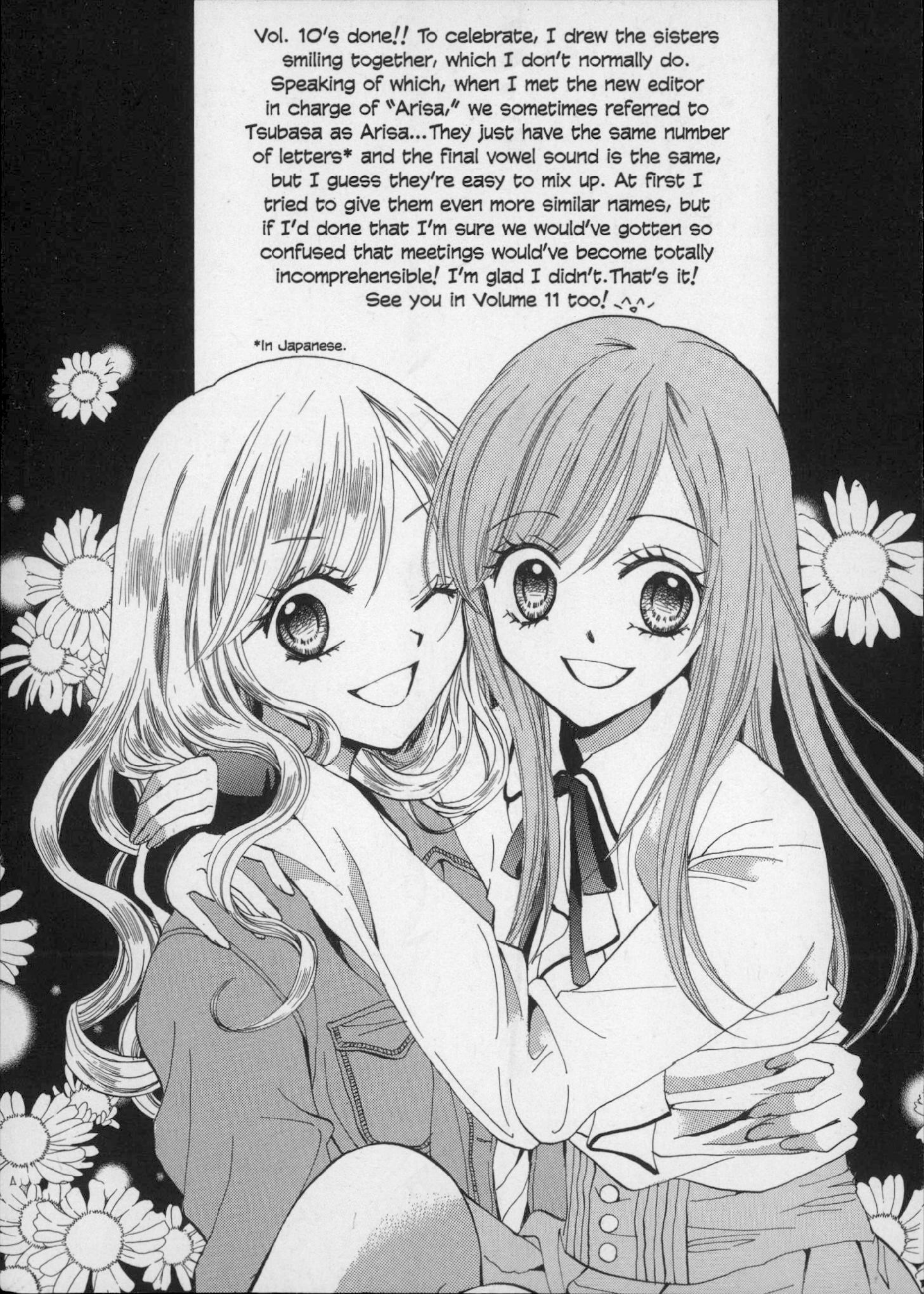

Translation Notes

Class 2-B:
In Japanese schools, classes stay in the same room all day and teachers for different subjects come to them. The "2" in Class 2-B indicates that this is a second-year class, and the "B" sets it apart from other second-year classes.

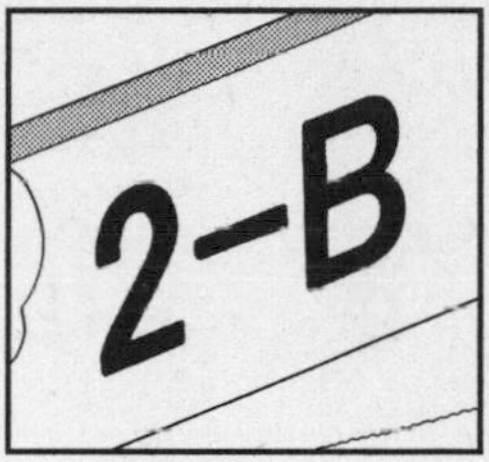
2-B

English testing, page 119:
Every Japanese student is required to take English classes, and scores on English tests like the TOEFL (Test of English as a Foreign Language) and TOEIC (Test of English for International Communication) are valuable résumé-builders for college applicants. In contrast to Europe, however, most Japanese can't really speak much English. Critics of English education in Japan say it puts too much emphasis on test scores and not enough on conversation skills.

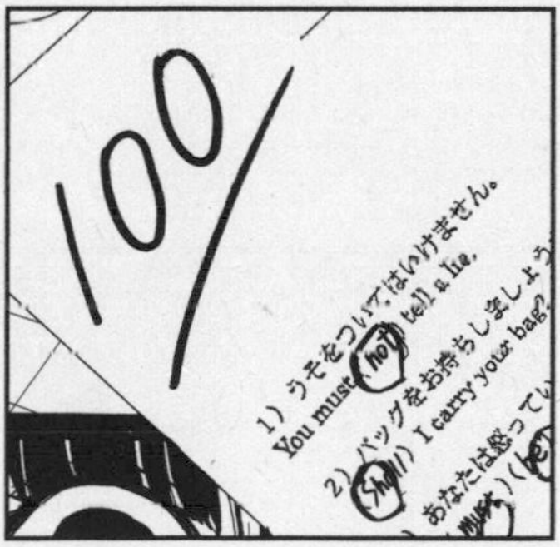
100

5,000 yen, page 130:
The bill Arisa's mom gives her is worth about $60. The portrait depicts Ichiyō Higuchi, a late 19th-century Japanese author.

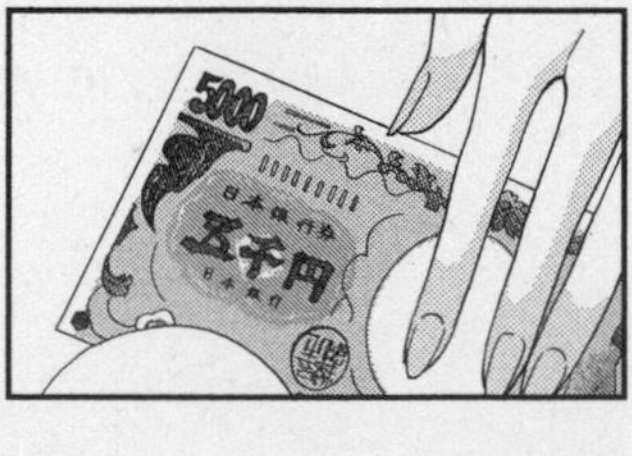
5000
五千円